Windows® 11

2nd Edition

by Alan Simpson
Original Edition by Andy Rathbone

A Wiley Brand

Windows® 11 For Dummies®, 2nd Edition

Published by: **John Wiley & Sons, Inc.**, 111 River Street, Hoboken, NJ 07030-5774, www.wiley.com

For general information on our other products and services, please contact our Customer Care Department within the U.S. at 877-762-2974, outside the U.S. at 317-572-3993, or fax 317-572-4002. For technical support, please visit https://hub.wiley.com/community/support/dummies.

Wiley publishes in a variety of print and electronic formats and by print-on-demand. Some material included with standard print versions of this book may not be included in e-books or in print-on-demand. If this book refers to media that is not included in the version you purchased, you may download this material at http://booksupport.wiley.com. For more information about Wiley products, visit www.wiley.com.

Library of Congress Control Number: 2024946905

ISBN 978-1-394-28904-2 (pbk); ISBN 978-1-394-28906-6 (ebk); ISBN 978-1-394-28905-9 (ebk)

SKY10087167_100824

Contents at a Glance

Table of Contents

Introduction

Welcome to *Windows 11 For Dummies*, 2nd Edition, the world's best-selling book about Windows 11!

This book's popularity probably boils down to one simple fact: Some people want to be Windows whizzes. They love interacting with dialogs. Some randomly press keys in the hope of discovering hidden, undocumented features. A few memorize long strings of computer commands while eating pizza.

And you? Well, you're no dummy, that's for sure. But when it comes to Windows and computers, the fascination isn't there. You want to do your work and then move on to something more important. You have no intention of changing, and there's nothing wrong with that.

That's where this book comes in handy. Instead of making you a whiz at Windows, it merely dishes out chunks of useful computing information when you need them. Instead of becoming a Windows expert, you'll know just enough to get by quickly and with a minimum of pain so that you can move on to the more pleasant things in life.

And you'll be able to do that whether you're dealing with a touchscreen tablet, laptop, or desktop computer.

About This Book

Instead of fancy computer jargon, this book uses plain English to cover subjects like the following:

>> Getting free instant tech help right from your computer

>> Keeping your computer safe and secure

>> Making sense of the Windows 11 Start menu

>> Finding, starting, and closing apps

>> Locating the file you saved or downloaded a while ago

>> Setting up a computer or tablet for the family to share

>> Copying information to and from USB drives and memory cards

>> Saving and sharing files from your smartphone or digital camera

>> Printing or scanning your work

>> Linking two or more computers with a network to share your internet connection, files, and a printer

>> Fixing Windows when it's misbehaving

There's nothing to memorize and nothing to learn. Just turn to the right page, read the brief explanation — bypassing the technical hoopla — and get back to work.

How to Use This Book

When something in Windows 11 2024 Update leaves you stumped, use this book as a reference, paging through the table of contents or index to the spot that deals with that particular bit of computer obscurity.

If you have to type something into the computer, you'll see easy-to-follow bold text like this:

Type **Mail** in the Search box.

In the preceding example, you type the word *Mail* and then press the keyboard's Enter key.

Key combination you should press look like this:

Press Ctrl+B.

That means you should hold down your keyboard's Control key while pressing your keyboard's B key.

This book doesn't wimp out by saying, "For further information, consult your manual." Windows doesn't even come with a manual. This book also doesn't contain information about running specific Windows programs, such as Microsoft

Word or Excel. Windows is complicated enough on its own! Luckily, other *Dummies* books explain most popular programs.

Don't feel abandoned, though. This book covers Windows in enough detail for you to get the job done. Plus, thanks to built-in artificial intelligence (AI), you can get answers to your technical questions just by clicking the Copilot icon at the bottom of your screen and asking your question there.

Most modern laptops come with a trackpad, which you can use instead of a mouse. However, unlike a mouse, the trackpad might not have buttons to click. You move the mouse pointer around the screen by *tracking* (gently moving your finger, without pressing down too much) along the trackpad surface. Then translate mouse terms as follows:

>> **When told to *click*, you should *tap*.** Just one gentle tap with one finger should to the trick.

>> **When told to double-click, *tap twice*.** Use one finger to gently tap two times in rapid succession.

>> **When told to *right-click* something,** tap gently using two fingers rather than one finger.

Windows 11 comes preinstalled on all new Windows desktop PCs and laptops and can also be used with *touchscreens*, those tablets, laptops, and desktop monitors that have screens you can control by touching them with your fingers. If you find yourself scratching your head over explanations aimed at mouse owners, remember these three touchscreen rules:

>> **When told to *click*, you should *tap*.** Quickly touching and releasing your finger on a button is the same as clicking it with a mouse.

>> **When told to double-click, *tap twice*.** Two touches in rapid succession does the trick.

>> **When told to *right-click* something, *hold down your finger on the item*. Then, when an icon appears, *lift your finger*.** The right-click menu appears onscreen. (That's what would have happened if you'd right-clicked the item with a mouse.) While you're looking at the pop-up menu, tap any of its listed items to have Windows carry out your bidding.

Foolish Assumptions

I don't assume that you're already a techie, with years of experience using older versions of Windows. I do assume that you might not be familiar with jargon such as files, folders, icons, upload, paste, and gigabytes. That's okay. I define every term when we introduce it.

Maybe you've used Mac computers in the past, but never Windows. No matter. This book takes it from the top and explains the stuff that other people assume you already know. So don't worry that you're already in over your head before you even get started.

About the only tech knowledge and experience I assume you do have is doing things online, such as using the internet for email, engaging with social media, shopping, and ordering take-out.

Icons Used in This Book

It just takes a glance at Windows to notice its *icons,* which are little push-button pictures for starting various apps. The icons in this book fit right in. They're even a little easier to figure out.

TECHNICAL STUFF

Watch out! This signpost warns you that pointless technical information is coming around the bend. Swerve away from this icon to stay safe from technical drivel.

TIP

This icon alerts you to juicy information that makes computing easier: a new method for keeping the cat from sleeping on top of your tablet, for example.

REMEMBER

Don't forget to remember these important points (or at least dog-ear the pages so you can look them up again later).

WARNING

The computer won't explode while you're performing the delicate operations associated with this icon. Still, wearing gloves and proceeding with caution is a good idea.

NEW

This icon alerts you to things that are new in Windows 11 2024 Update, including tips for making the best use of the free AI at your fingertips.

Beyond the Book

Like every *Dummies* book, this one comes with a free online cheat sheet that describes what's new in Windows 11 2024 Update and provides keyboard shortcuts. To get the cheat sheet, head for www.dummies.com and, using the Search box, search for **Windows 11 For Dummies Cheat Sheet.**

Where to Go from Here

Now you're ready for action. Give the pages a quick flip and scan a section or two that you might need later. Please remember that this is *your* book — your weapon against the computer nerds who've inflicted a complicated computer concept on you. Circle any paragraphs you find useful, highlight key concepts, add sticky notes, and doodle in the margins.

REMEMBER

The more you mark up your book, the easier it will be for you to find all the good stuff again. And the more techie buzzwords you come to understand, the easier it will be to get Copilot to answer your questions and do your work for you.

1

Getting Started with Windows 11 2024 Update

Understand the changes in Windows 11 2024 Update.

Start and use apps.

Catch up with the latest developments in AI.

Take control of your screen.

Manage your folders and files.

Chapter 1

What Is Windows 11 2024 Update?

There's a good chance you've heard about Windows: the boxes and windows that greet you whenever you turn on your computer. In fact, millions of people worldwide are puzzling over Windows as you read this book. Most new computers and laptops sold today come with Windows preinstalled, ready to toss colorful boxes onto the screen.

This chapter helps you understand why Windows lives inside your computer. I also introduce Microsoft's latest Windows version, Windows 11 2024 Update, and explain how this version differs from previous Windows versions.

What Is Windows, and Why Are You Using It?

Created and sold by a company called Microsoft, Windows isn't like your usual software that lets you calculate income taxes or send angry emails to politicians. No, Windows is an *operating system*, meaning it controls the way you work with your computer. It's been around since 1985, and the latest incarnation is called *Windows 11 2024 Update*, shown in Figure 1-1.

FIGURE 1-1:
Windows 11 2024
Update on a
typical PC —
yours might look
different.

The name *Windows* comes from all the windows it places on your computer screen. You can place several windows onscreen simultaneously and jump from window to window. Or you can enlarge one window to fill the entire screen.

Each window typically shows an open app. Windows comes with a bunch of free apps that let you do different things, such as write and print letters, browse the internet, play music, order takeout, and send your friends dimly lit photos of your latest meal.

TECHNICAL STUFF

Windows isn't the only OS (operating system) in town. Macs use an operating system named macOS (previously known as OS X). Apple's iPhones use iOS, and their iPads use iPadOS. Most non–Apple smartphones use Android. Some hardcore techie developers (the people who create apps) use Linux.

And why are you using Windows 11? Well, you probably didn't have much choice. If you're using a computer at work, it's probably a Windows PC. Aside from Apple's Mac computers, almost every computer, laptop, or Windows tablet sold after October 2021 comes with Windows 11 preinstalled. The 2024 Update is a free upgrade that installs automatically. So, if your computer is running Windows 11, chances are it's already using the 2024 Update version.

What's New in Windows 11 2024 Update?

The Windows 11 2024 Update version is virtually identical to Windows 11 released in 2021, including all the updates Microsoft released since that initial release date. Your existing skills will continue to apply. This 2024 update focuses on making the power of AI (artificial intelligence) freely available to everyone. The AI in Windows 11 2024 Update is called *Copilot in Windows*, but I refer to it as *Copilot*. Here's what you can achieve with Copilot:

>> **Instant answers and clever conversations:** Engage with Copilot Chat to swiftly get answers to a wide range of questions. I get you started with that task later in the chapter.

>> **Effortless typing:** Have something typed at a remarkable speed — around 1,000 words per minute — with zero errors, even on unfamiliar topics.

>> **Visual creations:** Describe any image you envision using plain English, and Copilot Designer will bring it to life, regardless of your artistic abilities.

>> **Easy videos and slideshows:** Craft videos and slideshows without needing advanced video-editing skills.

>> **Professional-grade social media content:** Quickly produce polished posts and videos for platforms such as Facebook, Instagram, and YouTube.

>> **Natural language commands:** Get instant answers and boss around AI using your voice and everyday language.

>> **Quality-of-life enhancements:** Honestly, I'm not exactly sure what that means, since I never thought of the quality of my own life as being related to computers or Windows. But apparently it has to do with improvements in battery usage, seamless phone connectivity, and enhanced teleconferencing via Teams.

 You can open Copilot in Windows any time by clicking its icon on the taskbar (and shown in the margin). Copilot appears, as shown in Figure 1-2. In Chapter 3, I explain how to get Copilot to answer your questions and do a lot of your typing. For now, if you want to put Copilot back into hiding, click X (close) in the top-right corner of Copilot's window.

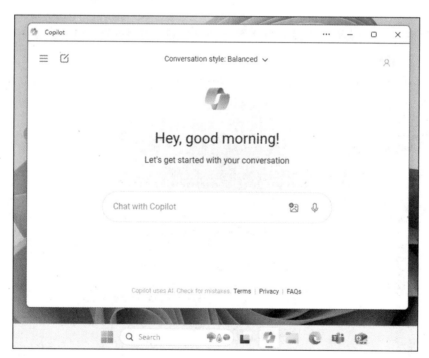

FIGURE 1-2: Copilot icon and open pane.

What's Missing from Windows 11 2024 Update?

If you upgraded from the original Windows 11, released in 2021, virtually nothing is missing in the 2024 update. If you instead upgraded from Windows 8 or 10, you'll find that the following features are missing:

>> **Timeline:** Windows 10 kept track of the apps and files you worked with for the past 30 days. A click of the Timeline button let you see them all, letting you quickly and easily jump back to, say, an unfinished file from last week. Windows 11 removes the feature and offers no replacement.

>> **Movable taskbar:** The Windows taskbar normally lives along the screen's bottom edge, but previous Windows versions let you move that taskbar to any edge you wanted. With Windows 11, the taskbar remains affixed to the bottom of your desktop, with no option to move it.

>> **Synced wallpaper:** In Windows 10, you could automatically sync your desktop wallpaper across multiple computers. To the dismay of computer decorators, Windows 11 killed that feature.

>> **Tablet mode:** Designed specifically for tablets with touchscreens, tablet mode quickly spaced your icons farther apart to accommodate thick fingertips. The Start screen and apps always filled the entire screen. Windows 11 dumps tablet mode because Windows 11 is automatically finger-friendly.

>> **Live tiles on the Start menu:** In Windows 10, the Start menu sometimes resembled a moving marquee, with animated tiles that changed their display. Windows 11 ditches the animated tiles in favor of a simpler menu that merely shows static icons. You also can no longer create folders on the Start menu for storing related items.

>> **Groove:** The Groove app for playing music has vanished in this version. Media Player is the preferred app for music.

>> **Internet Explorer:** Microsoft's elderly browser, Internet Explorer, disappeared from Windows 11 and has been replaced by Microsoft Edge.

>> **Cortana:** Microsoft fired its little robot that tried to help you work but mostly got in the way. You can still launch the Cortana app from the Start menu, but Cortana won't bother you otherwise.

>> **Paint 3D:** With Paint 3D, you could create three-dimensional images that rotated on the screen. Few people used it, and even fewer will notice that it's missing.

- **»** **Skype:** Microsoft paid billions for Skype, an app for making inexpensive (or free) phone calls using the internet, but then let the app languish. Skype has been replaced by Teams, an app for online collaboration and meetings. Microsoft added the chat portion of Teams in Windows 11 to compete with Zoom, which zoomed in popularity during the pandemic.

- **»** **OneNote:** Windows 10 came with free version of OneNote, an app for taking notes in a virtual school notebook. OneNote vanished from Windows 11, but compulsive note takers like me can still install it for free from the Microsoft Store.

TECHNICAL
STUFF

There never was a Windows 9 version. If you wonder why, just ask Copilot "Why did Microsoft skip a Windows 9 version?"

Can My Current PC Run Windows 11 2024 Update?

In mid-2024, the media buzzed about the AI PC, a new computer class. These PCs resemble our current Windows 10 and 11 computers but include an NPU (neural processing unit) alongside the traditional CPU (central processing unit) and GPU (graphics processing unit). Despite the impressive name, the NPU simply manages the additional processing that some aspects of AI demand, so the CPU and GPU don't have to.

An AI PC isn't necessary for running the Windows 11 2024 update or its AI features. Most computers already running Windows 10 or 11 should be able to cope with the update without issues.

TECHNICAL
STUFF

A handful of advanced AI features in Windows 11 2024 Update require an NPU. However, they're mostly related to AI Explorer, which tracks your File Explorer actions and makes them searchable using natural speech. You can do almost everything else in this book without the need for advanced hardware.

You can get detailed hardware requirements just by asking Copilot (Chapter 3) about *hardware requirements for Windows 24H2* (Microsoft's internal number for Windows 11 2024 Update). To check your current computer's specs, click the start icon and choose System ⇨ About (in Windows 10 or 11).

The Different Flavors of Windows 11

Microsoft offers several versions of Windows 11 2024 Update, but you'll probably want only one: the aptly titled Home version.

Small businesses will choose Windows 11 Pro, and large businesses will want Windows 11 Enterprise.

Here are some guidelines for choosing the version you need:

>> If you'll be using your PC at home or in your small business, pick up **Windows Home.**

>> If you need to connect to a domain through a work network — and you'll know if you're doing it — you want **Windows Pro.**

>> If you're a computer tech who works for businesses, go ahead and argue with your boss over whether you need **Windows Pro** or **Windows Enterprise.** The boss will make the decision based on whether the company is small (Windows Pro) or large (Windows Enterprise).

>> Progressive businesses can investigate **Windows 365**, a version of Windows that hosts *cloud PCs,* where every user can have a personalized version of Windows that runs on virtually any computer, even Mac computers.

Chapter **2**

Starting with the Start Menu

People use computers to enjoy their favorite apps. These apps might be for socializing online, staying informed, creating content, ordering take-out, writing code, and all kinds of other things. Opening an app usually begins with the Windows Start menu. Click the start icon or tap the Windows key on your keyboard, and the Start menu rises, offering access to all your apps. But before you can do even that, you need to turn the computer on and sign in. And when you've finished for the day, you'll need to leave the computer. You discover how to do all that in this chapter.

Being Welcomed to the World of Windows

Starting Windows is as easy as turning on your computer — Windows leaps onto the screen automatically with a flourish. But before you can begin working, Windows stops you cold: It displays what's called a *lock screen*, shown in Figure 2-1, with no entrance key dangling nearby.

FIGURE 2-1:
To move past
the lock screen,
press a key on
the keyboard or
drag up on the
screen with your
mouse or finger.

How do you unlock the lock screen? The answer depends on whether you're using a mouse, keyboard, or touchscreen:

» **Mouse:** On a desktop PC or laptop, click any mouse button or tap the trackpad.

» **Keyboard:** Press any key. Easy!

» **Touch:** Slide your finger *up* the glass. A quick flick of the finger will do.

When you're through the door, Windows wants you to *sign in*, as shown in Figure 2-2, by clicking your name and passing the security check.

When facing the Sign In screen, you have several options:

» **If you see your name or email address listed, type your password or PIN, or use a Windows Hello fingerprint reader or camera.** After verifying your identity, Windows lets you in and displays your desktop, just as you last left it. (I describe how to set up Windows Hello in Chapter 14.)

» **If you don't see your name but you have an account on the computer, look at the screen's lower-left corner.** There, Windows displays a list of all the account holders. Click your own account name to sign in.

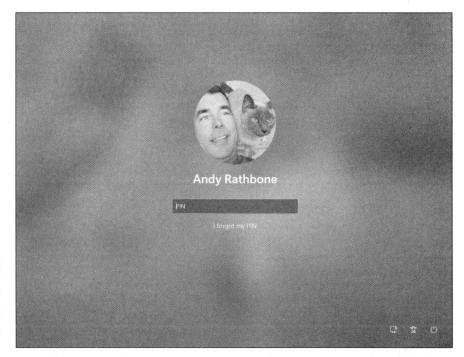

Andy Rathbone

PIN

I forgot my PIN

FIGURE 2-2:
Click your user
account name
and then type
your password or
PIN on the
next screen.

>> **If you bought a new computer and don't have a user account, you'll see a generic user account icon.** Click Sign Up, and Windows guides you through creating a Microsoft account on your computer.

>> **No account?** Find out who owns the computer and beg that person to set up an account for you.

If you need more information about user accounts, including creating new ones and managing old ones, flip ahead to Chapter 14.

Don't *want* to sign in at the Sign In screen? Two of the screen's bottom-right icons offer these other options:

>> **The figurine,** shown in Figure 2-2 and in the margin, customizes Windows for people with physical challenges with hearing, sight, or manual dexterity, all covered in Chapter 12. If you choose this icon by mistake, click or touch a different part of the screen to avoid changing any settings.

>> **The round icon,** shown in Figure 2-2 and in the margin, is the power icon. It lets you shut down or restart your PC, as well as put it to sleep — a power-saving state from which it can quickly awake. (If you've accidentally clicked the icon and shut down your PC, don't panic. Press the power button on your PC's case, and your PC returns to this screen.)

Understanding user accounts

Windows allows several people to work on the same computer, keeping everyone's work separate. To do that, it needs to know who's currently sitting in front of the keyboard. When you *sign in* — introduce yourself — by clicking your username and typing your password (refer to Figure 2-2), the Windows Start menu and desktop appear as you left them, ready for you to make your own personalized mess.

When you've finished working or feel like taking a break, sign out (explained later in this chapter, in the "Exiting Windows" section) so that someone else can use the computer. Later, when you sign back in, your files will be waiting for you.

REMEMBER

Although you may turn your work area into a mess, it's your *own* mess. When you return to the computer, your letters will be just as you saved them. Sue hasn't accidentally deleted your files or folders while playing *Words with Friends.* Bob's Start menu still contains links to his favorite ukulele websites. And no one else will be able to read your email.

Until you customize your username picture, you'll be a silhouette. To add a photo to your user account, open the Start menu and click your username, which is the text next to the icon directly above the start icon. Choose Change Account Settings from the pop-up menu. When the Settings menu's Your Info page appears, click the Open Camera button to take a quick shot with your computer's built-in camera. Still wearing your pajamas? Then choose the Browse Files button to choose a photo already stored in your Pictures folder.

Keeping your account private and secure

User accounts in Windows enable each person using the computer to personalize it to their own needs and keep their files separate and private.

Because Windows lets many people use the same computer, how do you stop Diane from reading Rob's love letters to Miley Cyrus? How can Grace keep Josh from deleting her *Star Wars* movie trailers? Using a *password* solves some of those problems, and Windows offers other security solutions, as well.

In fact, security is more important than ever in Windows because some accounts can be tied to a credit card. By typing a secret password when signing in, you enable your computer to recognize *you* and nobody else. When you protect your account, nobody can access your files. And nobody can rack up charges for computer games while you're away from home.

Also, if your computer is stolen, a strong password keeps the thieves from logging in to your account and stealing your files.

Windows allows you to sign in with either a Local account or a Microsoft account. A *Local account* enables you to access the PC but not various online services provided by Microsoft. A *Microsoft account* provides access to the computer as well as to cloud-based services provided by Microsoft so you can access files from any internet-connected compute. Chapter 14 explains user accounts in much greater detail. For now, just know that you can log into your Windows 11 PC using either type of account.

TIP

To change a password on a Microsoft account, visit your account's website at `https://account.microsoft.com`. After signing in, choose the Change Password option near your account name.

Holders of Local accounts, by contrast, can follow these steps on their own PC to set up or change the password:

1. **Click the start icon and then click the settings icon (shown in the margin), near the menu's top-left corner.**

The Settings app appears.

2. **Click the accounts icon (shown in the margin). When the Accounts pane appears, click Sign-in Options, along the pane's left edge.**

Options for signing in to your computer appear.

3. **Click the Password button (see Figure 2-3), and then click the Change button.**

You may need to type your existing password to gain entrance. Don't see the Password or Change button? Then you have a Microsoft account, and need to change your password online at `https://account.microsoft.com`.

4. **Type a password that will be easy to remember, and then write it down.**

Choose something like the name of your favorite vegetable or your dental floss brand. To beef up its security level, capitalize some letters and embed a number or two in the password, like **iH8Turnips** or **Floss2BKleen.** (Don't use one of these exact examples, though, because they've probably been added to every password cracker's arsenal by now.)

TIP

Forgotten passwords are a leading cause of hair-pulling frustration. If you still have hair, write down your passwords and keep them handy to avoid premature balding.

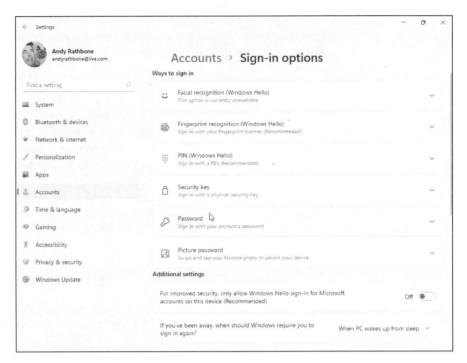

FIGURE 2-3:
Click the
Password button
and then click the
Change button
when it appears.

5. **If asked, type that same password in the Retype Password text box so Windows knows you're spelling it correctly.**

6. **In the Password Hint box, type a hint that reminds you — and only you — of your password.**

   Windows won't let you type your exact password as a hint. You have to be a bit more creative.

7. **Click the Next button and then click Finish.**

   Do you suspect you've botched something during this process? Click Cancel to return to Step 3 and either start over or exit.

After you've created the password, Windows begins asking for your password whenever you sign in. Here are some good things to know about passwords, in general:

» Passwords are case-sensitive. When typed as passwords, the words *Caviar* and *caviar* are not the same.

>> Afraid that you'll forget your password someday? Protect yourself now by writing your password down in a place that's easy to find. See Chapter 14 for ways to protect and reset passwords.

REMEMBER

>> When you change your Microsoft account password on your PC, that's for your online Microsoft account, not just the PC at which you're sitting. So you'll need to use that new password to sign in to Microsoft on every device you use but not to log into a local account on a computer or device. (I cover Microsoft accounts in this chapter's next section.)

>> Windows allows you to create a picture password in Step 4, where you drag a finger or mouse pointer over an onscreen photo in a certain sequence. Then, instead of entering a password, you redraw that sequence on the sign-in picture. (Picture passwords work much better on touchscreen tablets than desktop monitors.)

>> Another option that you may see in Step 4 is to create a PIN. A *PIN* is a code with four or more characters, like the one you punch into automated teller machines (ATMs). The disadvantage of a PIN? There's no password hint. Unlike Microsoft accounts, your PIN works only on the computer where it was created; it's not stored online, where hackers may find it.

TIP

>> Tired of constantly entering your password? Connect a Windows 11–compatible fingerprint reader or camera to your PC. (Some laptops, tablets, and keyboards have them built in.) Your computer quickly lets you in after you either scan your fingertip or gaze into your PC's camera. I describe how to sign in with Windows Hello in Chapter 14.

>> Forgotten your password *already?* When you type a password that doesn't work, Windows automatically displays your hint (if you created one), which should help remind you of your password. Careful, though — anyone can read your hint, so make sure it's something that makes sense only to you. As a last resort, insert your password reset disk, a job I cover in Chapter 14.

I explain much more about user accounts in Chapter 14.

Signing up for a Microsoft account

Whether you're signing in to Windows for the first time, trying to access some apps, or just trying to change a setting, you'll eventually see a screen similar to the one in Figure 2-4.

FIGURE 2-4:
You need a
Microsoft
account to
access many
Windows
features.

You can sign in to your computer with either a *Microsoft* account or a *Local* account. Although a Microsoft account makes Windows much easier to work with, each type of account serves different needs:

>> **Local account:** This account allows you to log onto the PC on which you created the account, but not onto other computer or online services. Local accounts work fine for people using Windows apps. However, Local account holders can't store files on OneDrive, where they're available from other PCs and devices. Local account holders also can't buy apps from the Microsoft Store app.

>> **Microsoft account:** Required to access many of Microsoft's services, a Microsoft account consists of simply an email address and a password. Microsoft account holders can store files on the internet with OneDrive, download apps from the Microsoft Store, and monitor their children's online activities. When you log in online to any PC with your Microsoft account, you find your email, browser favorites, OneDrive files, and settings automatically waiting for you.

You can sign in with a Microsoft account in one of the following two ways; I list the simplest method first:

>> **Use an existing Microsoft account.** If you already have a Microsoft account that was provided by your school or work, click Work or School Account. If already have a personal Microsoft account that you created previously, click Microsoft Account and sign in with your username and password for that account. If you don't have either of those account, follow the next step.

» **Sign up for a new Microsoft account.** If you don't have a Microsoft account, click Microsoft Account, and Microsoft takes you to a website where you can create an account. You can create an account also by browsing to `https://account.microsoft.com`. You can use any email address for a Microsoft account. You simply enter that email address, create a new password to go with it, and wham: You've created a Microsoft account.

Until you sign in with a Microsoft account, the nag screen in Figure 2-4 will haunt you whenever you try to access a Windows feature that requires a Microsoft account. (I explain how to convert a Local account into a Microsoft account in Chapter 14.)

TIP

When Windows asks for your *Windows password*, that's the password you might use to log into one PC or device. Your *Microsoft password* is the one you use to access Microsoft online services, from whatever computer or device you happen to be using at the moment.

When you first sign in to your new account, Windows may ask whether you want to find other PCs, devices, and content on your network. If you're using a home or work network, click Yes. (Doing so lets you print to network printers, for example, as well as share files with other networked computers.) If you're connecting to a *public* network, perhaps at a hotel, a coffee shop, or an airport, click No.

Figuring Out the Windows 11 Start Menu

In Windows, everything starts with the start icon and its Start menu. Whether you're ready to blow up spaceships, do your taxes, or check email, you start by clicking the start icon (shown in the margin) along the bottom edge of your screen. The Start menu leaps up with a list of your apps, shown in Figure 2-5.

In theory, you spot the name or icon for your desired app and click it; the app launches, and you're off to work. In reality, finding what you want on the Windows 11 Start menu can be a little more daunting.

In Windows 11, the Start menu contains the following four parts:

» **Search box:** This box lives across the top of the Start menu. Type what you're searching for — the name of a file or folder, or even some words contained in that file — in the Search box, and Windows will try to find it, whether it's on your PC or the internet.

Pinned   Search box

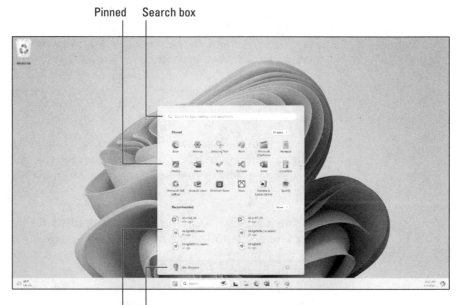

FIGURE 2-5:
The start icon is
always the
leftmost icon on
your taskbar,
which lives along
the bottom of
the screen.

Recommended   User name and power button

>> **Pinned:** Windows displays a selective list of pinned apps in this section. To see *all* your apps, click the All Apps button in the section's upper-right corner. I explain how to pin your own favorite apps here in this chapter's "Adding or removing Start menu items" section.

>> **Recommended:** Here, Windows initially lists some of its free apps to try. Over time, the Recommended section will list things you've used recently, or apps you open frequently.

>> **User account name and power icon:** The Start menu's bottom section lists your user account name. Opposite the name, the power icon awaits. Click it to put your computer to sleep, restart it, or shut it down for the day.

Click the magnifying glass or the Search box to the right of the start icon for a quick menu of your recently used apps.

TIP

Launching apps

Windows stocks the top half of your Start menu with icons for *apps*, programs for performing tasks. To see all the apps installed on your PC, click the All Apps button near the Start menu's upper-right corner. An alphabetical list of every installed app appears, ready for a mouse click or finger tap.

WHAT'S AN APP?

Microsoft Windows is an operating system, whose main purpose is to let you interact with the computer and run your favorite application programs. The term *application programs* is quite a mouthful and sounds nerdy. Being syllabically lazy by nature, we humans first shortened that to *applications,* then the word *program* became the preferred term. and now, in our modern enlightened era, the preferred term is the monosyllabic *app.*

Apps are the main reason you use a computer. There are apps for playing games, doing work, typing, goofing off online, making pictures and videos, and more. Pretty much anything you do on a computer, you do through an app. Many apps for work and play come with Windows, as I describe later in the chapter. But you can also purchase (or get for free) thousands of additional apps from the Microsoft Store and the internet.

Each name on the Start menu is a button for starting an app. Of course, Windows complicates things by offering several ways to launch an app:

>> **Mouse:** Move the mouse pointer over the icon and click the left mouse button or tap the trackpad.

>> **Keyboard:** Press the arrow keys until a box surrounds the desired icon. Then press the Enter key. (Press the Tab key to move between different sections of the Start menu.)

>> **Touchscreen:** Tap the icon with your finger.

No matter which app you've chosen, it jumps onto the screen, ready to inform you, entertain you, or if you're lucky, do both.

I explain the Start menu's built-in apps later in this chapter.

Finding something on the Start menu

You can scour the Start menu until your eagle eyes spot the app you need, and then you can pounce on it with a quick mouse click or finger tap. But when the thrill of the hunt wanes, you can use one of Windows shortcuts for finding apps within a crowded Start menu.

In particular, look for these items on the Start menu:

>> **Pinned section:** Windows stocks the Start menu's Pinned area with icons for popular apps, as well as ads for new ones. I explain how to add or remove pinned items later, in the "Adding or removing Start menu items" section.

>> **Recommended section:** When you open the Start menu, it automatically stocks the list's bottom half with your most recently installed apps or recently used documents. Click one to launch it.

>> **All Apps button:** To see an alphabetical list of *all* the apps on your PC, click the All Apps button.

TIP

There's a good chance that you'll spot your desired item on the Start menu without much digging. But when an app proves to be particularly elusive, try these tricks:

>> After opening the Start menu, keyboard owners can simply begin typing the name of their desired app. As you type, Windows lists all the apps matching what you've typed so far, eventually narrowing down the search to the runaway.

>> If the apps you see don't reflect the way you work, it's time to customize the Start menu to meet your needs. Head for the upcoming "Customizing the Start menu" section.

Viewing, closing, or returning to open apps

In the olden days, computers could run only one app at a time, and that app hogged the entire screen. To switch to another app, you had to exit the app you were using before starting the other app. Not so with modern computing. Microsoft Windows gets its name from the fact that every app you open runs in its own window, and you're not limited to running one app at a time. Regardless of whether the app is a game, a typing app, a browser for goofing off online, or something else, it exists inside a window, and that window will contain the main components shown in Figure 2-6.

Once the app is up and running inside a window, the taskbar at the bottom of the screen displays a *taskbar icon* for the app. The icon matches the app icon, which appears in the upper-left corner of the app window. A line below the taskbar icon indicates that the app is open. Click that taskbar icon to hide and restore the app window as convenient.

Taskbar icons appear along the bottom of the screen even when no apps are open. That's because you can pin buttons for frequently used apps to the taskbar so that they're always available.

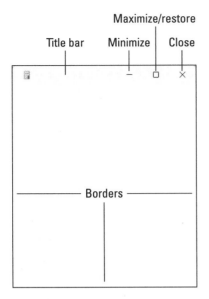

Maximize/restore

Title bar   Minimize   Close

Borders

FIGURE 2-6:
Every open
window has these
components.

You can control the size and position of an app on your screen by using the doo-dads pointed out in Figure 2-6 as follows:

>> To enlarge a window to fill the screen, click its maximize/restore icon or double-click its title bar.

>> To return a full-screen window to its previous size, click the maximize/restore icon again (which now shows two squares), or double-click its title bar again.

>> To move a window to a new location, drag its title bar.

To drag with a mouse or trackpad, make sure the tip of the mouse pointer is touching the title bar of the window you want to move. Then hold down the left mouse button or press down on your trackpad (or screen, if you're using a touchscreen) while moving the mouse.

>> To resize a window, put the mouse pointer to an edge (border) or a corner until the mouse pointer turns to a two-headed arrow. Then drag in the direction you want to size the window. Release the mouse button when the window is the size you want.

>> Optionally, you can drag a window to the top of the screen, or press Windows+Z to see suggested layouts. Then click a layout sample.

>> To get an app out of the way without closing it, minimize its window by clicking its minimize icon. Or just click the app's taskbar icon.

>> To bring a minimized window back to the desktop, click its taskbar icon.

TIP

- **»** To minimize all open windows, press Windows+M. Use the taskbar to bring them back individually as needed.

- **»** To see all currently open apps, click the task view icon shown in the margin and just to the right of the Search box in the taskbar, or hold down the Windows key and press the Tab key.

- **»** To see a jump list of other actions for a taskbar icon, right-click the app's taskbar icon.

- **»** To close an app you're no longer using, click its close icon (X). Use the Start menu to restart it in the future.

If everything I just told you seems overwhelming, don't worry. Chapter 4 covers it all in more depth. Or just ask Copilot, "How do I move and size open windows in Windows 11?"

Getting to know your free apps

The Windows Start menu comes stocked with several free apps, each represented by an icon. Clicking All Apps button on the Start menu lists them all.

Here are some of the most popular free Windows 11 apps, which you now own, ready to be launched with a click or a tap:

- **»** **Accessibility:** This app offers a set of tools for overcoming challenges posed by sensory or physical impairments.

- **»** **Calculator:** With a toggle among standard, scientific, and a variety of converter modes, this app will please grade schoolers, math majors, chefs, and physicists.

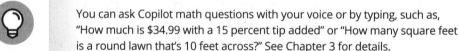

TIP

  You can ask Copilot math questions with your voice or by typing, such as, "How much is $34.99 with a 15 percent tip added" or "How many square feet is a round lawn that's 10 feet across?" See Chapter 3 for details.

- **»** **Camera:** Covered in Chapter 17, the Camera app lets you snap photos with the camera built into most laptops, tablets, and some desktop PCs.

- **»** **Clock:** Not just your typical wall timepiece, Clock offers timers, a stopwatch, alarms, and a world clock. You can stick it on your desktop so it never gets lost.

- **»** **File Explorer:** This app helps you manage your files by moving, copying, deleting, or searching for them. I cover all these tasks in Chapter 5.

- >> **Get Help:** Click here to begin your journey through Microsoft's official technical support channels, all covered in Chapter 22.

- >> **Get Started:** This app walks you through Windows 11 and also introduces Microsoft's paid services, such as OneDrive.

- >> **Media Player:** Covered in Chapter 18, this app plays music and videos.

- >> **Microsoft Clipchamp:** A terrific app for easily creating professional-grade slideshows and videos.

- >> **Microsoft Edge:** A web browser (like Google Chrome or Safari). I cover Microsoft Edge and web browsing in Chapter 9.

- >> **Microsoft Store:** Covered in Chapter 6, the Microsoft Store is the only way to add more apps on your Start menu. The Microsoft Store also carries some apps you can install on your Windows desktop and Android phone, as described in Chapter 3.

- >> **Microsoft Teams:** Seems like just about everyone uses this app for online meetings these days.

- >> **Microsoft To Do:** A super handy to-do list for day-to-day reminders.

- >> **Notepad:** A basic app for writing text, as well as a place to put all the smart stuff AI types for you, to save in a file or print on paper.

- >> **Outlook:** An optional app for sending and receiving email and managing contacts.

- >> **OneDrive:** The Microsoft internet cubbyhole where you can store your files. By storing them online in OneDrive, covered in Chapter 5, you can access them from nearly any internet-connected computer, phone (both Android and Apple), or tablet.

- >> **Paint:** A handy app for saving, cropping, resizing, editing, and removing the background from photos and pictures. It also has some built-in AI that lets you draw a picture just by describing it in words — no artistic talent or skill required.

- >> **Photos:** Covered in Chapter 17, the Photos app displays photos and videos stored throughout your computer.

- >> **Settings:** In the Windows 11 Settings app, you can tailor almost anything to your tastes and work needs. (I cover the Settings app in Chapter 12.)

- >> **Snipping Tool:** The go-to app for taking screenshots and recording the action on your screen for videos.

- >> **Solitaire & Casual Games:** The quintessential collection of computer timewasters, and a lot of ads for buying more of them.

- >> **Sound Recorder:** If your computer has a microphone, here is what you can record your voice or any other sound worthy of recording.

- **» Sticky Notes:** Like the yellow sticky notes we all rely on, only these are on your computer screen.

- **» Weather:** This weather station forecasts a week's worth of weather in your area, but only if you grant it permission to access your location information. (Unless your computer has a GPS — Global Positioning System — the app narrows your location by closest major city rather than street address.)

- **» Windows Security:** Click this to access the built-in antivirus app. Flip ahead to Chapter 11 for more details.

- **» Windows Tools:** A treasure trove of uber-nerdy techie tools for tinkering with Windows.

Adding or removing Start menu items

Microsoft dumped a random assortment of icons on the Windows 11 Start menu's *Pinned* area — the rows of icons that fill the top half of the Start menu. The resulting jumble consumes lots of real estate, includes advertisements, and is probably not tailored to your interests or work habits. This section shows how you can fix that shortcoming by removing, or *unpinning*, the extra icons from the Pinned area of the Start menu, and adding, or *pinning*, the ones you use most often.

Removing icons from the Start menu is easy, so we begin there. To remove an unwanted or unused icons from the Start menu, right-click it and choose Unpin from Start from the pop-up menu. The unloved icon vanishes without fuss, freeing up some prime real estate. This doesn't *uninstall* (remove) the app, mind you; unpinned items can still be found in the Start menu's All Apps area.

On a touchscreen, hold down your finger on the unwanted icon. When the pop-up menu appears, choose Unpin from Start to remove the icon.

After removing the unwanted items, spend some time *adding* items to the Start menu, making them as easy to reach as a pencil holder on an office desk. To add apps to the Start menu, follow these steps:

1. **Click the start icon to display the Start menu.**

   The Start menu presents an alphabetical list of all your installed apps, even those you've just unpinned from the Start menu.

2. **Click the All Apps button.**

3. **Right-click the icon for the app that you want to appear in the Pinned area of the Start menu, and then choose Pin to Start.**

Each selected app icon appears as a new pinned Start menu icon. Repeat until you've added all the items you want.

The Start menu icons aren't limited to apps. From the desktop or even in File Manager, right-click any oft-used folder, file, or other item you want added to the Start menu and then choose Pin to Start from the pop-up menu. When you're through, the Pinned area of your Start menu will have grown considerably with all your newly added destinations.

TIP

Can't find a newly installed app? Chances are it's hiding in the Start menu's All Apps area. If you want it visible in the Pinned area near the Start menu's top edge, you need to pin it there yourself.

Now that you've stuffed your Start menu's Pinned area with your favorite desktop destinations, head to the next section to finish organizing.

Customizing the Start menu

The Start menu contains mostly *icons* —pictures that represent apps on your PC. The icons consume a lot of space, but they're not organized. How can you find your favorite stuff?

Give yourself a fighting chance by organizing your Start menu. The following steps begin with a small dose of organization: removing unwanted apps and adding your favorite apps to the Start menu's Pinned area. These steps won't uninstall any apps; they all remain safely on your PC. However, the Start menu's Pinned area will be full of apps that match your *own* interests.

But no matter how organized you want to be, follow these steps to begin turning that haphazard Start menu into your own organized list:

1. **Remove icons you don't need from the Pinned area.**

   Spot an icon you don't need? Right-click it and choose Unpin from Start from the pop-up menu. Repeat until you've removed all the icons you don't use. (On a touchscreen, hold down your finger on an unwanted app and then tap Unpin from Start from the pop-up menu.)

REMEMBER

   Choosing Unpin from Start doesn't *uninstall* the app; removing the icon merely removes that item's icon from the Start menu's Pinned area. In fact, if you accidentally remove the icon for a favorite app, you can easily put it back in Step 3.

2. **In the Start menu's Pinned area, move related icons next to each other.**

As an example, you might want to keep your people-oriented apps — Mail and Calendar — next to each other and on the top row, as shown in Figure 2-7. To move an icon to a new location, move the mouse pointer over the icon, and then hold down the left mouse button as you drag the icon to the desired spot. As you drag the icon, other icons automatically move out of the way to make room for the newcomer.

FIGURE 2-7:
Your Start menu may be easier to work with when the Pinned area shows only your favorite icons.

TIP

On a trackpad, tap with two fingers to right-click. On a touchscreen, hold down your finger on the icon; when the pop-up menu appears, drag the icon to its new position.

When you've dragged an icon to the desired spot, lift your finger or release the mouse button to set the icon into its new place.

3. **Add icons for the apps, folders, and files you need.**

I explain how to add icons for apps, folders, and files earlier, in the "Adding or removing Start menu items" section.

TIP

Newly added items appear at the bottom of the Start menu's Pinned area. To move an icon quickly to the top, right-click it and choose Move to Top from the pop-up menu.

PERSONALIZING THE START MENU

The Windows 11 Settings app offers additional ways to tweak the Start menu. To find the Start menu settings, click the start icon, choose the settings icon, and click Personalization in the left column. When the Personalization page appears, click Start in the pane on the right. You'll see the following options for the layout of your Start menu:

- **More Pins:** Choose this layout if you have a lot of pinned apps, and don't care for Microsoft's recommendations.

- **Default:** The Start menu you get automatically, shown earlier in this chapter.

- **More Recommendations:** If you don't have many pinned apps, and prefer recommendations, choose this layout.

Below the Layout options are some settings you can turn on or off:

- **Show Recently Added Apps:** With this option on, newly installed apps will automatically appear in the Start menu's Pinned area — a boon for those who hate to organize.

- **Show Most Used Apps:** Another perk for the lazy, leave this option on, and the Start menu's Pinned area will be automatically stocked with your most-used apps.

- **Show Recommended Files in Start, Recent Files in File Explorer, and Items in Jump Lists:** That's a lot of tech talk. Just leave this option turned on if you want easy access to recently opened documents.

- **Show Account-Related Notifications:** Turning this option off keeps alerts related to your Microsoft account to a minimum, displaying only alerts that need attention soon.

- **Folders:** The Start menu's bottom edge normally lists your account name, a lot of empty space, and a power icon. Click here to fill that empty space with links to your favorite folders and other things. You can add or remove links to Settings, File Explorer, Documents, Downloads, and other commonly used folders.

There's no right or wrong way to set these. Stick with the default settings or experiment to see which settings work for you. The settings are on-and-off toggles, so you can always return and flip the toggle again if a change doesn't meet your needs.

Exiting Windows

Ah! Sometimes the most pleasant thing you'll do with Windows is to stop using it. Technically, you can't really exit Windows because it is on if your computer is on. Instead, you decide how you want to leave your computer unattended.

Temporarily leaving your computer

If you'll be away for a day or less and aren't worried about someone else using your computer, the easiest thing to do is just walk away. I do this all the time, leaving my computers on and online, 24/7, for months or years. For a laptop, I'll close the cover. If you'll be away for a while and have a charger handy, you might as well plug in the charger while you're at it.

Many workplaces frown on just walking away from your computer because doing so gives other people easy access to your computer. To thwart such activity, you can lock the screen. You can press Windows+L, or you can click the start icon, click the power icon near the bottom right of the Start menu, and choose Lock. Doing so brings up the lock screen. Any would-be thieves who don't know your username and password will be locked out. But you can log in and everything will be just as you left it.

If you're gone for more than five minutes, Windows will automatically shut off your screen to conserve power. If you're gone for more than 15 minutes, Windows will put your computer to sleep (not in the veterinary sense of the term) to conserve more energy. But when you return, just jiggle the mouse or tap a keyboard key to bring Windows back to life.

TIP

You can change the settings for conserving power by using System settings. See Chapter 12.

If you share a computer with others and will be gone for longer than a bathroom break, you can sign out of your account. Click the start icon, click your account picture or name on the Start menu, click the three dots in the upper-right corner of the pop-up menu that appears, and then choose Sign Out to log out of the computer, as shown in Figure 2-8.

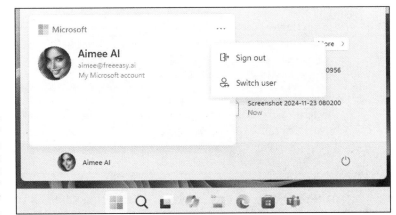

FIGURE 2-8:
Click your
account picture
or name near the
Start menu's
lower-left corner
to display
these options.

Leaving your computer for the day

When you're finished computing for the day — or perhaps you just want to shut down the laptop while on the subway or that flight to Rome — Windows offers three ways to handle the situation.

 Click the start icon and then click the power icon (shown in the margin). The Power icon's pop-up menu offers four settings, as shown in Figure 2-9.

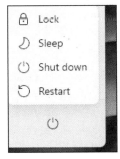

FIGURE 2-9:
The power icon's
pop-up menu
options include
Lock, Sleep,
Shut Down,
and Restart.

Here's the rundown on your options:

>> **Lock:** Displays the lock screen, which prevents other people from accessing your desktop.

>> **Sleep:** Puts the computer into a sleep state immediately, to conserve power. Later, when you return to your PC, Windows quickly presents everything — even your unsaved work — as if you'd never left. And if the power goes out, your PC will still wake up with everything saved, but it will take a few more seconds.

» **Shut Down:** Turns off your computer completely. If you're using a desktop computer and need to relocate it, you should choose this option before unplugging the computer. It's also a good choice if you need to leave your laptop stored somewhere without charging it.

» **Restart:** *Reboots* your computer, which is something you may have to do to activate certain kinds of updates. It's also a last-resort cure-all for any problems that cause your computer to go berserk or *hang* (become woefully unresponsive).

So that's the day-to-day stuff that goes with using a computer at home or at work. Next, mosey over to Chapter 3, where you get into all the stuff you can do while you're sitting at the computer.

Chapter **3**

The Traditional Desktop and Modern AI

W hen you sign in to your computer, the Windows desktop warmly welcomes you. The largest part of the screen is the desktop. Across the bottom of the screen is the taskbar, a useful tool that serves many purposes. In this chapter, I take you on a whirlwind tour of the desktop and taskbar.

The real star of the show in Windows 11 2024 Update is AI (artificial intelligence), now freely available right in Windows. In this chapter, you learn how to get instant answers from Copilot and also see how to make Copilot do your writing and typing.

Jazzing up Your Desktop

Exactly how your desktop looks depends on several factors. If no apps are open, it will probably look something like Figure 3-1. However, your desktop may display a different picture and may have more icons.

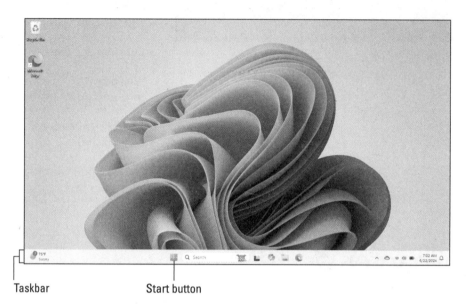

FIGURE 3-1:
The Windows 11
desktop, with the
taskbar across
the bottom.

Taskbar   Start button

Personalizing Windows is all about making it your own by decorating it with pictures, adding colors, and rearranging items on the screen. All the settings for personalizing Windows reside in an area aptly named Personalization. To get to the Personalization area, you can do one of the following:

» Click the start icon, and then click Settings. In the Settings window, click Personalization. (This is the method I use throughout the chapter.)

» Right-click the desktop and then click Personalize.

» If your keyboard has a Windows key (usually near the lower-left corner), press Windows+I. Then click Personalization in the left column.

As shown in Figure 3-2, you have many choices for personalizing Windows. I describe the settings you'll probably want to use first when setting up the screen your way.

Choosing a dark or light theme

A *theme* consists mainly of pictures and colors and determines the overall look and feel of your computer screen. Choosing between a light or dark theme for your screen is a great way to get started making Windows your own. On the Personalization page, click Themes to display the screen shown in Figure 3-3.

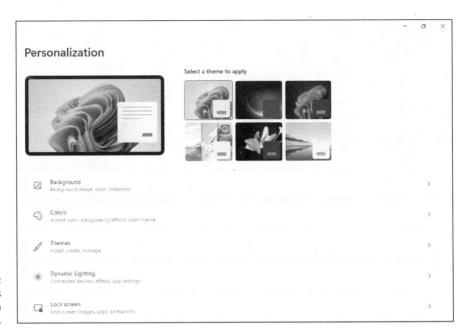

FIGURE 3-2:
Windows
Personalization
screen.

FIGURE 3-3:
The Themes
page in
Personalization.

The name of your current theme, if any, appears to the far right of the Current Theme section; the current theme in the figure is Windows (light). The thumbnails (little pictures) display suggested themes. To check out a theme, simply click the thumbnail. The theme is applied immediately, so you can see how it looks. Feel free to try them all. Don't worry, you're not making a lifelong commitment. You can change your selected theme any time you want.

TIP

If you have a visual impairment that requires high contrast, click Contrast Themes under Related Settings, and choose from one of the available themes presented on your screen.

To see more themes, click Browse Themes and choose from others in the Microsoft Store. Note that not all themes are free.

When you find a theme you like, close the Personalization page by clicking X (close) near the top-right corner. You'll get an even better view at how things look with the Settings page out of the way. If you're not thrilled with the look, just choose a different theme.

Beautifying with accent colors

Any theme you apply to your desktop will have accent colors that are applied to the taskbar, Start menu, and (optionally) open window title bars and borders. To change your accent colors, go to the Personalization page and click Colors. The screen shown in Figure 3-4 appears.

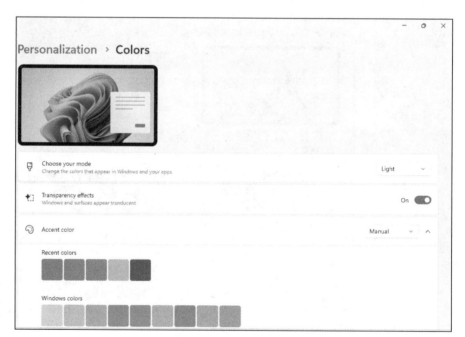

FIGURE 3-4:
Color choices for your Windows theme.

Regardless of what theme you've chosen, you can set a general mode for your desktop and open app windows. Click the button to the right in the Choose Your Mode section, and then choose Light or Dark for the default Windows mode (background), and default app mode (foreground).

For an ultra-modern look on your screen, you can turn on transparency effects. Doing so makes the background colors of window title bars and some other elements translucent, so you can partially see anything behind the item. But if you prefer everything opaque with no see-through, turn off the Transparency Effects option.

To choose an accent color, first set the Accent Color drop-down to Manual. Then click a color under Recent Colors or Windows Colors. Or for even more colors, scroll down to Custom Colors, click View Colors, and choose a color and shade from the color picker.

TECHNICAL
STUFF

If you're familiar with color RGB numbers or hex codes for colors, instead of using the color picker you can choose a color by typing its RGB number or six-digit hex code preceded with a hash (#) character.

Finally, scroll down a bit more and choose where you want the accent colors to appear. If you're using a Light color mode, the Show Accent Color on Start and Taskbar option will be disabled (dimmed), so you can't change that. But if you're using a Dark or Custom mode, you can turn the mode off if you don't want the accent color to apply to the Start menu and the taskbar. To apply accent colors to window title bars and borders, set the Show Accent Color on Title Bars and Window Borders on.

To apply what you've chosen so far and see how it all looks, close the Personalization page by clicking X in its upper-right corner. If all looks good, you're done. But if you're horrified by the garish monster you've accidentally created, just go back to the top of this section and take another shot. No harm in trying things out!

If you suspect that your own taste in colors is dubious, set the Accent Color drop-down menu to Automatic. Windows will then choose colors based on your theme.

Wallpapering your desktop

Your Windows desktop can display a picture, a wallpaper pattern, a slide show, or a simple solid color. If you're bored with the current background, choose something different. Once again, you use Personalization settings for this task. So click the start icon and choose Settings and then Personalization, or just right-click the desktop and choose Personalize. Then click Background to reveal the new set of options shown in Figure 3-5.

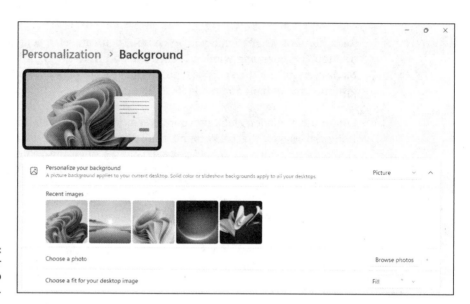

FIGURE 3-5:
Design your
desktop
background.

Your first step is to choose the type of background from the drop-down menu in the Personalize Your Background section:

**TECHNICAL
STUFF**

>> **Picture:** Choose a single picture for your background by clicking a photo under Recent Images. Or if you want to use your own photo, click Browse Photos, navigate to and select the photo you want to use, and then click Choose Picture.

If you're not familiar with navigating through folders and the like, don't fret. I explain how all that works in Chapter 5.

>> **Solid Color:** Choose a single color for your background. For example, some people prefer a solid black background behind all their open windows. As with the accent color, you can also click Custom Colors and use the color picker, RGB numbers, or hex codes to define your preferred color.

>> **Slideshow:** Choose a folder containing the pictures you want your desktop to display, and then set a time interval and other options for the slideshow.

>> **Windows Spotlight:** Let Windows automatically choose the background from Microsoft's selection of scenic photos. The image will change periodically, so you won't get bored by any one image.

You can change your mind at any time by returning to the Personalization page. There are lots of other ways to personalize Windows too, as I explain in Chapter 12. For now, this should be enough to get you comfortable with your screen.

Bellying Up to the Taskbar

Believe it or not, your best ally in using your computer amicably, rather than through strife and struggle, is the taskbar, that bar that's always stretched across the bottom of your computer screen. Turning it into your trusty sidekick now will save you from many of computing's most frustrating moments.

The taskbar is divided into three main sections, pointed out in Figure 3-6. You explore its best features in this section.

FIGURE 3-6:
The Windows
11 taskbar.

Personalizing your taskbar

First things first: If your taskbar doesn't look like the one in Figure 3-6, or your taskbar tends to slide out of view at times, use the Personalization features to take control of things:

1. **Click the start icon, Settings, and then Personalization.**

2. **Scroll down, if necessary, and click Taskbar.**

    You see options for choosing what's visible on your taskbar.

    As an alternative to going through the Start menu, you can right-click an empty spot on the taskbar and choose Taskbar Settings.

TIP

3. **Make sure Search is set to Search Box, and that Task View and Widgets are both on.**

    If you change your mind about those choices, don't worry. This chapter will also show you how to remove any unwanted doodads.

4. **Click Taskbar Behaviors to expand that section.**

    If your taskbar tends to slide out of view and you don't want it to do that, click Taskbar Behaviors and deselect Automatically Hide the Taskbar.

5. **Click X (close) in the upper-right corner to close the Personalization page.**

Your taskbar should now resemble the one in Figure 3-6 (unless you intentionally chose to hide something) and should always remain visible on the screen.

Fidgeting with widgets

On the left side of the taskbar is the widgets area. You'll probably see weather information or stock market news there. Click the left side of the taskbar, on the weather widget, to display a larger Widgets window, as shown in Figure 3-7.

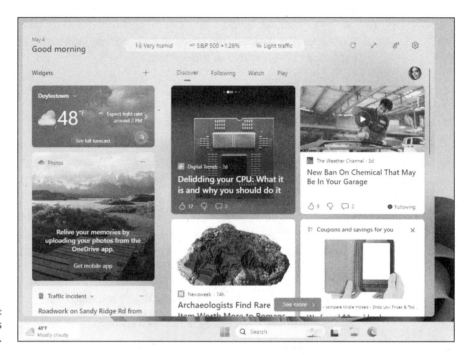

FIGURE 3-7:
The Widgets pane.

The left side of the Widgets pane shows *pinned widget,* which are always visible when you open the Widgets pane. You can pin widgets to get current information about weather, news, sports, stock prices, traffic, and more.

To the right of the pinned widgets are news stories, ads, coupons, and such — mostly just advertisements, really, designed to look like news.

The left side of that pane is where your pinned widgets live. Click the + sign next to the Widgets heading to see a list of widgets you can explore. When you click a widget's name, a preview appears to the right. If you like that widget, click Pin below it to add it to the left side of your Widgets pane. Feel free to pin as many widgets as you like. Then click the X near the upper-right corner of the Pin Widgets window to close it.

Each widget in your Widgets pane has three dots near its upper-right corner. Click those three dots for a widget to see your choices. Most pinned widgets give you at least these two options:

>> **Customize Widget:** If the widget has additional options, click Customize to tailor the widget.

>> **Unpin widget:** Click this option to remove the widget from the left column where it's currently displayed.

If you change your mind about an unpinned widget and want it back, click + again and re-pin the widget.

If you prefer to have nothing at the left side of your taskbar, right-click an empty spot on the taskbar and choose Taskbar Settings. Under Taskbar items, set the Widgets slider off.

Where the Action Is: The Center Section of the Taskbar

The area of the taskbar that you'll use most frequently is the center area, where the start icon, Search box, and taskbar icons reside. As you know, clicking the start icon opens the Start menu, the place for opening any app on your computer.

You use the Search box to search for apps, settings, recently opened documents — just about anything. As you type in the Search box, options that resemble what you've typed so far appear. When you see what you're looking for, just click it.

The Search box also keeps track of things you've done lately. Simply click on or near the magnifying glass to display a list of recently used apps. When you see what you want, just click it. (And again, ignore the plethora of ads that appear to the right of the list.)

Pinning (and unpinning) taskbar icons

When it comes to convenience, the taskbar icon to the right of the Search box are your number-one pal. Any time you open an app, a taskbar icon representing the app appears on the taskbar. If it's an app you use often, you can pin its icon to the taskbar, so that the app is always easy to find. Just right-click the app's icon on the Start menu and choose Pin to Taskbar, as shown in Figure 3-8.

A pinned taskbar icon remains on the taskbar after you close the corresponding app. To re-open the app, just click its taskbar icon. You don't have to go through the Start menu.

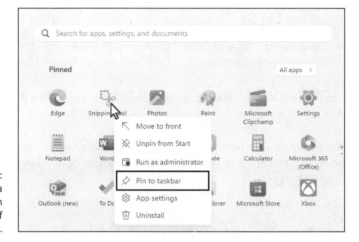

FIGURE 3-8:
Right-click a
Start menu icon
for a list of
useful tasks.

TIP

Right-clicking an open app's taskbar icon and then choosing Close Window is a handy alternative to clicking the app window's X icon (close).

You can drag pinned taskbar icons left and right to reorganize them. To move a taskbar icon, position the mouse pointer on the icon, and hold down the mouse button (or press down on the trackpad) while moving the icon left or right. When the taskbar icon is where you want it, release the mouse pointer or lift your finger from the trackpad.

If you lose interest in an app, you can remove its pinned taskbar icon to make room for others. Right-click the app's pinned taskbar icon and choose Unpin from Taskbar. You can still start the app from the Start menu. And when you later open that app, its taskbar icon will remain visible until you close the app.

Jumping for joy with jump lists

Things that you create with computers, such as written documents, pictures, and videos, are collectively known as *documents* or *docs* (as opposed to apps, which are the programs used to create the documents). If you right-click an app's taskbar icon, a *jump list* of recently opened documents appears. Click a listed document to open it and the app at the same time.

You can even pin documents to a jump list. This feature is handy when you want ready access to a document that has been bumped off the list by more recent documents. To pin a document to a jump list, put the mouse pointer on the document's filename in the jump list and then click the pin icon that appears to the right of the name.

TIP

If the document you want to pin isn't in the jump list, open the document. Doing so puts the document in the jump list so you'll then be able to pin it.

You can also right-click a document in the jump list to display a list of options, as shown in Figure 3-9. Depending on the app, you can open, edit, or print the document. You can remove it from the jump list or open the folder in which the document is contained. If you're a content creator who is constantly juggling documents, jump lists will be a boon to your productivity.

FIGURE 3-9:
Right-click a document in a jump list to see more options.

Making apps appear and disappear like magic

When things get too cluttered on your screen, you can quickly minimize an app window by clicking its taskbar icon. The window disappears from the screen so you can see everything that was behind it. When you're ready to bring the app window back, just click its taskbar icon again. The window pops up, right where you left it. Couldn't be easier.

If you want to make all open windows disappear and reappear at once, do the following:

1. **Right-click the taskbar and choose Settings.**

2. **Scroll down, if necessary, and click Taskbar Behaviors to expand that section.**

3. **Select the option that reads Select the Far Corner of the Taskbar to Show the Desktop.**

4. **Close the Personalization window.**

To test your new powers, make sure you have some open windows on your screen. Then click the far-right edge of the taskbar a few times to watch everything appear and disappear with a simple mouse click. Feel free to say "Abracadabra" when impressing your friends with this.

TIP

You can minimize all open windows also by pressing Windows+M.

Moving the start icon to the left

For decades, the Windows start icon lived on the left side of the taskbar. If you find yourself still heading there to click it, you're not alone. To go back to the original arrangement, right-click the taskbar and choose Taskbar Settings. Click Taskbar Behaviors to expand that section, and change Taskbar Alignment to Left. If Widgets is turned on in Taskbar Settings, the weather widget will change to a taskbar icon to the right of the Task View icon or Search box.

Clicking the Taskbar's Sensitive Areas

Like a crafty card player, the taskbar comes with a few tips and tricks. On the right side of the taskbar is the *system tray*, containing tools that let you reach inside your computer and tinker with things such as the speaker volume, Wi-Fi connection, and wireless Bluetooth devices. If you click one of the icons just to the left of the date and time, a Quick Settings window pops up, as shown in Figure 3-10.

If the arrow is pointing up at the left side of the tray (as it is in Figure 3-10), clicking it will reveal still more icons.

FIGURE 3-10:
Click an icon to
the left of the
date and time for
an expanded
view of system
tray icons.

Adjusting screen brightness and sound volume

Two things you might find yourself wanting to adjust often are the screen bright-ness and the volume. You can do so right from the system tray. Click on whatever icon appears just to the left of time and date to reveal the Quick Settings window (refer to Figure 3-10). To adjust the screen brightness, move the slider next to the sun icon. To change the volume, use the slider next to the speaker icon.

Preparing the system tray

The icons you see in your system tray depend on your computer. Here is the low-down on some likely suspects:

 >> **Bluetooth:** If you have a wireless Bluetooth device connected to your computer, such as earbuds or a wireless mouse, click this icon to see what's what.

 >> **Safely remove hardware:** If you have a USB drive or similar storage device plugged into a USB port, click this icon and choose the Eject or Safely Remove option before you yank the device from its port. Any files you may have left opened will be safely tucked away on the drive before removal.

 >> **Wired network:** Found mostly in work environments, this icon appears when your computer is connected to the internet or other PCs through a wired network. Not connected? The icon turns into a circle with a line through it.

>> **Wireless network:** This icon appears when your PC has Wi-Fi capability to connect to a network and the internet wirelessly. (You can see this icon between the cloud and speaker icons in Figure 3-10.) If you're already connected, the more waves you see on the icon, the stronger your wireless signal. You can also click here to join any available Wi-Fi network. (I explain how to connect to wireless networks in Chapter 9.)

>> **Volume:** Click or tap the tiny speaker icon to adjust your PC's volume, using the speaker slider that appears above the icon.

>> **Task Manager:** Coveted by computer technicians, this program can end misbehaving programs, monitor background tasks, track your PC's performance, and do other stuff of techie dreams. To take a peek, right-click an empty spot on the taskbar and choose Task Manager.

>> **Windows Update:** When you spot this icon, Windows Update wants you to restart your computer so it can finish installing an update. Before starting an update, close all open apps and files, and plan to be unable to use the computer for up to an hour.

>> **OneDrive:** Clicking this icon gives you access to your personal OneDrive storage space in the cloud.

>> **Power, outlet:** Your laptop or tablet is plugged into an electrical outlet and is charging its battery.

>> **Power, battery:** Your laptop or tablet is running on batteries only. Rest your mouse pointer over the icon to see how much power remains.

You can choose which notification icons should always be visible by right-clicking a blank portion of the taskbar and choosing Taskbar Settings. When the Taskbar Settings page opens, click Other System Tray Icons to see options like those in Figure 3-11. Choose which icons should appear in your system tray by clicking their on/off toggles. If you choose more icons than can fit, click ∧ on the left side of the system tray to see them all.

Viewing notifications

Clicking the date and time area in the system tray provides quick access to a calendar and a list of notifications, as shown in Figure 3-12. You can also click the bell icon to display notifications sent to your computer via the internet. If you don't see the calendar, click ∧ to the right of the current date to slide the calendar into view.

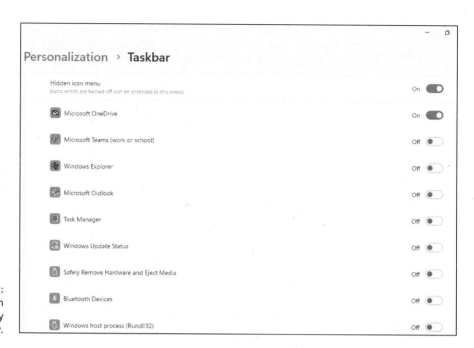

FIGURE 3-11:
Choose which
system tray
icons to display.

Mouse pointer
on notification

FIGURE 3-12:
Click the time and
date area to see
the Notifications
pane and
the calendar.

Notifications may list information about your latest emails as well as the time of an upcoming appointment, news headlines, virus scan results, and other informational tidbits. A notification slides into view in the lower-right corner of the screen, hoping your eyes will dart to and absorb it. Then it disappears, piling up in the Notifications pane.

You can deal with notifications in a variety of ways:

>> **Ignore the notifications.** You needn't look at the Notifications pane. The notifications will simply pile up unread, with no damage done. Most notifications are more informational than urgent.

>> **Clear the notifications.** If you grow weary of seeing a pile of notifications, click the Clear All button in the Notifications pane's upper-right corner. Whoosh, gone!

>> **Close a notification.** You can close a single notification by clicking X in its upper-right corner.

>> **Stop seeing a notification.** Move the pointer over the annoying message. Click the three dots that appear in the message's upper-right corner and then select Turn Off All Notifications.

>> **Decide which apps can bug you with notifications.** Click the three dots in any notification's upper-right corner. When the drop-down menu appears, click Go to Notification Settings. Use the toggle switches to choose which apps can and can't disturb you with their latest news.

Silencing notifications

In our age of information overload, getting your computer to shut up for a while can be a refuge. To stop notifications from requesting your attention, you can silence them indefinitely or set a timer to turn notifications back on automatically after a preset time.

 To silence notifications without a timer, click the date and time icon or bell icon and then click the tiny bell with *zz* near the top-right corner of the panel that slides open. Doing so turns on do not disturb mode. When you're ready to face new incoming information, click the bell icon in the system tray again.

 If you want to fine-tune your notifications, click Notification Settings after turning on do not disturb mode. Or click the start icon and choose Settings, then System, and then Notifications. You'll see many more options, most of which are self-explanatory.

TIP

As an alternative to permanently silencing notifications, you can set up a focus session (yes, that's its name) in which you turn on do not disturb mode for a limited time. To get started, click the date and time icon or the bell icon and look to the very bottom of the panel that appears. You'll see a time, such as 30 min. That's how long the focus session will last. Use – and + next to the time to increase or decrease that time duration (sadly, infinity is not an option).

Next, to start the session, click the word Focus or the triangle next to it. A disturbing timer will pop onto the screen, counting down the minutes remaining for your focus session. The bell next to the date and time will again show zz to indicate that you're in do not disturb mode. When the time is up, equally disturbing sounds and on-screen messages will let you know your focus session is over, and the bell will lose its sleepy zz symbol.

Stumbling into the Age of AI

Late in November 2022, a little-known company named OpenAI stunned the world with ChatGPT, an artificial intelligence app that could chat with you (like chatting on a smartphone) in plain English. Within five days, over a million people had subscribed to the service — the fastest technology adoption rate in history. (Before that, Instagram held the record by achieving 1 million subscribers in about two and a half months.)

Microsoft was so impressed by ChatGPT that they tossed OpenAI a cool $13 billion (yes, a million dollars, 13,000 times over). Lucky for you, all that AI wonderfulness is now built into Microsoft's Windows 11 2024 Update. You can use ChatGPT for free, whenever you like, right from the comfort of your own computer.

Meeting your AI Copilot

Most of the AI capabilities of Windows 11 2024 update are contained in Copilot. An apt name, since AI is artificial intelligence, not real intelligence. AI can't make conscious, intelligent decisions about anything. Nor can it predict the future, solve your personal problems, or tell you how to get rich quick. Even with AI onboard, you're still the pilot of your own life and creative endeavors. Copilot is like a know-it-all trusty sidekick who can answer your factual questions, write your text, improve your writing, summarize long documents, draw your pictures, and even assemble your videos.

Most of the time Copilot minds its own business, awaiting your commands via its icon in the taskbar. Click that icon and the Copilot window opens. That window's appearance will vary, depending on how you've used Copilot in the past, but it should resemble Figure 3-13.

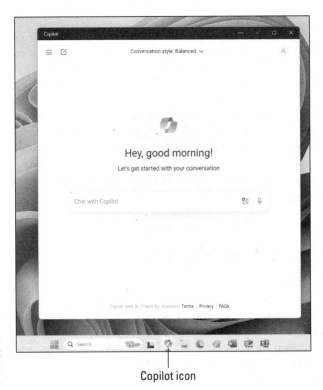

FIGURE 3-13:
Copilot chat
interface open on
the desktop.

Copilot icon

TIP

Some modern keyboards have a Copilot key that you can tap to open and close Copilot.

Asking AI questions

Perhaps the most common use of AI is to simply ask questions. In the chat interface (refer to Figure 3-13), just type your question as if you were asking a person. No special commands or magic incantations to puzzle over. Regular old English is fine.

Your questions should be of a factual nature — the kind of stuff you search for online. Personal questions, predictions about the future, and such generally don't work. Remember, Copilot is offering artificial intelligence, not genius, clairvoyance, therapy, or a close personal relationship.

TIP

You can include a picture, screenshot, or document file with your question, which is handy if your question is about something you see in a photo or on your screen, or you want Copilot to explain or summarize a lengthy article. I explain how that works in Chapter 16.

When you've finished typing your question, press Enter or click the circled up-pointing arrow to the right of what you just typed. Be patient. Copilot might need a few seconds to formulate its answer, which will appear below your question. If you mistyped your original question or don't like what Copilot is telling you, you can cancel your question by clicking the circled square below the text that Copilot is typing.

After Copilot answers your question, you may see numbered buttons with website names and perhaps thumbnail images of web pages. You can click any one of those buttons or thumbnails to get more information about your initial question.

To see more options, touch the mouse pointer on any text that Copilot wrote. The following icons appear, as shown in Figure 3-14:

» **Copy icon:** Click to copy the answer. Then you can paste it anyplace you can type, including in apps such as Notepad, Microsoft Word, and Google Docs.

» **Share icon:** Click to share the answer with others via the web, email, or various social media sites.

» **Speaker icon:** Click if you'd like Copilot to read its answer aloud. Make sure your computer's speakers are not muted.

» **More icon:** Click the three dots to see even more options. If Copilot did well, click the thumbs up icon. Otherwise, click the thumbs down icon. Giving feedback helps Copilot improve its answers. Click the Export option if you want to save Copilot's answers to a Microsoft Word file, a PDF, or a plain text file.

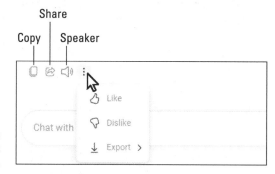

FIGURE 3-14:
Copilot
answer icons.

TIP

Some Copilot output, especially computer code, song lyrics, and other lengthy content, appears in its own shaded box in the Copilot output. To copy just the content in the shaded box, click the copy icon in the upper-right corner of that box.

Asking questions is a great way to get instant answers to all your tech questions without pestering cranky tech nerds. But keep in mind that you can ask Copilot *anything*, not just tech stuff. If you can't think of anything offhand, try some of the following questions. (Note that you don't have to include the question mark.)

> What's a good recipe for strawberry shortcake?
>
> When and where is next year's Superbowl?
>
> If I drive from L.A. to Dallas to Miami and then to Bangor Maine, how many miles is that?
>
> How much is $147.25 with 6.5 percent sales tax added?
>
> How do I move my Windows 11 start icon to the left side?
>
> What is dead internet theory?
>
> How much wood would a woodchuck chuck if a woodchuck could chuck wood?

Okay, that last one was a trick question. But go ahead and submit it anyway. Copilot will be happy to take a crack at it.

If Copilot's first answer to your question isn't what you expected, you can continue the conversation by typing in the next text box. The process is similar to talking to another person. Sometimes you need to converse back-and-forth for a while, to zero in on the best answer to your question.

ISN'T AI EVIL?

There's no shortage of "The end is near" folks ready to instill AI dread into anyone who will listen. For AI, the preferred doomsday scenarios are

- AI will take all the jobs
- AI will destroy humanity

You needn't worry about AI taking any jobs. AI is lazy and oblivious and has no goals, desires, or ambition (like many humans). Like any other app, Copilot is basically an electronic circuit that sits around doing absolutely nothing until some person uses it. However, it is fair to say that *people who know how to use AI* to maximize their own creativity and productivity will have a big advantage in many job markets. If you're building a career and future, learning to use AI now is your best investment.

The second threat is a proverbial doozie. The end-of-humanity scenario has some roots in a book titled *Superintelligence* by philosopher Nick Bostrom. (Yes, there are still people in the world who hold the job title of philosopher.) In that book, Bostrom ponders the many unintended consequences of creating a machine that's a thousand times smarter than any human, and how that machine might view us dopey humans. For now, you can put that fear on the back burner. Chances of people creating such a machine during your lifetime are slim to none.

Making AI do your writing

With Copilot, you're not limited to asking questions. You can ask it to write anything for you: homework assignments, emails, social media posts, blog posts, video scripts, poems, book outlines, song lyrics, research papers with citations, essays, book summaries, newsletter articles, limericks, haikus, sermons — anything you've been tasked to write yourself.

When using Copilot as a tool for your creative writing, tailor its response to your intended audience by choosing a conversation style. To start a new topic with your chosen conversation style, click the new chat icon, labeled in Figure 3-15. Then choose your conversation style from the drop-down menu at the top-center of the window.

FIGURE 3-15:
Choose a
conversation
style for your
Copilot output.

Your conversation styles choices follow:

>> **Creative:** If you're writing to entertain or be light and friendly, choosing More Creative will get you casual and light-hearted responses.

>> **Balanced:** If you're writing for business or fact-based informational content, More Balanced will give you answers that are neither too lighthearted nor overlay pedantic.

>> **Precise:** For scientific, academic, or technical information, More Precise is your best bet for getting just the facts with minimal frills.

After you've chosen your conversation style, tell Copilot exactly what you want it to type. Don't expect Copilot to write an entire book or a long paper. It's limited to short documents a few pages in length. (See Chapter 16 for details.) If you can't think of something for Copilot to type, try some of these prompts:

Write a group email reminding co-workers not to leave a mess in the community kitchen.

Write a Shakespearian sonnet about pizza and bananas.

Write an outline for a research paper about microplastics.

Write lyrics for a song lamenting the heartbreak of flatulence.

Write a list of 12 ways Copilot can help you.

Write a limerick about leprechauns and daffodils.

If school, your job, or your social life require *any* form of writing, just ask Copilot to type your first draft. It's not really cheating. You're just doing normal research the way it will be done by everyone from now on. Treat whatever Copilot writes for you as food for thought. You can copy and paste Copilot's output into Notepad, Microsoft Word, Google Docs, or any other typing app, and then work with it to make it your own.

Communicating with AI using your voice

If your typing skills aren't great and you talk better than you type, try communicating with Copilot with your voice. Make sure your microphone isn't muted, and then click the use microphone icon (labeled in Figure 3-15) in Copilot's Ask Me Anything box.

COPILOT OUTSIDE WINDOWS 11

It's nice to have Copilot at your beck and call in Windows 11 2024 update. Clicking Copilot's icon, or tapping the Copilot key (if you have one) on your keyboard will get you started immediately. However, Copilot is always available on your Mac, phone, and other devices too.

If you use Microsoft Edge as your browser, clicking the Copilot icon near the upper-right corner of the browser window opens Copilot inside Microsoft Edge. If you're using another browser, browse to www.bing.com/chat for more AI fun with Copilot.

Copilot isn't the only free AI in town. Last time I checked, the following sites were still free or had a free tier: ChatGPT (https://chatgpt.com), Claude (https://claude.ai), Gemini (https://gemini.google.com). For even more sites, search the web for *free ai*.

When "I'm Listening" replaces "Ask Me Anything", speak your question or command. You can then press Enter, click the right-facing arrowhead, or just keep quiet for a few seconds, and Copilot will get to work serving up whatever you need. When Copilot is finished, you can click the speaker icon under its output to have the answer read back to you by voice.

You can continue the voice conversation for as long as the microphone icon is highlighted or pulsating. To make AI stop listening, click the microphone icon. When you want to resume voice control, click the microphone icon again.

You can move Copilot's window by dragging its title bar. Size the window by dragging any corner or edge. Use the minimize and maximize/restore icons in the usual manner, and close the app by clicking its close icon (X) in the upper-right corner. (See Chapter 2 if you're not familiar with these icons.)

Clicking the menu icon near the top-left corner opens a list of topics related to your previous questions, as shown in Figure 3-16. To remove an item, touch the mouse pointer to the item, and then click the three dots that appear and choose Delete. Clicking the three dots also gives you the option to rename, share, or export Copilot's answer to a separate file.

To read Copilot's answer to a previous question, just click the topic name in the left column. If the answer is partially blocked by the menu, click X (close) in the top-right corner of the menu bar to close the pane.

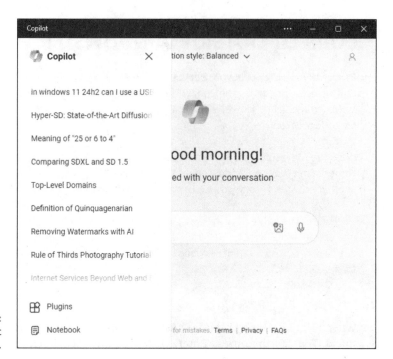

FIGURE 3-16:
Your recent
activity in Copilot.

What if I lose Copilot?

If you don't see a Copilot icon on your taskbar, try these steps to get it back:

1. **Click the start icon, and then click All Apps.**
2. **Scroll down to the letter C, right-click Copilot, choose More, and then click Pin to Taskbar.**

If you can't find Copilot in the Start menu, don't worry. You can download it from the Microsoft Store. In the Search box next to the Start menu, type **store**. Then click Microsoft Store. In the Microsoft Store app that opens, type **Copilot** in the search box at the top of the window. Then download Microsoft Copilot when you see it.

That should be enough to get you started with Copilot. There's plenty more fun to be had with Copilot, as you see throughout the rest of the book. Welcome to the Age of AI!

Chapter **4**

Taking Control of Your Desktop

The Windows Start menu contains icons and an occasional button. It's easy to see what you're poking at with a finger or mouse. The Windows desktop, by contrast, includes lots of movable windows, each with miniscule, monochrome buttons, tiny lettering, unlabeled buttons, and pencil-thin borders. The windows come with way too many parts, some with confusing names that you're expected to remember. To give you a hand, this chapter provides a lesson in basic Windows desktop anatomy, as well as tools and techniques to control the size and position of every open window on your desktop.

Dissecting a Typical Desktop Window

Figure 4-1 places a typical window on the slab, with all its parts labeled. Those doodads offer hidden gems that let you turn a confusing mess of piled-up windows into something usable. You visited these tools briefly in Chapter 2. I show them again here so you can refer to this figure when reading the sections that follow, where you'll finally take control of your open apps and desktop.

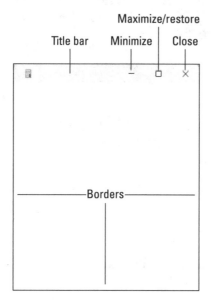

Maximize/restore

Title bar   Minimize   Close

————Borders————

FIGURE 4-1:
Here's how
ever-precise
computer nerds
address the
different parts
of a window.

Mastering the drag and drop

Before I get to the specifics of wrangling open desktop windows, however, you need to know some more terminology and skills. Although the phrase *drag and drop* sounds as if it's straight out of a Mafia guidebook, it's a nonviolent mouse trick used throughout Windows. Dragging and dropping allows you to move and resize app windows on your desktop.

To drag with a mouse, put the mouse pointer on the area or item you want to drag and then hold down the left mouse button as you move the mouse. With a track-pad, put the mouse pointer on the thing you want to drag. Press down, and keep pressing down as you move the mouse pointer. Lift your finger when the item you're dragging is in place.

TIP

Helpful tip department: Did you start dragging something and realize midstream that you're dragging the wrong item? Don't let go of the mouse button or stop pressing — instead, press Esc to cancel the action. Whew!

Using the scroll bar to move inside a window

The scroll bar, which resembles a cutaway of an elevator shaft (see Figure 4-2), rests along the edge of all overstuffed windows. By *overstuffed,* I mean any window that isn't large enough to display all its contents. If a window doesn't have a scroll bar, that means there is no place to scroll to.

FIGURE 4-2:
Horizontal
and vertical
scroll bars.

Scroll bars

Inside the shaft of a scroll bar, an elevator — technically, the *scroll box* — rides along as you move through the window's contents. In fact, by glancing at the box's position in the scroll bar, you can tell whether you're viewing items in the window's beginning, middle, or end.

By clicking in various places on the scroll bar, you can quickly move to different parts of the window:

>> To scroll slowly, click the arrow at the top or bottom of the scroll bar.

>> Click inside the scroll bar in the direction you want to view. On a *vertical* scroll bar, for example, click above the scroll box to move your view up one page. Similarly, click below the scroll box to move your view down a page.

>> To move around in a hurry, drag the scroll box inside the scroll bar. As you drag, the window's contents race past. When you see the spot you want, release the mouse button to stay at that viewing position.

>> If you're using a trackpad, use two fingers on the trackpad. Up and down to scroll vertically. Left and right to scroll horizontally.

>> Are you using a mouse that has a trackpad or a wheel embedded in the poor critter's back? Just track your finger along the trackpad or spin the mouse wheel in the direction you want to scroll. The elevator moves inside the scroll bar, shifting your view accordingly. To scroll sideways, hold down the Shift key while scrolling.

If you're typing, you can move up and down through text one line at a time by pressing the up and down arrow keys, respectively. To scroll larger distances without reaching for the mouse, use these keys to scroll about:

>> **Scroll in screenful-sized chunks:** Press PgUp (page up) to scroll up, and press PgDn (page down) to scroll down.

>> **Jump to the end:** Press Ctrl+End.

>> **Jump to the top:** Press Ctrl+Home.

>> **Scroll to the start of a line of text:** Click the line of text and press the Home key.

>> **Scroll to the end of a line of text:** Click the text and press the End key.

Scrolling inside a section

Inside any open window, you might come across an area that has its own scrolling capabilities, usually for scrolling left and right. Some windows may have their own scroll bar. But more commonly, when you rest the mouse pointer on the item, you'll see arrow on one side or both sides, as shown in Figure 4-3. Just click the arrow that points in the direction you want to scroll.

Scroll buttons

FIGURE 4-3:
Scroll arrows may
appear when you
touch the mouse
pointer
to an item.

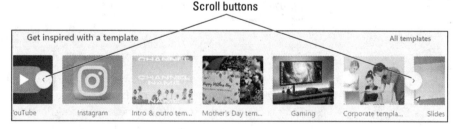

Zooming in, zooming out

If you already have your app window open to full screen but you still have to scroll to see everything, you may be able to just change the magnification of the item inside the window so you see everything without the need to scroll. This capability applies to many but not all apps. Figure 4-4 shows an example where only a portion of a photo is displayed. The scroll bars at the edge of the window tell you that there's more to be seen.

Scroll bars when zoomed in

No scroll bars

FIGURE 4-4:
Scroll bars
indicate that you
aren't seeing
everything.

Rather than scrolling around to see what's missing from your view of the photo, you can change the photo's magnification so that the entire photo fits on the screen.

Many apps have a View menu with options for changing the magnification (or *zoom level*). If you're using a mouse that has a wheel, try the following:

>> **Zoom in:** Hold down the Ctrl key while scrolling up.

>> **Zoom out:** Hold down the Ctrl key while scrolling down.

If you're using a trackpad, do this:

>> **Zoom in:** Place two fingers close together on the trackpad, and then spread them.

>> **Zoom out:** Place two fingers spread apart on the trackpad, and then bring your fingers together.

For more trackpad terminology, ask Copilot to "Explain Windows 11 trackpad gestures" (the keyword there is "gestures").

If you're typing and don't feel like reaching for the mouse, use the following shortcut keys to zoom in and out:

>> **Zoom in:** Hold down the Ctrl key and tap the + key repeatedly.

>> **Zoom out:** Hold down the Ctrl key and tap the – (hyphen) key repeatedly.

>> **Zoom to 100 percent:** Hold down the Ctrl key and tap the number zero (not the letter O) to zoom to 100 percent or the default magnification for your app.

Keep in mind that not all apps offer zooming. If you try to zoom and nothing works, don't assume that something is broken or that you're not doing it correctly.

Sizing a Window to Your Liking

Just about any open window can be as large as your entire desktop, invisibly small, or any size in between. Resize a window to whatever works for you. This section explains how.

Making a window fill the entire desktop

Sooner or later, you'll grow tired of all this multiwindow mumbo-jumbo. Why can't you just make one window fill the screen? Well, you can.

To make any desktop window grow as large as possible, click its maximize/restore icon (when it looks like one large square, as shown in the margin). Or double-click an empty spot on the title bar. The window leaps up to fill the entire desktop, covering up all the other windows.

To reduce the pumped-up window back to its former size, click its maximize/restore icon (which now shows two smaller squares, as shown in the margin) or double-click the window's title bar again. The window quickly shrinks to its former size, and you can see the things that it covered.

Making a window bigger or smaller

Like big lazy dogs, windows tend to flop on top of one another. To space your windows more evenly, you can resize them by dragging and dropping their edges or corners. It works like this:

1. **Put the tip of the mouse pointer on the border or a corner of the window you want to resize, until the mouse pointer turns to a two-headed arrow, as shown in Figure 4-5.**

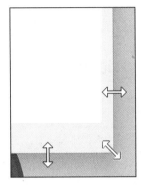

FIGURE 4-5:
Two-headed
mouse pointer
arrows, for
sizing a window.

2. **Drag in any direction indicated by the arrows, keeping your finger pressed down on the mouse button or trackpad.**

3. **When you're happy with the window's new size, release your finger on the mouse button or the trackpad.**

   The window settles down into its new size.

Sizing a window to half (or a quarter) of the screen size

If you think that dragging window borders and corners is tedious, you won't get any argument from me. Here are some tips to make quick work of sizing a window:

>> To make a window half the screen width, drag its title bar left or right until the mouse pointer hits the very edge of the screen. When you see a blurry area that's half the screen width, release the mouse button.

>> To make a window one fourth the screen size, drag the window's title bar until the mouse pointer touches a corner of the screen. When you see a blurry area, release the mouse button.

When the window is sized and in place, any other open windows will automatically be rearranged so as not to share the same screen space. To return those windows to their previous size and position, click inside the window you just positioned. You can also click one of the other windows to size it to the remaining available screen space.

TIP

If you want to size and position multiple windows in one fell swoop, see the section "Snapping multiple open windows into shape," later in this chapter.

Hiding a window without losing your place

If you want to get a window out of your way entirely, without losing your place in that window, make sure you minimize the window rather than close it. Minimizing is easy:

>> To minimize (hide) a window, click the window's minimize icon. The window disappears, but its taskbar icon remains in the taskbar.

>> To bring the minimized window back to its former glory, just click its taskbar icon. Easy Parcheesi.

TIP

Too busy to reach for the mouse? Maximize the current window by pressing Windows+up arrow. Press Windows+down arrow to return the window to its previous size. To minimize an open window, press Alt + spacebar +N.

Maneuvering Windows Around the Desktop

A terrible dealer at the poker table, Windows tosses windows around the desktop in a seemingly random way. Programs cover each other or sometimes dangle off the desktop. The following sections show you how to gather all your windows into a neat pile, placing your favorite window on the top of the stack. Or if you prefer, you can lay them all down like a poker hand. As an added bonus, you can make them automatically open to any size you want.

Moving a window to the top of the pile

The open window that's on top of the pile and not covered by any other open windows is the *active window*, and it receives any keystrokes you or your cat happen to type. If you try typing something into an open app window and nothing happens, that app probably isn't in the active window.

You can make any open window the active window in several ways:

TIP

>> Click the window. Windows immediately brings the window to the top of the pile.

>> On the taskbar, click the icon for the window you want. If the window disappears, it was already the active window, so you just minimized it. No biggie. Just click the same taskbar icon again to make that app's window the active window.

>> Hold down the Alt key while tapping the Tab key. With each tap of the Tab key, a small window pops up, displaying a thumbnail of each open window on your desktop. When your press of the Tab key highlights your favorite window, release the Alt key and your window leaps to the forefront.

>> Click the task view icon (shown in the margin) or press Windows+Tab to place thumbnails on the screen. Click the desired miniature window, and it rises to the top, ready for action. I cover the task view icon in more detail later in this chapter.

Moving a window from here to there

Sometimes you want to move a window to a different place on the desktop. Perhaps part of the window hangs off the edge, and you want it centered. Or maybe you want one window closer to another.

You can move a window by dragging and dropping its title bar. As you drag the window's title bar, the window follows across the screen. When you're happy with the window's position, drop the window in place.

TECHNICAL
STUFF

Here's a historical tidbit: Title bars used to contain the title of the app or program, hence the name *title bar*. Now, many apps leave out the title. Nevertheless, you can still tug these apps around by dragging their title bar, just as before.

Snapping multiple open windows into place

The aptly named snap layouts feature is a great way to get multiple open windows sized and positioned in one quick step. There are three ways to access these layouts. But if you have a main window you want to position specifically, try this:

1. **Drag the title bar of your selected window all the way to the top center of the screen, so that the mouse pointer touches the screen edge and a panel of layout thumbnails drops down, as shown in Figure 4-6. Don't release the mouse button yet.**

FIGURE 4-6:
Snap layouts let you size and position open windows the easy way.

2. **Keeping the mouse button held down, drag downward a little, until the mouse pointer is inside the panel with the thumbnails.**

3. **Drag the mouse pointer left and right, touching each box.**

    A blank window appears indicating where the window will be if you release the mouse button.

4. **When you find a good size and position for the window you're dragging, leave the mouse pointer on that square and release the mouse button.**

The window you're dragging snaps into place on your screen. Any other open windows fill the remaining empty boxes in the layout.

Another way to arrange multiple windows is to click anywhere on the window you want to reposition. Then touch (but don't click) that window's maximize icon. The snap layouts appear as shown in Figure 4-7. Click the square into which you want to place the current window. The current window takes on the size and shape of the box in the layout.

Lastly, you can press Windows+Z to display the snap layouts. Click a layout in which to size and position your open windows.

Mastering task view

Task view displays thumbnails of all currently open windows, as shown in Figure 4-8. To bring an open window to the forefront, simply click its thumbnail. To open task view, simply click the task view icon on the taskbar.

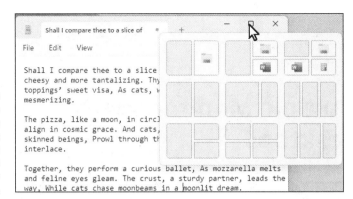

FIGURE 4-7:
You can also
hover the mouse
pointer over a
window's
maximize icon to
display the
snap layouts.

Task view icon

FIGURE 4-8:
Task view
displays open
apps as
thumbnails.

You can also use task view from the keyboard, rather than by clicking the task view icon. Here's how:

>> Press Windows+Tab to display the app thumbnails. Use the left and right arrow keys to move the highlight to any available thumbnail. Press Enter to select a thumbnail.

>> Press Alt+Tab. This method retains compatibility with older Windows versions, where you can keep holding down the Alt key and tapping the Tab key to move through the thumbnails. When your desired app's thumbnail is highlighted, release the Tab and Alt keys.

Task view also provides access to another hidden gem: virtual desktops, which I tell you all about next.

Faking Multiple Monitors with Virtual Desktops

Virtual claustrophobia is a term I just made up to describe the feeling you get when your computer screen feels too cramped and you desperately need elbow room. One cure is to add a second monitor, so you have two screens instead of one. But multiple monitors aren't necessarily an ideal solution for everyone.

A free and easy alternative to multiple monitors is virtual desktops. Each *virtual desktop* is a screen of its own, just like when you have two or more monitors. However, with virtual desktops, you can see only one screen at a time. Still, it's not a bad deal, because you can display thumbnails of all your virtual desktops and switch from one to another with ease.

Creating and using virtual desktops in Windows 11 is easy:

1. Click the task view icon (to the right of the taskbar's Search box).

A bar slides up showing thumbnails for the current desktops, plus a blank thumbnail labeled New Desktop.

2. To create a virtual desktop, click + inside New Desktop.

A second desktop, named Desktop 2 appears as on Figure 4-9.

FIGURE 4-9: Virtual desktops named Desktop 1 and Desktop 2.

If you started with a blank screen, the new desktop looks exactly like the first one. So, what's the big deal? Well, each virtual desktop can have its own open windows. So rather than sizing app windows down into tiny squares on one desktop, you can have each of those apps open in larger windows across multiple desktops.

To switch from one desktop to another, click the task view icon, and then click whichever desktop you want. That desktop fills your screen. Now you can open any apps you like on the desktop.

For example, open Copilot on Desktop 2. Then click the task view icon and click Desktop 1. You now have an entire desktop on which you can pile up more open windows. You can open Notepad, Paint, a graphics editing app, or another app on Desktop 1.

Finally, generate Copilot content on Desktop 2. Copy that content, and paste it into the text or graphics editor on Desktop 1. That way, you don't need to have all three apps squeezed onto a single screen.

You can switch between virtual desktops pressing Windows+Ctrl+left arrow or Windows+Ctrl+right arrow. To move an open window from one virtual desktop to another, open task view by clicking the task view icon or by pressing Windows+Tab. Then drag the app's thumbnail to the thumbnail of the desktop where you want to place that app.

Chapter **5**

Storing and Organizing Files

f you do any kind of writing on your computer, or download pictures and videos from your phone or camera, or download files from the internet, you're familiar with files. Every written document, photo, song, and video you save is saved as a *document file*, also called simply a *file* or *doc.*

The average hard disk in a computer has enough space to store many thousands of files. As your file collection grows, however, managing your files becomes more challenging and it's easy to lose track of them. To help, Windows includes an app named File Explorer. As its name implies, File Explorer lets you rummage through (explore) your files. But more importantly, File Explorer lets you create, organize, rename, and delete files. You get chummy with File Explorer in this chapter. But before we go there, I want to clarify some major tech terms.

Understanding Drives, Folders, and Files

Working with files on computers starts with understanding the terms *drive*, *folder*, and *file*. Think of a drive as a drawer in a filing cabinet, filled with manila file folders, as shown in Figure 5-1. Each of those folders contains documents.

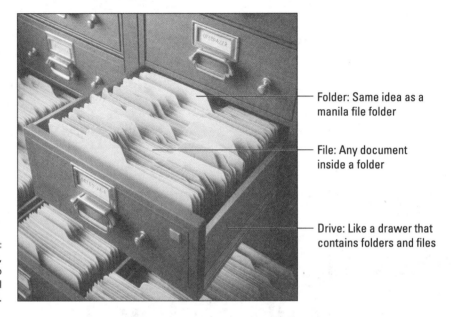

Folder: Same idea as a manila file folder

File: Any document inside a folder

Drive: Like a drawer that contains folders and files

FIGURE 5-1:
How drive, folder, and file relate to a traditional filing cabinet.

Here's how the filing cabinet analogy relates to a computer:

» A **drive** is a physical device like a hard drive inside your computer or a USB drive that you can hold in your hand and plug into a computer. The drive can store files, and those files can be organized into folders.

» A **folder** in Windows is like a manila file folder in a filing cabinet drawer. Each folder groups files that belong together. You can create folders and organize your files however you like.

» A **file** is like a single document inside a manila folder. But with computers, a single file might contain a written document, a photo, a song, a video, a spreadsheet — basically anything you can create on or download to a computer.

In a filing cabinet, you use your hands to create folders, organize files, and so forth. In Windows, you use File Explorer for these tasks.

Exploring Your Computer

File Explorer is so commonly used, it has its own pinned taskbar icon. That icon looks like a manila file folder, as shown in Figure 5-2, so it should be easy to recognize.

FIGURE 5-2:
Open File
Explorer by using
its taskbar icon.

File Explorer

Here are three ways you can open File Explorer:

>> Click the File Explorer icon on the taskbar.

>> Press Windows+E on your keyboard.

>> Click the start icon and search for File Explorer on the Start menu (though I don't know why you'd want to go through these extra steps).

When you open File Explorer, a screen similar to Figure 5-3 appears, though you will have different drives, folders, and files.

Here's a quick rundown of what's shown on the screen:

>> **Title bar:** As in other open windows, the title bar is at the top of File Explorer. You can move the File Explorer window by dragging its title bar, and size the window by dragging any corner or edge. These basic techniques are described in Chapter 4.

>> **Address bar:** The address bar shows the location of the file you're viewing and helps you navigate drives and folders.

>> **Toolbar:** The toolbar contains icons for tools to move, copy, rename, and delete files. Officially it's called the command bar (yawn).

>> **Navigation pane:** In this pane, you tell File Explorer what you want to explore.

>> **Content pane:** The content pane contains icons for files and folders in whatever drive or folder you happen to be exploring. The content pane is also called file list view (even though the icons aren't always displayed in a list).

Address bar   Title bar   Toolbar

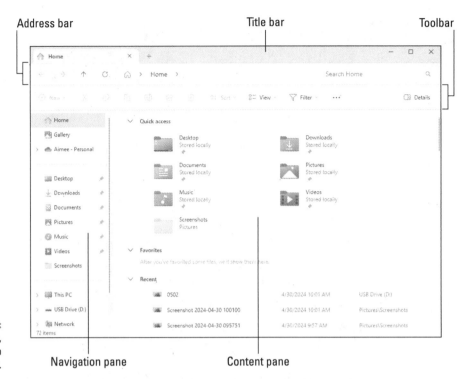

FIGURE 5-3:
File Explorer,
open on
the desktop.

Navigation pane   Content pane

Unlike most apps, File Explorer doesn't display its name and icon in its title bar. Instead, it shows the name of the location you're currently viewing. In Figure 5-3, for example, I selected Home in the navigation pane, so the title bar displays Home (and the content pane shows the contents of Home).

Figuring out navigation pane icons

The left side of File Explorer's window divides icons into three groups: special, folders, and drives, as shown in Figure 5-4. Knowing what these represent can make dealing with File Explorer a lot easier.

Let's start from the bottom. The drives section provides access to drives that are available to you:

» **This PC:** If you expand This PC, you'll probably see Local Disk (C:), which is the hard drive in your computer. Windows names the drive C: for simple identification.

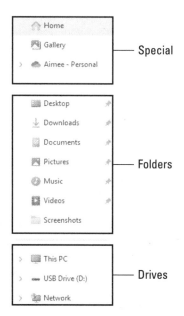

Special

Folders

Drives

FIGURE 5-4:
Sections in File
Explorer's
navigation pane.

>> **USB Drive:** If you have a flash drive or similar device plugged into your computer, an icon for that drive also appears. In Figure 5-4, I have a USB drive plugged into my laptop. In the navigation pane, it's called USB Drive and Windows has assigned it the name D:.

>> **Network:** If your computer is part of an office network or a home network, the Network icon lets you poke around the drives and folders on other computers within your network.

Next up is the folders section. This is where you can access folders on your hard drive, including built-in folders that Windows created for you. The name of each folder suggests what it contains: Pictures, Music, Videos, and so forth. Click a folder name, and the content pane on the right changes to display the contents of the folder you just clicked.

NEW

The special section at the top contains icons that aren't related to a folder or drive. Rather, they're specialized alternatives to simplify navigation as follows:

>> **Home:** This icon is sort of a convenience store for files and folders. It provides quick access to frequently used folders, any items you marked as favorites, and a list of files you've opened recently.

>> **Gallery:** This icon provides quick access to recent photos regardless of where they happen to be stored.

>> **Cloud:** The cloud icon, which might also display your username, represents OneDrive, an optional cloud drive. I assume your head is spinning with terminology, so I describe OneDrive later in the chapter.

Understanding this terminology makes it a lot easier to find, organize, and manage your files. Now put on your hard hat and get ready to go spelunking among your computer's drives, folders, and files.

Exploring your hard drive

Most of the files you've saved in the past are probably on your hard drive. That's true for files you download from the internet or a connected device. To explore files and folders on your hard drive, you don't need to connect anything to your computer — just open File Explorer. The folder names you see in the folders section, such as Desktop, Downloads, and Documents, are all on your hard drive.

To open any folder, click its icon in the navigation pane. The folders and files in that folder leap to the contents pane. For example, if you opened your Pictures folder, all the picture files stored in that folder would be visible. In Figure 5-5, the Pictures folder contains lots of pictures as well as a subfolder named Screenshots.

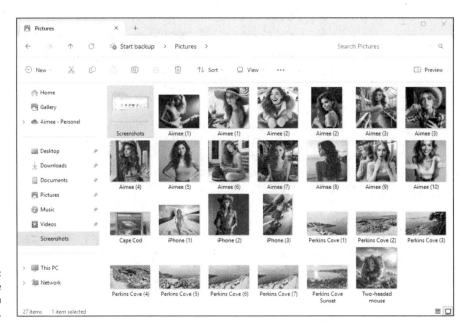

FIGURE 5-5:
Viewing the contents of a Pictures folder.

TIP

In Figure 5-5, you can tell that Screenshots is a folder and not a file because its icon looks like a manila file folder.

Seeing files on another drive

Your hard drive is inside your computer, so just opening File Explorer is enough to view its contents. To see what files are on an external device, such as a USB drive or a memory card, or in a phone or camera, connect the device to the computer. For most external storage devices, you just plug the device into a USB port on the computer.

When you first plug in a device, something may or may not happen on the screen, depending on what you plugged in. If the screen displays options, typically you want to choose the option to open the drive and view its contents. Regardless of what happens immediately after you plug in the device, an icon for it should appear in the drives section at the bottom of the navigation pane. For example, in Figure 5-6, I connected a video camera (Insta360 D:) and a USB drive (E:).

Drive letters are assigned to devices when you connect them. so don't expect them to always be the same. For example, when I had only my USB drive connected, it was automatically given the drive letter D:. Later, when I removed that drive, plugged in a camera first and the USB drive second. the camera was given D: and the USB drive became E:.

FIGURE 5-6:
A camera and a
USB drive are
connected to
this computer.

WHEN EXTERNAL DEVICES DRIVE YOU BONKERS

Dealing with external devices can be aggravating, especially when you plug in the device and it starts doing something you hadn't intended. That business of a device doing something on its own is called *autoplay* (yes, even *that* has a name). The good news is, you're not stuck with it.

You can change what happens when you plug in a specific device via Settings in Windows. Click the start icon, choose Settings, click Bluetooth & Devices. If you don't want autoplay for anything you plug into your computer, turn off the Use AutoPlay for All Media and Devices switch. Or leave that option on and choose autoplay defaults for individual devices, such as removable drives and memory cards. For any device type listed on your screen, click the drop-down menu and choose what you want to have happen whenever you plug in that type of device. If you set AutoPlay to Ask Me Every Time, you'll always be given a choice of what you want to do right after you plug in the device.

Once you connect a device to the computer and its name appears in File Explorer's navigation pane, you can manage its folders and files exactly as you would on your hard drive. All of the management tips and tricks you learn in this chapter apply.

Note that in Figure 5-6, Insta360 (D:) is selected. (Its name is highlighted in the navigation pane and appears in a tab near the upper-left corner.) In the content pane to the right is an icon for a folder named DCIM (Digital Camera Images), which is a common folder in devices that can store photos and videos. Double-clicking the folder opens the folder and reveals its contents, as with any other folder.

Keen-eyed observers might also notice a new option, Eject, in the toolbar near the top. Before removing any device you've plugged into the computer, you should always click Eject (or right-click the drive's icon in the navigation pane and choose Eject) to make sure the device's files are closed and safely tucked away before you yank the device from your computer. Windows will display a Safe to Remove notification in the lower-right corner of the screen to let you know when you can unplug the device.

Seeing what's inside a folder

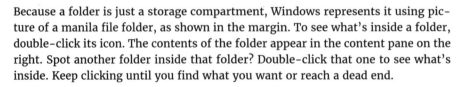

Because a folder is just a storage compartment, Windows represents it using picture of a manila file folder, as shown in the margin. To see what's inside a folder, double-click its icon. The contents of the folder appear in the content pane on the right. Spot another folder inside that folder? Double-click that one to see what's inside. Keep clicking until you find what you want or reach a dead end.

Reached a dead end? If you mistakenly end up in the wrong folder, back your way out as if you're browsing the web. Click the back arrow at the window's top-left corner (and shown in the margin). You'll see the contents of the folder you just left. If you keep clicking the back arrow, you'll end up where you started.

The address bar — that wide word-filled box near the top of the window — provides another quick way to jump to different places in your PC. As you move from folder to folder, the folder's address bar keeps track of your trek. Note the arrows between the folder names. They provide shortcuts to other folders and windows. If you click an arrow, a menu appears, listing the places you can jump to from that point. For example, I have a folder named Classical inside my Music folder. Clicking the arrow after Classical, as shown in Figure 5-7, lists the folders in the Classical folder.

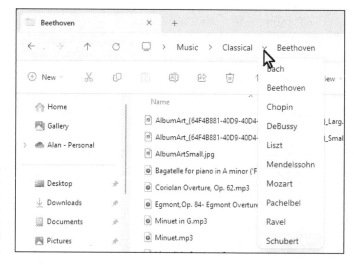

FIGURE 5-7: Click the arrow after the folder's name to jump to any other place within that same folder.

WHAT'S ALL THIS PATH STUFF?

A *path* is merely the file's address, similar to your street address. When a letter is mailed to your house, for example, it travels to your country, state, city, street, and (with any luck) apartment or house. A computer path does the same thing. In File Explorer's address bar, you see a series of names separated by > arrows. But if you click just to the right of that, you see the same information presented another way, looking something like this:

```
C:\Users\aimee\Pictures\Screenshots
```

(continued)

(continued)

That's the location of the current folder from the computer's perspective. The C:\ means the folder is on the computer's internal hard disk. Every person who has a user account on the current computer has their own folder in the Users folder on the hard drive. So, for example, Users\aimee just means "inside aimee's user account." Finally, \Pictures\ Screenshots are the folder names as they appear in File Explorer. So C:\Users\aimee\ Pictures\Screenshots refers to the Screenshots folder in Aimee's user account on the hard drive (C:).

TIP

Here are some more tips for finding your way into and out of folders:

>> Sometimes a folder contains too many files or folders to fit in the window. To see more files, click that window's scroll bars along its bottom or right edge. (I cover scroll bars in Chapter 4.)

>> As you burrow deeply into folders, the address bar keeps track of each folder you visited along the way. If you want to go back to a folder, just click its name there.

>> Click the up arrow in the address bar (shown in the margin) to move your view up one folder. Keep clicking the arrow and you'll eventually wind up at a recognizable place: your desktop.

>> Can't find a particular file or folder? Start typing its name in the Search box next to the start icon. That Search box can find lost files, folders, email, and nearly anything else hiding in your PC as well as on the internet.

>> When faced with a long list of files, click anywhere in the list. Then quickly type the first letter or two of the filename you're looking for. Windows jumps up or down the list to the first name beginning with those letters.

Opening files from File Explorer

You can open any file from File Explorer by double-clicking the file's icon or name. Windows automatically opens the file in whatever app is currently defined as the default app for that file type. If you get an oddball file for which Windows has no default app, it will let you know and give you some choices. If you're not confident that you know the file's contents, it might be best not to open the file at all, unless it came from a trustworthy source.

If you're comfortable enough with your own knowledge of apps and file types, you can override the default app that opens when you double-click a document file's icon. Just don't double-click the icon. Instead, right-click it, choose Open With, and then click whichever app you prefer to use.

Sorting and previewing files in File Explorer

The Sort, View, and Preview icons (see Figure 5-8) give you plenty of options for organizing and viewing your content. Click Sort to choose a sort order. For example, sorting by Name lists files in alphabetical order by name. Choosing Date puts them in date-modified order. The default is descending order, which means the files you've saved most recently are listed near the top (which is great if you forget the name of a file you recently saved).

↑↓ Sort ˅   ⬚ View ˅   • • •   ⬚ Preview

Click View if you want to see files in different ways. The various icon views, such as Extra Large Icons, display pictures, videos, and songs as thumbnail images rather than just a filename. The other options display more textual information about files, which can be helpful depending on the kinds of files you're viewing.

Click the Preview icon to open a preview pane on the right side of the File Explorer window. Then click the name or icon of the file you want to see, and its contents appear in the preview pane, without opening the file. You can widen or narrow the preview pane by dragging its inner border left and right, respectively. To put the preview pane back into hiding, just click Preview in the toolbar again.

Viewing filename extensions

A *filename extension* consists of one or more letters preceded by a dot (period) at the end of the filename. The extension tells the computer how the information inside the file is encoded. There are thousands of filename extensions. Some of the more commonly used follow:

>> **.png:** A picture (png stands for Portable Network Graphics)

>> **.jpg:** A picture (jpg stands for Joint Photographic Experts Group)

>> **.mp4:** A video

>> **.mp3:** Music

>> **.txt:** Text

>> **.pdf:** A Portable Document Format (text and pictures)

- » **.docx:** A Microsoft Word document

- » **.xlsx:** A Microsoft Excel spreadsheet

- » **.zip:** A compressed file or folder

If you want to see filename extensions in File Explorer, click the View icon in File Explorer, click Show, and then click Filename Extensions. Follow the same procedure to put file extensions back into hiding.

NEW

If you're curious about a filename extension, just ask Copilot for help. For example, you can ask Copilot "What is the .jpeg extension?" or "What are some common filename extensions?" or "What app can open .tiff files?" or "How do I work with .zip files?"

Working with Files and Folders

As your collection of files grows, you may want to organize the files to make things easier to find. You organize paper files into different folders, and perhaps even different filing cabinets if you work in a large company. You may want to move files from one folder to another, or get rid of an old file you no longer need. The term *managing files* refers to all the things you can do to keep files organized, so that they're easy to find. This section describes all the different ways you can manage files in File Explorer.

Creating a folder

To store new information in a file cabinet, you grab a manila folder, scrawl a name across the top, and start stuffing it with information. To store new information in Windows — notes for your autobiography, for example — you create a folder, type a name for it, and start stuffing it with files.

When creating a folder, first open the folder where you want to place the new folder. For example, suppose you are tired of scrolling around in your Pictures folder, looking for a particular picture. You decide to organize the photos into folders, with a folder for each vacation. In that case, you'd open the Pictures folder first. Then click New in the Pictures folder's upper-left corner, and choose Folder from the drop-down menu. A new folder appears, ready for you to type its name.

You can create a folder also with this quick and foolproof method:

1. **Right-click a blank spot inside your folder (or on the desktop) and choose New.**

   The all-powerful right-click shoots a menu out to the side.

2. **Choose Folder.**

   A new folder appears.

3. **Type a new name for the folder.**

   A newly created folder bears the boring name New Folder. When you begin typing, Windows erases the old name and fills in your new name.

4. **Save the new name by pressing Enter or clicking somewhere away from the name you just typed.**

 If you mess up the name or didn't seem to get a chance to type it, right-click the misnamed folder, choose the rename icon (shown in the margin and at the top of the context menu that pops up), and type the new name. When naming your files, keep the name short and to the point. Stick with letters, numbers, hyphens, and underscores. The "Using legal folder names and filenames" sidebar spells out the details.

USING LEGAL FOLDER NAMES AND FILENAMES

Windows is pretty picky about what you can name a file or folder. If you stick to plain old letters and numbers, you're fine. But don't try to stick any of the following characters in there:

: / \ * | < > ? "

If you try to use any of those characters, Windows bounces an error message to the screen, and you have to try again. Here are some illegal filenames:

1/2 of my Homework

JOB:2

(continued)

(continued)

ONE<TWO

He's no "Gentleman"

These names are legal:

Half of my Term Paper

JOB=2

Two is Bigger than One

A #@$%) Scoundrel

Renaming a file or folder

Sick of a filename or folder name? Then change it. Just right-click the offending icon and choose the rename icon (shown in the margin) from the top edge of the pop-up menu. Windows highlights the file's old name, which disappears as you begin typing the new one. When you're done, press Enter or click the desktop.

Or you can click the filename or folder name to select it, wait a second, and click the name again to change it. Yet another method: Click the filename and press F2. Here are some things to keep in mind when renaming files:

» When you rename a file, only its name changes. The file's contents, size, and location remain the same.

TIP

» To rename large groups of files simultaneously, select them all, right-click the first one, and then click the rename icon. Type the new name and press Enter. Windows renames that file plus all the other selected files, adding numbers as it goes. For example, if you renamed the first file cat, Windows renames the others cat(2), cat(3), cat(4), and so on. It's a handy way to rename a group of photographs after a special event.

» Renaming some folders confuses Windows, especially if those folders contain apps. And please don't rename your main folders: Downloads, Documents, Pictures, Music, or Videos. (Doing so can cause under-the-hood problems that you don't want to deal with.)

» For power users who need to rename groups of files based on specific words or patterns within filenames, Microsoft offers PowerToys PowerRename. For more information, just ask Copilot.

TIP

>> Windows won't let you rename a file or folder if one of your apps currently uses it. Closing the app usually fixes the problem.

Selecting bunches of files or folders

Although selecting a file, a folder, or another object may seem boring, it swings the door wide open for further tasks: deleting, renaming, moving, copying, and performing other file-juggling tricks discussed in the rest of this chapter.

To gather several files or folders sitting next to each other in a list, click the first one, and then hold down the Shift key as you click the last one. Those two items are highlighted, along with every file and folder sitting between them.

When the files you want to select aren't next to each other, use the Ctrl key instead. Click the first file or folder that you want to select. Then hold down Ctrl and click the other files you want to select. If you make a mistake, keep holding down Ctrl and click a selected file a second time to deselect it. To deselect all files, click anywhere without holding down the Ctrl key.

TIP

Windows lets you *lasso* files and folders, as well. Point slightly above the first file or folder you want to select. Then, while holding down the mouse button, drag the mouse pointer through all the files you want to select. The mouse creates a colored lasso surrounding your files. Let go of the mouse button and the lasso disappears, leaving all the surrounded files highlighted (selected).

Here are a few things you can do with a bunch of files you've selected:

>> Drag and drop armfuls of files in the same way that you drag a single file.

>> Cut or copy and paste these armfuls into new locations using any of the methods described in the "Copying or moving files and folders" section, later in this chapter.

>> Delete these armfuls of goods with a press of the Delete key. (They all drop into the recycle bin and are available for emergency retrieval.) You can find the recycle bin's icon on the desktop. Or type *recycle* in the Search box next to the start icon, and click Recycle Bin on the Start menu.

TIP

To quickly select all the files in a folder, click the folder's see more icon (three dots in the folder's upper-right corner) and choose Select All. No icon? Select them by pressing Ctrl+A. Here's another nifty trick: To grab all but a few files, press Ctrl+A and, while still holding down Ctrl, click the ones you don't want to deselect them.

Getting rid of a file or folder

 Sooner or later, you'll want to delete a file that's no longer important — yesterday's lottery picks, for example, or a particularly embarrassing digital photo. To delete a file or folder, right-click its name or icon. Then click the delete icon (shown in the margin) at the top edge of the pop-up menu. This surprisingly simple trick works for files, folders, shortcuts, and just about anything else in Windows.

To delete in a hurry, click the offending object and press the delete key. Dragging and dropping a file or folder to the recycle bin does the same thing.

WARNING

You can delete entire folders, including any files or folders stuffed inside those folders. Just be sure you select the correct folder before you delete it and all its contents. Deleted something by mistake? It's waiting to be recovered in the recycle bin.

If you don't recognize a file, that doesn't mean you should delete it. Some files are required for Windows to function properly. When you are wondering whether to delete a file, consider the following:

>> Be extra sure that you know what you're doing when deleting a file whose icon depicts a gear. These files are usually sensitive hidden files that belong to apps, and the computer wants you to leave them alone. (Other than that, they're not particularly exciting, despite the action-oriented gears.)

 >> Icons with arrows in their corners (like the one in the margin) are shortcuts, which let you open other files. But the shortcut itself doesn't contain the file that opens. (I cover shortcuts in Chapter 6.) Deleting a shortcut deletes only the icon. The file or app itself remains.

 In a pinch, just ask Copilot "How do I delete files?" or "How do I undelete a file?"

TIP

What if you delete a file or folder and want it back? Don't worry, the deleted item isn't gone forever. More likely, it's in your recycle bin, which is like the waste-paper basket under your desk. You can fish it back out of there, as I explain next.

Dumpster diving in the recycle bin

The recycle bin, represented by a wastebasket in the upper-left corner of your desktop (and shown in the margin), works much like a real recycle bin. It lets you retrieve the discarded desktop files you thought you'd never need. If you don't have a recycle bin icon on your desktop, don't worry, Just start typing *recycle* in the Search box next to the start icon, and click Recycle Bin when it appears in the menu.

If you deleted something by accident or just changed your mind and want it back, you can pull it out of the recycle bin. Click the recycle bin icon to see your recently deleted items. Right-click the item you want and choose Restore. The handy recycle bin returns your precious item to the same spot where you deleted it. (You can also resuscitate deleted items by dragging them to your desktop or any other folder; drag 'em back into the recycle bin to delete them again.)

TIP

The recycle bin can get crowded. If you're searching frantically for a recently deleted file, you can tell the recycle bin to sort everything by the date and time you deleted it. Right-click an empty area inside the recycle bin, choose Sort By, and then choose Date Deleted from the pop-up menu.

TIP

To delete something permanently, just delete it from inside the recycle bin by clicking it and pressing the Delete key. To delete everything in the recycle bin, right-click the recycle bin icon and choose Empty Recycle Bin.

To bypass the recycle bin when deleting files, hold down Shift while pressing Delete. Poof! The deleted object disappears, ne'er to be seen again — a handy trick when dealing with sensitive items, such as credit-card numbers or bleary-eyed selfies.

The recycle bin serves as an intelligent wastebasket. Here are a few other ways it shines:

>> The recycle bin icon changes from an empty wastepaper basket to a full one (as shown in the margin) as soon as it's holding a deleted file.

>> The recycle bin keeps your deleted files until they consume about 5 percent of your computer's storage capacity. Then the recycle bin automatically purges the oldest deleted files to make room for the new. If you're low on hard drive space, shrink the bin's size by right-clicking the recycle bin and choosing Properties. Decrease the Custom Size number to purge the bin more quickly; increase the number, and the recycle bin hangs onto files a little longer.

WARNING

>> The recycle bin saves only items deleted from your computer's drives. That means it won't save anything deleted from a memory card, phone, MP3 player, flash drive, or digital camera.

>> Already emptied the recycle bin? You might still be able to retrieve the then-trashed-now-treasured item from the Windows File History backup, covered in Chapter 13.

WARNING

If you delete something from someone else's computer over a network, it can't be retrieved. The recycle bin holds only items deleted from your computer. (For some awful reason, the recycle bin on the other person's computer doesn't save the item either.) Be careful, and make sure every computer on your network has a backup system in place.

Copying or moving files and folders

To copy or move files to different folders on your hard drive, it's sometimes easiest to use your mouse to drag them there. For example, here's how to move a file to a different folder on your desktop. In this case, I'm moving the Traveler file from the House folder to the Morocco folder.

1. **Align the two windows next to each other.**

The windows can be any size. But if you drag one window all the way to the left side of the screen and the other window all the way to the right, the two windows should end up side-by-side, each about half the screen width.

2. **Right-click the file you want to move or file, keeping the mouse button depressed, and drag the item to the destination folder.**

As you see in Figure 5-9, I'm dragging the Traveler file from the House folder to the Morocco folder.

Moving the mouse drags the file along with it, and Windows explains that you're moving the file, as shown in Figure 5-9. (Be sure to hold down the right mouse button the entire time.)

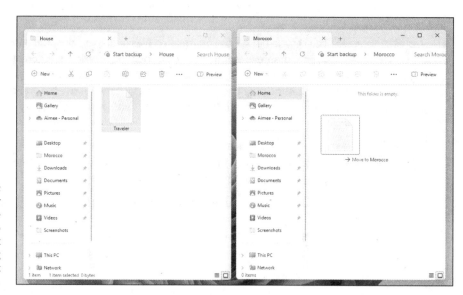

FIGURE 5-9:
To move a file or folder from one window to another, drag it while holding down the right mouse button.

3. **Release the mouse button and choose Copy Here, Move Here, or Create Shortcuts Here from the pop-up menu.**

REMEMBER

Always drag icons while holding down the *right* mouse button. Windows is then gracious enough to give you a menu of options when you position the icon, so you can choose to copy, move, or create a shortcut. If you hold down the *left* mouse button, Windows sometimes doesn't know whether you want to copy or move.

Windows offers a few other ways to copy or move files. Depending on your screen's current layout, some of the following onscreen tools may be easier than dragging and dropping:

>> **Right-click menu:** Right-click a file or folder and choose the Cut icon or the Copy icon, depending on whether you want to move or copy the item. Then right-click inside your destination folder and click the Paste icon. It's simple, it always works, and you needn't bother placing any windows side by side.

>> **File Explorer command:** In File Explorer, click your file or folder, and then click the Copy icon or the Move icon from the toolbar near the top of File Explorer. Then click inside that item's destination and click the Paste icon to neatly deposit the item into its new location.

>> **Navigation pane:** Described in Chapter 4, this panel along File Explorer's left edge lists popular locations — drives, networks, OneDrive, and oft-used folders. You can drag and drop items into a folder on the navigation pane, sparing yourself the hassle of opening a destination folder.

NEW

If you forget any of this, just ask Copilot "How do I copy files?" or "How do I move files?"

WARNING

After you install an app on your computer, don't ever move that app's folder because doing so might break the app, and you'll have to reinstall it. However, feel free to move an app's shortcut. (Shortcut icons contain an arrow in their lower-left corner.) If you no longer need the app, head to the Start menu, right-click the unloved app, and choose Uninstall from the pop-up menu.

Seeing more information about files and folders

When you create a file or folder, Windows scrawls a bunch of hidden information about it, such as the date you created it, its size, and even more trivial stuff. Sometimes Windows lets you add your own secret information, including reviews for your music files or thumbnail pictures for your folders.

You can safely ignore most of this information. Other times, tweaking the information is the only way to solve a problem.

To see what Windows is calling your files and folders behind your back, right-click the item and choose Properties from the pop-up menu. Choosing Properties on a picture, for example, brings up bunches of detail, as shown in Figure 5-10. Here's what each tab means:

>> **General:** This first tab shows the file's type, the app that opens it, the file's location, its size, and much more.

NEW

If you're perplexed by all the techie KB, MB, GB, and gigabytes stuff, just ask Copilot "What are KB, MB, GB, and TB in computing?" or "What's a byte?"

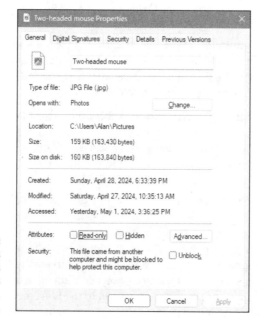

FIGURE 5-10:
A file's Properties window shows which app opens it, the file's size, and other details.

>> **Digital Signatures:** This tab shows any digital signature associated with the file. Digital signing is an advanced technology that can be used to authenticate files that contain sensitive information. You probably would never use these on a personal computer. But if you're curious, you can just ask Copilot what digital signatures are all about.

>> **Security:** On this tab, you control *permissions,* which are rules determining who may access the file and what they may do with it. System administrators earn high wages for understanding this type of stuff.

>> **Details:** True to its name, this tab reveals arcane details about a file. On digital photos, for example, the tab lists EXIF (Exchangeable Image File Format) data: the camera model, f-stop, aperture, focal length, and other items loved by photographers. On songs, the tab displays the song's *ID3 tag* (IDentify MP3), which includes the artist, album title, year, track number, genre, and length.

>> **Previous Versions:** After you set up the Windows File History backup system, this tab lists all the previously saved versions of this file, ready for retrieval with a click. I cover File History in Chapter 13.

You can override the default app for opening a file by right-clicking the file's icon, choosing Open With, and then choosing the app you want to use. To permanently change the default app for a file type, use the Change button in the Properties dialog box shown in Figure 5-10.

Normally, these tidbits of information remain hidden unless you right-click a file or folder and choose Properties. But what if you want to see details about all the files in a folder, perhaps to find pictures taken on a certain day? For that, switch your folder's view to Details by following these steps:

1. **Click the View icon in File Explorer's toolbar.**

   A menu appears, listing the umpteen ways a folder can display your files.

2. **Click Details.**

   The screen changes to show the names of your files, with details about them stretching to the right in orderly columns.

>> If you can't remember the purpose of a folder's toolbar icon, rest your mouse pointer over it. Windows usually displays a helpful box summing up the icon's mission.

>> Switch among views until you find one that fits what you're trying to accomplish, such as seeing a particular photo's creation date or seeing thumbnails of every photo in a folder. Different views work better for different folders; there's no right view.

>> Folders usually display files sorted alphabetically. To sort them differently, right-click a blank spot in the folder and choose Sort By. A pop-up menu lets you choose to sort items by size, name, type, and other details. Or click the sort and group options icon (shown in the margin), which lives atop every folder to see the same options.

TIP

>> When the excitement of the Sort By menu wears off, try clicking the words at the top of each sorted column. Click Size, for example, to sort the items based on size. Click a second time to reverse the sort order. The arrow centered at the top of the heading points up when the items are in ascending order and points down when the items are in descending order.

TIP

>> You can add columns to Details view. Right-click a column header you don't need, and a drop-down menu appears, letting you choose a different criterion. (I always add a Date Taken column to my photos, so I can sort my photos by the date I snapped them.)

Working with Flash Drives and Memory Cards

Digital camera owners eventually become acquainted with *memory cards* — those plastic squares that replaced rolls of film. Windows can read digital photos directly from the camera after you find its cable and plug it into your PC. But Windows can also grab photos straight off the memory card, a method praised by those who've lost their camera's cables.

The same holds true for smartphones and tablets, which also use the cards, as well as some audio recorders and digital gaming devices.

The secret to using memory cards is a *memory card reader* — a slot-filled box that stays plugged into your PC. Slide your memory card into the slot, and your PC can read the card's files, just like reading files from any other folder.

Most office supply and electronics stores sell memory card readers that accept most popular memory card formats. If you're buying online, search for *card reader* or *memory card reader*. Note that some tablets, laptops, and PCs include built-in memory card readers.

The beauty of card readers is that there's nothing new to figure out: Windows treats your inserted card just like an ordinary folder. Insert your card, and a folder appears on your screen to show your digital camera's photos. The same drag-and-drop and cut-and-paste rules covered earlier in this chapter still apply, letting you move pictures or other files off the card and into your Pictures folder.

 USB drives — also known as *flash drives* or *thumb drives* — work just like memory card readers. Plug the flash drive into one of your PC's USB ports, and the drive appears in File Explorer as an icon (shown in the margin), ready to be opened with a double-click. Skip back to this chapter's "Copying or moving files and folders" section for step-by-step instructions on transferring the flash drive's contents to your PC.

![Warning icon]

WARNING

Formatting a card or flash drive wipes out all its information. Never format a card or flash drive unless you don't care about the information it currently holds.

If Windows complains that a newly inserted card isn't formatted, right-click its drive and choose Format. (This problem happens most often with new or damaged cards.)

When creating a music USB drive for your car, format it using the exFAT or FAT32 option, unless instructed otherwise in your car's user manual. Use NTFS for drives you intend to use only in Windows computers.

OneDrive: Your Cubbyhole in the Clouds

When you're sitting in front of your computer, you probably save your files on the hard drive inside your computer because it's the easiest place to put them. But if you need to use those files on another computer, you must copy them to an external drive and then connect the external drive to the other computer.

But how can you access your files if you've forgotten to bring along the files? How can you grab your home files from work and vice versa? What if you're using your laptop in front of the TV and a file you need is on your desktop computer in another room? How can you get your PC's files with your smartphone?

Microsoft's answer to those questions is *OneDrive*, a private file storage space on the internet that's built into Windows. With OneDrive, your files are available from any computer with an internet connection. You can even grab them from phones or tablets that run iOS or Android: Microsoft offers a free OneDrive app for both operating systems.

If you change a file stored on OneDrive, the updated file is available on all your computers and devices. OneDrive automatically keeps everything in sync. You need only the following to put OneDrive to work:

>> **Microsoft account:** You need a Microsoft account to upload, view, or retrieve your files from OneDrive. Chances are good that you created a Microsoft account when you created your account on your Windows PC. (I describe Microsoft accounts in Chapter 2.)

>> **An internet connection:** Without an internet connection, your OneDrive files remain floating in the cloud, away from you and your computer. (You can avoid that problem by choosing to keep all your OneDrive files stored on your computer as well as in the cloud.)

>> **Patience:** Uploading files takes longer than downloading files. Although you can upload small files fairly quickly, larger files such as digital photos or movies take much longer to upload.

Before I go any deeper into this, let's clear up some tech terms you're bound to come across. First, let's talk about the cloud versus the internet. The *internet* is a huge network covering the entire globe, allowing virtually everyone access to all that it has to offer. But not everyone on the internet is nice. You really don't need to be putting your personal important files out there.

You can think of the term *cloud* as referring to a location on the internet that only your computers can access. In the cloud, you needn't worry about the general public wandering in and rummaging through your stuff. Your cloud files can be reached via the internet, but only by you and people with whom you intentionally share files.

If you envision the cloud as a literal cloud, floating above your well-grounded computer, the difference between *upload* and *download* is much easier to understand (see Figure 5-11). *Upload* means copy from your computer up to the cloud, and *download* means copy to your computer from the outside world.

As always, if you forget any of the terminology, you can ask Copilot "What is the difference between upload and download?"

NEW

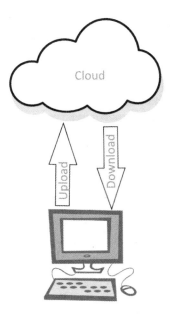

FIGURE 5-11:
Upload means to copy from your PC to an external device, and download means to copy from an external device (or the internet) to your PC.

Backing up files

In addition to making your files easier to access, OneDrive can perform another important task: backing up your files. Suppose you have a treasured photo or important information for work stored on your PC. Due to no fault of your own, the PC gets lost, stolen, or destroyed. You lose all its files — not just the PC. For many users, losing the files is worse than losing the PC.

People learned long ago that having only one copy of an important file is never a good idea when using computers. If you have two copies in two different places, you're much safer. So if you back up your files to OneDrive and lose your PC, those files are on OneDrive.

When you open a built-in folder, such as the Pictures folder, you might notice Start Backup at the beginning of the address bar, as shown in Figure 5-12.

FIGURE 5-12:
The Start Backup button in File Explorer lets you quickly set up OneDrive as a backup device.

When you click Start Backup, Windows takes you through some simple steps so you can decide which types of files you want to back up automatically. (Most people want to back up documents and pictures.) When you have finished following the onscreen instructions, the OneDrive icon next to your username in File Explorer's navigation pane will have an arrow next to it. Click that arrow to see the folders now in your OneDrive, as shown in Figure 5-13.

Backups of local folders

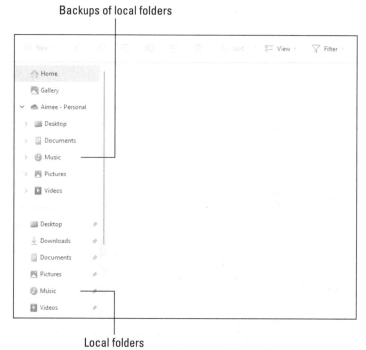

FIGURE 5-13:
Folders under
OneDrive
replicate folders
on your
hard drive.

Local folders

Each folder in OneDrive is a duplicate of a local folder. And as you add or change files in your local folders, the backups stay in sync automatically. If your computer is lost, stolen, or damaged and you lose all your local files, go into your OneDrive using a different computer and all your "lost" files will be there waiting for you.

That's the simplest way to use OneDrive. If you never see the Start Backup button in File Explorer, chances are your OneDrive is already set up. Or maybe you don't have that option under your current account because the computer owner set you up with a guest account with limited access. Read on to learn more ways to use OneDrive.

Changing OneDrive settings

Everyone gets 5GB (5 gigabytes) of OneDrive storage for free. If you don't want to pay for more OneDrive storage, keep the folders and file types you back up to a minimum. Text documents tend to take up the least space; image, sound, and video files can use up space quickly. You can change your OneDrive settings so that OneDrive backs up documents and perhaps pictures too but not larger sound and video files.

The OneDrive icon is in the system tray near the lower-right corner of your screen, usually near the Wi-Fi or speaker icon. It looks like a cloud, and displays *OneDrive* when you rest the tip of the mouse pointer on the icon. To change your OneDrive settings, right-click the cloud icon and choose Settings from the menu that pops up. If you don't see Settings, click the gear icon in the upper-right corner and then choose Settings. The screen shown in Figure 5-14 appears.

FIGURE 5-14: The Account options in the OneDrive Settings screen.

Here's a quick summary of the options in the OneDrive Settings screen. The Sync and Backup option on the left controls how much of your content is backed up automatically and how often its synced. When you click Sync and Backup, you'll see the options shown in Figure 5-15.

Click Manage Backup to change which folders are backed up automatically. In the new window that opens, use the toggle to the right of a folder's name to select it for automatic backup.

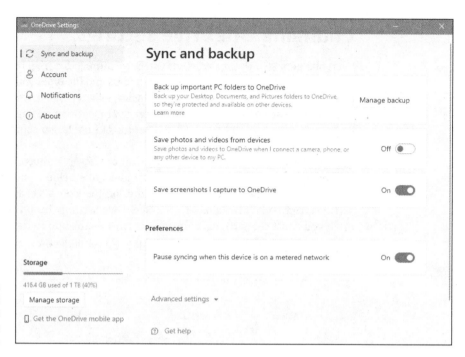

FIGURE 5-15:
Sync and
Backup options
in OneDrive
settings.

In the Preferences section of Sync and Backup, you can turn on Pause Syncing When This Device Is in Battery Saver Mode to prevent syncing from draining your battery too quickly. Also, if you use a metered network, where you're charged by the amount of data you transfer while connected, turn on Pause Syncing When This Device Is on a Metered Network.

Under Advanced Settings, you can limit upload and download rates if your web browsing and other networking activities are too slow when OneDrive is syncing. Reducing those rates will slow down syncing but free up network bandwidth for other online activities.

Under the Excluded File Extensions heading (you may need to scroll down to see it), click Exclude if you want to avoid backing up certain file types. For example, .mp4 videos tend to be huge, so you could avoid backing up just that type of file. Under Files On-Demand, you can click Free Up Disk Space to minimize local storage and conserve disk space. You can still access your OneDrive files from those devices, but the files won't be copied to your internal hard drive and take up all your local storage space.

Going back to the Account option in OneDrive Settings (refer to Figure 5-14), click Choose Folders to select which folders you want to replicate between OneDrive and your computer or device. You can conserve disk space by choosing only folders that contain files you work with often. You can also determine how quickly your Personal Vault folder (described next) locks itself automatically.

The Notifications option in the left column enables you to choose which OneDrive notifications appear on your desktop. And the About option provides technical information and options for getting help. Of course, you can ask Copilot any questions about OneDrive that pop into your head too.

Opening and saving files from OneDrive

The navigation pane in File Explorer provides a link to OneDrive, so you can explore OneDrive's folders and files as you do on your local hard drive. The icon sports a cloud, your username, and the word *Personal* (for your personal OneDrive), as shown in Figure 5-16. When you click the OneDrive icon, the main pane on the right shows folder and files stored on OneDrive. Optionally, click > to the left of the OneDrive icon to display a list of folders on OneDrive in the navigation pane. Then click the name of any OneDrive folder in the navigation pane to see that folder's contents in the main pane to the right.

OneDrive icon

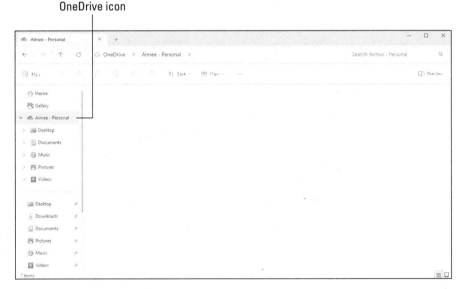

FIGURE 5-16:
OneDrive's icon in
File Explorer's
navigation pane.

ONEDRIVE'S PERSONAL VAULT

A *personal vault* is a fancy term for what looks and acts like a regular OneDrive folder but with one big difference: To open it, you need to pass a second layer of security. A personal vault is a perfect place to store sensitive files because they can be accessed only by people who can pass the second layer of security.

Personal vault security could be as simple as running your fingertip over a fingerprint reader or looking into a camera. (I cover Windows Hello fingerprint readers and face cameras in Chapter 14.) You can also enter a PIN, or a secret code sent to you through email or a phone message.

After 20 minutes of inactivity, the personal vault automatically locks itself, keeping your most sensitive files secure yet accessible.

You have nothing new to learn with OneDrive; its folders work like any other folder on your computer:

>> To edit a file stored in a OneDrive folder, double-click it.

>> To save something new inside a OneDrive folder, save it to a folder inside OneDrive — its Documents folder, for example. Don't just save it to the Documents folder on your PC.

>> To delete something from OneDrive, right-click it and choose Delete. The item moves to your desktop's recycle bin, where you can retrieve it later if necessary.

No matter what changes you make to your files and folders in your computer's OneDrive folder, Windows automatically changes the internet's copies to match as soon as your computer finds an internet connection.

Later, when you visit OneDrive using anything with a web browser — a smartphone, tablet, or even another PC — your up-to-date files are waiting for you to peruse.

Understanding which files live on OneDrive, your PC, or both places

Windows lets you see the names of every file and folder you've stored on OneDrive. Then you can quickly open a OneDrive file or folder even if it's not stored locally on your PC. OneDrive simply grabs the file from the internet and places it onto your computer (assuming you have a working internet connection at the time, of course).

OneDrive's files-on-demand feature lets you see all your files on all your devices. Yet it lets you save space on devices that don't have much storage space. For example, you can sync your entire music collection only on devices with lots of storage space. But your devices that lack storage can still see the music and, if you have an internet connection, play it whenever you like.

You can even see thumbnails of more than 300 different file types — even if they're not stored on your computer.

To turn on OneDrive's files-on-demand feature, follow these steps:

1. **In the taskbar's notification area, right-click the OneDrive icon and choose Settings from the pop-up menu.**

2. **Click Sync and Backup and choose Advanced Settings.**

3. **Scroll down to the Files On-Demand section, and click Free Up Disk Space.**

4. **Click Continue.**

The OneDrive system tray window slides up, explaining what files on demand means, to remind you that files are no longer synced automatically. You can click Got It! when you tire of seeing that message.

Now, even though your OneDrive files aren't saved on your PC, you can see their names when you open a folder on OneDrive, as shown in Figure 5-17.

FIGURE 5-17:
OneDrive
files-on-demand
feature displays
the name of
every stored file
and folder, as
well as its status.

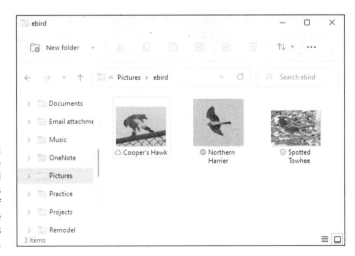

The key to understanding files on demand is to look at the icon next to the filename:

» **Online only:** The file is available only online; you need an internet connection to access it.

» **Locally available:** You opened an online-only file, so now it's available on your PC. Any edits you make change the copy stored on OneDrive. If you need to free up space and remove the file from your PC, right-click it and choose Free Up Space. A copy remains on OneDrive, and the file's icon on your PC changes to online only.

» **Always keep on this device:** The file is always available on your PC, even without an internet connection.

To change the status of a file, right-click it. You can then choose one of the following settings:

» **View Online:** Downloads the file or folder to your PC and opens it for you to view or edit.

» **Always Keep On This Device:** Downloads the file or folder to your PC but doesn't open it. This option is handy for grabbing folders that you want to have available even when you don't have an internet connection.

» **Free Up Space:** Deletes the file from your device, freeing up storage space. However, the file is stored on OneDrive, where you can fetch it again whenever you have an internet connection.

TIP

The following tips will help you decide whether files on demand is worth turning on and how to use it on different devices:

» If your device has plenty of storage space, as do most desktop PCs, don't bother with files on demand. Instead, click Account in OneDrive Settings left column, click Choose Folder, and then select the Make All Files Available check box.

» If your device doesn't have much storage but you want to see the names of all your OneDrive files and folders, turn on files on demand. Then, when you have an internet connection and need a file or folder, just open it as if it lived on your PC. Windows quickly downloads and opens it.

By assessing your needs, your device's storage limits, and the availability of your internet connection, you can customize OneDrive's files-on-demand feature to meet the storage capacity of all your devices.

Accessing OneDrive from the internet

Sometimes you may need to access OneDrive when you're not sitting in front of your computer. Or you may need to reach a OneDrive file that's not synced on your PC. To help you in either situation, Microsoft offers OneDrive access from any web browser.

When you need your files, drop by any computer, visit the OneDrive website at `https://onedrive.live.com/`, and if asked, sign in with your Microsoft account name and password. The OneDrive website appears, as shown in Figure 5-18.

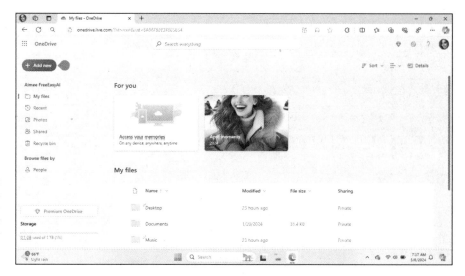

FIGURE 5-18: You can access your OneDrive files from any computer or device with a web browser.

After you sign in to the OneDrive website, you can add, delete, move, and rename files, as well as create folders and move files between folders. You can even edit some files directly online. (OneDrive even contains a recycle bin for retrieving mistakenly deleted OneDrive files, whether they were deleted online or on your phone, PC, or other device.)

It's much easier to manage your files directly from the folder on your computer, but if you're away from your computer, the OneDrive website is a handy fallback.

The OneDrive website also lets you share files by emailing people links to them. You can also share OneDrive files with friends directly from your PC: Right-click the file or folder you want to share, choose OneDrive, and then choose Share from the pop-up menu. A window appears, where you can enter the email address of the person who should receive a link to the shared item. When the recipient clicks the link in the email, they're taken online to view the file or folder's contents.

If you use OneDrive regularly, and have a Mac computer or an Apple and Android smartphone or tablet, note that Microsoft offers free OneDrive apps for iOS, iPadOS, and Android operating systems.

2

Working with Apps and Files

IN THIS CHAPTER

» Opening an app or a document

» Changing which app opens
which document

» Installing, uninstalling, and
updating apps

» Creating a shortcut

» Cutting, copying, and pasting

Chapter **6**

Playing with Apps and Documents

I n Windows, *apps* are your tools: Load an app, and you can add numbers, arrange words, shoot spaceships, alter pictures, play music, create videos. *Documents,* by contrast, are the things you create with apps, such as tax forms, heartfelt apologies, pictures, music, and videos.

In this chapter, you learn how to find, download, and install an app from the Start menu's Microsoft Store app, and then start the app from the Start menu in Windows.

As you flip through this chapter's pages, you figure out how to make your preferred app open your files. You also create desktop shortcuts — buttons that let you quickly open favorite files, folders, and apps.

The chapter ends with the section "Absolutely Essential Guide to Cutting, Copying, and Pasting." Put those skills under your belt, and you'll know how to manipulate words in a word processor, move files between folders, copy files from your camera to your PC, and send files to and from flash drives.

Starting an App

The Start menu, shown in Figure 6-1, is home to icons for starting apps, and a list of recently opened documents. Icons under the Pinned heading all represent apps. When your computer is new, you might see some app icons under Recommended, simply because you haven't opened many documents yet. But over time, the Recommended section's icons will all represent documents. If none of this sounds familiar, take a look at Chapter 2.

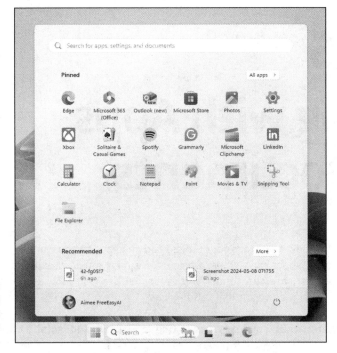

FIGURE 6-1:
On the Start menu, click the icon for the app you want to open.

If you just want to launch an app, follow these steps:

1. **Open the Start menu.**

   Summon the Start menu by clicking or tapping the start icon on the taskbar. Or if your hands are already on the keyboard, press the Windows key.

2. **If you spot the icon for your app under the Pinned heading, click or tap it.**

   You can skip the rest of these steps.

   Don't see an icon for your sought-after app on the Start menu's list? Move to the next step.

3. **To see more icons, page down the Start screen's right side. On a touch-screen, slide your finger up the screen, over the icons.**

   If you have more than one page of pinned app icons, a vertical stack of dots appears to the right of the app icons. Click a dot to move from page to page.

   Still don't see your app listed? Head for Step 4.

4. **View all your apps by clicking the All Apps button.**

   All your apps are listed alphabetically. If you want to add one of those apps to your pinned icons, right-click the app's icon and choose Pin to Start. If you just want to open the app, click its icon.

NEW

If you *still* can't find your app on the admittedly crowded Start menu, click in the Search box, located along the top edge of the Start menu, and start typing the name of the app. After you type the first letter, the Search box expands into its own window and begins presenting a list of names containing that letter. Type a second or third letter, and the list shrinks accordingly to match that sequence. When the window lists your desired app, open it with a click (or a tap on a touchscreen).

These are all the ways you can start an app from the Start menu. You can also pin icons for favorite apps to your desktop. Once you've pinned an app's icon to the desktop, you can open the app by double-clicking its icon. You don't need to go through the Start menu.

Opening a Document

Documents are the things you view, play, create, and edit using apps. You might use Notepad for text documents, Photos and Paint for pictures, Clipchamp for videos. Opening a document means to display the document in its app so you can view, play, or change the document.

To open a recent document, you can click the document's icon under Recommended on the Start menu.

You can open any document using File Explorer as well. Open File Explorer, as discussed in Chapter 5, navigate to the folder (or drive) in which the document is stored, and double-click the document's icon.

Yet another way to open a document is to open the app first, and then open the document from the app.

Like Tupperware, the Windows desktop is a big fan of standardization. Almost all Windows apps load their documents — which are stored as *files* — the same way. First you open the app. Then in the app, follow these steps:

1. **Click File on the app's *menu bar,* that row of words along the app's top.**

   If your app hides its menu bar, pressing the Alt key often reveals it. If you still can't find a menu bar, you may need to go through the app's ribbon. Ask Copilot, "How to I open files in *app*?" replacing *app* with the name of the app you're using.

2. **When the File menu drops down, choose Open.**

   Windows gives you a sense of déjà vu with the Open dialog box, shown in Figure 6-2. It looks (and works) like File Explorer, which I cover in Chapter 5. There's one big difference, however: This time, the main window in the middle displays only files that your particular app knows how to open. If you've never saved any files with the current app, you won't see any files to open.

3. **Click the file name or icon for the document you want to open, and then click the Open button.**

   On a touchscreen, tap the document to open it.

TIP

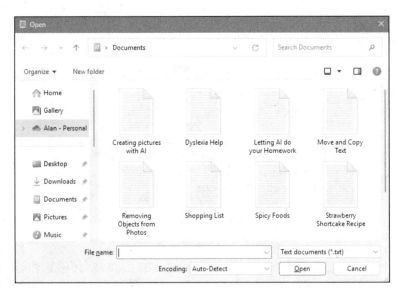

FIGURE 6-2:
The Open dialog box for an app.

When you're in the Open dialog box, you can also do the following:

TIP

>> Double-click a desired file's name to open it immediately, automatically closing the Open dialog box.

>> Humans store things in the garage, but computers store their files in neatly labeled compartments called *folders*. (Double-click a folder to see what's stored inside. If you spot your file, open it with a double-click.) If browsing folders gives you trouble, go to the folders section in Chapter 5 for a refresher.

>> If your file isn't visible in the current folder, use the navigation pane (on the left side of the Open dialog box) to browse to the folder in which the document is contained.

Once opened, the document appears in its app, where you can view and edit the document.

WHEN DEVELOPERS FIGHT OVER FILE TYPES

When not fighting over fast food, developers (the techies who create apps) fight over *formats* — ways to pack information into a file. To tiptoe around the format wars, most apps let you open files stored in several different types of formats.

For example, look at the drop-down list box in the bottom-right corner of Figure 6-2. It currently lists Text Documents (*.txt), the format used by the Notepad text editor built into Windows. To see files stored in *other* formats, click in that box and choose a different format. The Open box quickly updates its list to show files from that new format instead.

And how can you see a list of *all* your folder's files in that menu, regardless of their format? Select All Files in the drop-down list. That switches the view to display all of that particular folder's files. However, your app will probably choke while trying to open them.

For example, Notepad may include some digital photos in its All Files view. But if you try to open a photo, Notepad dutifully displays the photo as obscure coding symbols. (If you mistakenly open a photo in an app and *don't* see the photo, don't try to save what you opened). If the app is like Notepad, saving the file ruins the photo. Simply turn tail and exit immediately with a click on the Cancel button. Or if the file is already open, close the app (with the usual X in the top-right corner) and choose No when asked if you want to save.

Saving a Document

Saving a document means retaining any changes you made to the document while you had it open. Or if you just created a document from scratch, saving it will save the entire document, so you can re-use it in the future.

Many apps have an Auto Save option, visible in the top-left corner. When that option is on, any changes you make to the document are saved automatically as you work.

Thanks to Microsoft snapping the whip, a Save command appears in nearly every Windows app. Here are a few ways to save a file:

- >> Click File on the top menu and choose Save.
- >> Click the save icon (shown in the margin).
- >> Press Ctrl+S.

If you're saving something for the first time, Windows asks you to think up a name for your document. Type something descriptive using only letters, numbers, and spaces between the words. (If you try to use one of the illegal characters I describe in Chapter 5, the Windows police step in, politely requesting that you use a different name.)

Here are some general tips for saving documents:

REMEMBER

- >> You can save files to any folder or flash drive. But files are much easier to find down the road when they stay in one of your four main folders: Documents, Music, Pictures, or Videos. (Those folders are listed on the left edge of every folder — in the navigation pane — making it easy to place files inside them.)

- >> Choose descriptive filenames for your work. Windows gives you 255 characters to work with. A file named *January 2024 Fidget Spinner Sales* is easier to relocate than one named *Stuff*.

- >> If you want to access your current file from other devices, perhaps your phone, tablet, or another PC, save it to the Documents folder on OneDrive. Choose OneDrive from the Save window's left edge, choose the OneDrive Documents folder, and then click the Save button.

WHAT'S THE DIFFERENCE BETWEEN SAVE AND SAVE AS?

Huh? Save as *what?* A chemical compound? Nah, the Save As command just enables you to save your work with a different name or in a different location.

Suppose that you open the Ode to Jazz file and change a few sentences. You want to save your new changes, but you don't want to lose the original words. Preserve both versions by selecting Save As and typing the new name, Tentative Additions to Ode to Jazz.

When you're saving something for the first time, the Save and Save As commands are identical: Both make you choose a fresh name and location for your work.

Perhaps just as important, the Save As command also lets you save a file in a different format. You can save your original file in your normal format and also save a copy in a different format for a friend clinging to older software that requires a format from yesteryear.

REMEMBER

>> If you are working on something important (and most things are important) and don't have AutoSave turned on, click the app's Save command or press Ctrl+S every few minutes to save any recent changes that you want to keep. Apps make you choose a name and location for a file when you first save it; subsequent saves are much speedier.

NEW

If you need help, ask Copilot. For example, ask it, "How do I save a document in Notepad?" or "How do I open a picture in Paint?"

Choosing Which App Should Open Which File

Most of the time, Windows automatically knows which app should open which file. Open a file, and Windows tells the correct app to jump in and let you view its contents.

But sometimes Windows doesn't choose your preferred app. When the wrong app opens your file, here's how to make the right app open it instead:

1. **Right-click your problematic file, and choose Open With from the pop-up menu.**

   As shown in Figure 6-3, Windows lists a few capable apps, including ones you've used in the past to open that file.

FIGURE 6-3:
Windows lists some apps that opened that type of file before.

2. **Click Choose Another App.**

   The window that appears, lists more apps, with the currently assigned apps at the top of the list, as shown in Figure 6-4.

3. **Click the app you want to use.**

4. **Click Always if you think you'll always want to use the selected app to open that type of file or choose Just Once to open the file in that app now.**

Select an app to open this .jpeg file

Suggested apps

Paint

Photos

Snipping Tool

More options

Notepad

Windows Media Player Legacy

Word

Browse apps in the Microsoft Store

Choose an app on your PC

Always   Just once

FIGURE 6-4:
Choose the app
you want, and
click Always or
Just Once at
the bottom.

THE AWKWARD WORLD OF FILE ASSOCIATIONS

Every Windows app slaps a secret code known as a file extension onto the name of every file it creates. The *file extension* works like a cattle brand: When you double-click the file, Windows eyeballs the extension and automatically summons the proper app to open the file. The app that opens when you double-click a file's icon is called the *default app* for that file type. For example, Notepad (a simple text editor that comes free with Windows) is the default app for text files with a .txt extension. So, when you double-click a file with a .txt extension, Notepad opens to display the file (unless you've changed the default app for .txt documents).

Windows normally doesn't display these extensions, isolating users from such inner mechanisms for safety reasons. If somebody accidentally changes or removes an extension, Windows won't know how to open that file.

(continued)

(continued)

If you're curious about what an extension looks like, sneak a peek by following these steps:

1. **Click the View button in the toolbar above any folder.**

   A drop-down menu appears, showing different ways to view that folder's contents.

2. **Choose Show ⇨ File Name Extensions.**

   The files inside the folder immediately change to show their extensions — a handy thing to know in technical emergencies, especially if you get into content creation, which involves working with many different types of files.

3. **Repeat these steps to stop showing file name extensions.**

Please don't change a file's extension unless you know exactly what you're doing. Windows will forget which app to use for opening the file, potentially leaving the file inaccessible until you change the extension back to what it was originally.

Navigating the Microsoft Store

 You can purchase and download apps from the Microsoft Store app, available with a click on the taskbar's Microsoft Store icon (shown in the margin). If you've removed that taskbar icon, just type *store* in the Search box next to the start icon, or tell Copilot to "Open the Microsoft Store."

Apps can be created and sold by large companies or hobbyists working in their spare time. It's difficult to tell beforehand which one will give you the most support should things go wrong.

Adding apps from the Microsoft Store app

When you're tired of the apps bundled with Windows or you need a new app to fill a special need, follow these steps to bring one into your computer:

1. **Click the start icon, and then click the Microsoft Store app from the Start menu.**

    The Microsoft Store app jumps to the screen, as shown in Figure 6-5. If you prefer, you can instead click the Microsoft Store app (shown in the margin) from the taskbar along the bottom of your screen.

Although the Microsoft Store changes its layout frequently, it usually opens to show its Spotlight category along the top edge, where Microsoft highlights a few chosen apps. Keep scrolling down the window to see links to popular apps, as well as apps that are trending, or rising in popularity.

To see more, point near the Microsoft Store app's left edge to see the top few apps in each category: Apps, Gaming, Arcade, Entertainment, and AI Hub. (You can also buy or rent movies and computer gadgets from the Microsoft Store app.)

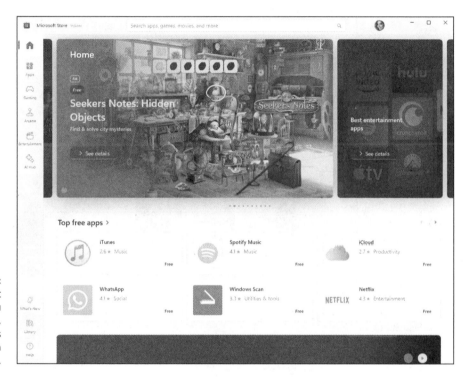

FIGURE 6-5:
The Microsoft Store app lets you download free, trial, or paid apps to launch from your Start menu.

2. **To narrow your search, click a category.**

The Store lists its offerings based on your chosen category.

TIP

Save some time by scrolling down to the Top Free Apps section, if you spot one. If you see an interesting free app, click it. Click the Install button to install the app and get the hang of the process. (To buy a paid app, click the button that lists its price.)

Didn't find the right app? Head to the next step.

3. Search for a particular app by typing a keyword in the Search box across the upper edge and pressing Enter.

Shown in Figure 6-6, the Search box narrows down the apps by the keyword. When you press Enter, the Microsoft Store app lists all matching apps, games, artists, albums, movies, and TV shows.

REMEMBER

Like the Microsoft Store app, almost all searchable apps include a built-in Search box.

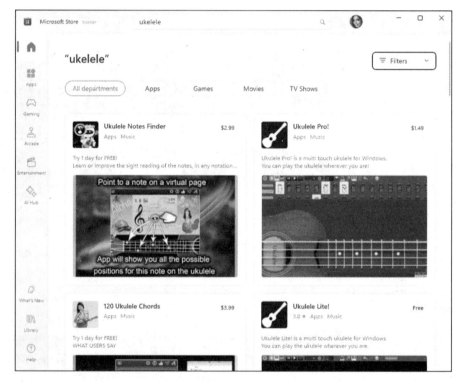

FIGURE 6-6:
Type a keyword in the Search box and press Enter to see relevant apps.

4. Sort the listed apps.

The buttons along the search results top let you fine-tune your app search. Click the Apps button, for example, to further sort your search by only apps; similarly, the Games, Movies, and TV Shows buttons limit your search to those categories.

5. Click an app to read a more detailed description.

A page opens to show more detailed information, including its price, pictures, reviews left by customers, and more technical information.

6. **Click the Get or Price button.**

    When you find a free app that you can't live without, grab it with a click on its adjacent Get button. To buy a paid app, click the button that lists its price. The price will be charged to the credit card linked to your Microsoft account. If you haven't yet entered a card, Microsoft walks you through the process.

TECHNICAL STUFF

    The Microsoft Store may ask you to choose which drive to use for installing your app. Most people choose their C: drive; owners of tablets with limited storage may prefer to choose their memory card, which is usually the D: drive. (Tiny tablets traditionally come with tiny C: drives.)

    No matter what you download from the Microsoft Store, the new item appears on your Start menu's alphabetical All Apps list as quickly as your internet connection speed allows.

To add an app's icon to the pinned area of the Start menu, click All Apps, right-click the app's name, and choose Pin to Start. I explain how to customize your Start menu further in Chapter 2.

Uninstalling apps

Downloaded a dud? To uninstall an app from the Start menu, right-click its icon. When the pop-up menu appears, click Uninstall.

Uninstalling an app removes that app only from your account's Start menu. Your action won't affect other account holders on your PC who may have installed the app. You won't get a refund for an app you've uninstalled.

UPDATING YOUR APPS

Software manufacturers constantly tweak their apps, smoothing rough spots, adding features, and plugging security holes. Whenever you connect with the internet, Windows examines your installed apps. If any are out of date, Windows automatically downloads and applies any waiting updates.

If you're using a cellular connection, don't worry: Apps don't update when you're using a metered internet connection like those found on cellphones. Windows resumes updating the apps as soon as you connect to a Wi-Fi or wired internet connection.

(continued)

(continued)

Don't want automatic updates, perhaps when traveling through areas with a slow or expensive internet connection? You can temporarily turn off automatic updating by following these steps:

1. **From the Microsoft Store app, click your account icon and choose App Settings from the drop-down menu.**

   Your account icon is your round user account photo, located in the Microsoft Store app's upper-right corner next to the Search box.

2. **When the Settings screen appears, click to make sure the App Updates toggle is set off.**

   Your changes take place immediately. When you reach a more reliable internet connection, be sure to set the toggle back on; otherwise, your apps won't update.

When the App Updates toggle is on, all your apps update. You can't keep individual apps from updating, unfortunately. That's why I recommend that you keep your apps set to update automatically. If you try to stop one from updating, you could miss out on security patches as well as improvements to all your other apps.

Taking the Lazy Way with a Desktop Shortcut

As you work, you'll constantly find yourself traveling between the desktop and the Start menu. When you grow tired of meandering through the woods to find an app, a folder, a disc drive, a document, or even a website, create a desktop *shortcut* — an icon that takes you directly to the object of your desires.

 Because a shortcut is a mere icon that launches something else, shortcuts are safe, convenient, and disposable. And they're easy to tell apart from the original because they have an arrow lodged in their lower-left corner, as you can see on the folder shortcut shown in the margin.

To skip the Start menu, follow these instructions to create desktop shortcuts to your oft-used items:

>> **Folders or documents:** From File Explorer, right-click a favorite folder or document and choose Show More Options. When the pop-up menu appears, choose Send To, and select the Desktop (Create Shortcut) option. The shortcut appears on your desktop.

- **Websites:** When viewing a website in Microsoft Edge, look for the icon in front of the website's address in the browser's address bar. Drag and drop that icon to your desktop for quick access later.

- **Storage areas:** Open File Explorer with a click of its icon (shown in the margin) on the desktop's taskbar. Then, while holding down the right mouse button, drag and drop nearly anything you want to the desktop. Release the mouse button and choose Create Shortcuts Here from the pop-up menu. This technique works for drives, folders, files, and even network locations.

Here are some more tips for desktop shortcuts:

- Want to send a desktop shortcut to the Start menu? Right-click the desktop shortcut and choose Pin to Start.

WARNING

- Feel free to move shortcuts from place to place, but *don't* move the items they launch. If you do, the shortcut won't be able to find the item, causing Windows to panic and search (usually in vain) for the relocated goods.

- Want to see which app a shortcut will launch? Right-click the shortcut and click Open File Location. The shortcut quickly takes you to its leader.

Absolutely Essential Guide to Cutting, Copying, and Pasting

Windows took a tip from the kindergartners and made cut and paste an integral part of computing life. You can electronically cut or copy just about anything and then paste it just about anyplace else with little fuss and even less mess.

For example, you can copy a photo and paste it onto your party invitation flyers. You can move files by cutting them from one folder and pasting them into another. You can cut and paste your digital camera's photos into a folder in your Pictures folder. And you can easily cut and paste paragraphs to different locations in a word processor.

The beauty of the Windows desktop is that, with all those windows onscreen at the same time, you can easily grab bits and pieces from any of them and paste all the parts into a new window.

Don't overlook copying and pasting for small stuff. Copying a name and an address is much faster and more accurate than typing them into a letter by hand. Or when someone emails you a web address that does nothing when you click it (because it's not a link), you can copy and paste it directly into your browser's address bar. It's easy to copy most items displayed on websites, too (much to the dismay of many professional photographers).

The quick 'n' dirty guide to cut, copy, and paste

In compliance with the Don't Bore Me with Details Department, here's a quick guide to the three basic steps used for cutting, copying, and pasting:

1. **Select the item to cut or copy.**

   You can select a few words, a paragraph, an entire page, a file, a group of files, a web address, or just about any other item on your computer.

2. **Right-click your selection, and choose the Cut or Copy icon from the top of the pop-up menu, depending on your needs.**

   Use Cut when you want to move something. Use Copy when you want to duplicate something, leaving the original intact. Keyboard shortcut: Hold down Ctrl and press X to cut or C to copy.

3. **Right-click the item's destination, and then choose Paste.**

   You can right-click inside a document, a folder, another app, or some other place in your computer. Keyboard shortcut: Hold down Ctrl and press V to paste.

As always, Copilot can help you with any copy-and-paste task you have. For example, ask Copilot, "How do I copy and paste text?" or "How do I copy and paste files?" or "How do I move a file to a different location?"

The next three sections explain each of these three steps in more detail.

Selecting things to cut or copy

Before you can shuttle pieces of information to new places, you have to tell Windows exactly what you want to grab. The easiest way to provide this info is to *select* the information with a mouse. In most cases, selecting involves one swift trick with the mouse, which then highlights whatever you've selected:

» **To select text in a document, an email, a website, or a spreadsheet:** Put the mouse pointer or cursor at the beginning of the information you want and hold down the mouse button. Then move the mouse to the end of the information and release the button. That's it! That lassoing action selects all the stuff between where you clicked and released, as shown in Figure 6-7. Chapter 16 discusses selecting text in detail.

TIP

On a touchscreen, double-tap one word to select it. To select more than one word, double-tap the first word but keep your finger pressed on the glass with your second tap. Then slide your finger along the glass until you've reached the area where the highlighting should stop. Done? Remove your finger to select that portion of text.

WARNING

Be careful after you highlight a bunch of text. If you accidentally press the K key, for example, the app replaces your highlighted text with the letter *k*. To reverse that calamity, choose Undo from the app's Edit menu (or press Ctrl+Z, which is the magical keyboard shortcut for undo).

FIGURE 6-7:
Windows highlights the selected text, changing its color for easy visibility.

» **To select any files or folders:** Simply click a file or folder icon to select it. To select *several* items, try these tricks:

- **If all the files are in a row (contiguous):** Click the first item in the bunch, hold down the Shift key, and then select the last item. Windows highlights the first and last items as well as everything in between.

- **If the files *aren't* in a row (noncontiguous): Click the first file or folder you want to select, and then Ctrl+click any others you want to select.**

After you select something, cut it or copy it *immediately.* If you absentmindedly click the mouse someplace else, your highlighted text or file reverts to its boring self, and you have to start over. If you just want to delete the selected item(s), press the Delete key. Alternatively, right-click the item and choose Delete from the pop-up menu.

If all this select, cut, copy, and paste terminology leaves you flummoxed, try to remember the keyword *select.* Then you can ask Copilot, "How do I select text?" or "How do I select icons?"

Cutting or copying your selected goods

After you select some information (which I describe in the preceding section, in case you just arrived), you're ready to start playing with it. You can cut it or copy it. (Or just press Delete to delete it.)

This bears repeating. After selecting something, right-click it. (On a touchscreen, touch it and hold down your finger.) When the menu appears, choose Cut or Copy, depending on your needs, as shown in Figure 6-8. Then right-click your destination and choose Paste.

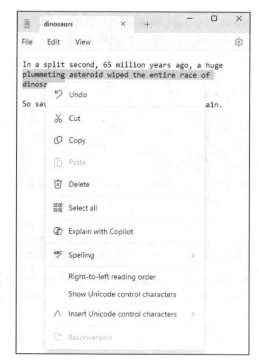

FIGURE 6-8:
To copy information into another window, right-click your selection and choose Copy.

The Cut and Copy options differ drastically. How do you know which one to choose? Use Cut when you want to *move* (relocate) a file. Use Copy when you want to *duplicate* a file.

Pasting information to another place

Any time you select and copy or cut something, a copy of that item is placed in the Windows clipboard, which is an area of the computer's memory. Once you have the information in the clipboard, it stays there until you cut or copy something else. While the item in still in the clipboard, you can paste that information nearly anyplace.

Pasting is straightforward:

1. **If you're pasting icons, open the folder or drive in which you want to paste the item(s). If you're working with text, click the spot where you would have otherwise typed the text yourself.**

2. **Right-click the mouse and choose Paste from the pop-up menu, or press Ctrl+V.**

   Presto! The item you just cut or copied leaps into its new spot.

Here are some general things worth knowing about pasting:

>> The Paste command inserts a *copy* of the information that's sitting on the clipboard. The information stays on the clipboard, so you can keep pasting the same thing into other places if you want.

>> To paste on a touchscreen, hold down your finger where you'd like to paste the information. When the menu pops up, tap Paste.

>> Some apps, including File Explorer, have toolbars along their tops, offering additional one-click access to the versatile Cut, Copy, and Paste icons, as shown in Figure 6-9. (To keep you from having to move your hand too much, they also appear along the top of some pop-up menus.)

If this cut, copy, paste terminology leaves your head spinning, just ask Copilot, "How do I copy and paste text?" or "How do I copy and paste files?"

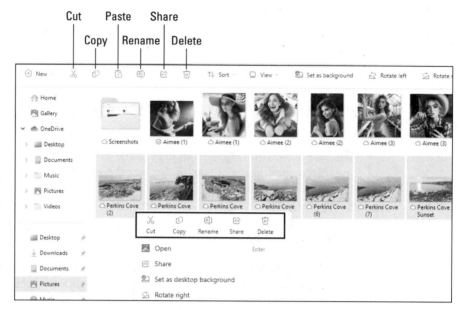

FIGURE 6-9:
Throughout
Windows 11 2024
Update, look for
the Cut, Copy,
and Paste icons
along the top
or bottom of
its many
pop-up menus.

Undoing what you've just done

If you complete an action and suddenly realize you've made a mistake, don't panic. Windows offers a way for you to undo your last action, which quickly pours the spilled milk back into the carton.

Simply press Ctrl+Z. The last mistake you made is reversed, sparing you from further shame. (Clicking an app's undo icon, if you can find one, does the same thing.)

And if you mistakenly undo something that really should have stayed in place, press Ctrl+Y. That undoes your last undo, putting it back in place.

NEW

If you forget how to undo or redo, just ask Copilot, "How do I undo (or redo) in Windows?" Replace *Windows* with the name of the specific app you're using, as needed.

IN THIS CHAPTER

» Finding currently running apps

» Finding lost desktop
   windows and files

» Finding lost apps, emails, songs,
   photos, and documents

» Finding stuff based on their details

Chapter **7**

Finding the Lost

Sooner or later, Windows gives you that head-scratching feeling. "Gosh," you say as you drum nervous fingers, "that stuff was *right there* a second ago. Where did it go?" When you can't seem to find a desired item anywhere, you can use Windows to *search* for the missing item. This chapter explains how.

Finding Currently Running Apps

The Windows desktop lets you run apps in windows, keeping everything neatly self-contained. But even then, those windows tend to overlap, hiding the ones beneath.

How do you find and return to an app you just used? How do you easily jump between them, perhaps glancing at a report while creating a spreadsheet?

Windows offers a quick solution to the problem: It can shrink all your running apps into miniature windows called *thumbnails,* and show you the lineup, as displayed in Figure 7-1. Click the app you want, and it returns to active duty at its normal size.

FIGURE 7-1:
Click the task
view icon to see
all your currently
running apps.

To see the list of your open apps (and to close unwanted ones, if desired), employ any of these tricks:

>> **Mouse:** Click the taskbar's task view icon (shown in the margin) to see thumbnails of all your open apps. To switch to an app, click its thumbnail. To close an app, right-click its thumbnail and choose Close. (You can also click the X in the thumbnail's upper-right corner.)

>> **Keyboard:** Press Windows+Tab to see the list of your open apps (refer to Figure 7-1). Press the left- or right-arrow key to select different thumbnails. When you've selected your desired window, press Enter, and the app fills the screen. Or press Delete to close the selected app.

Windows 11 no longer allows touchscreen owners to slide their finger gently inward from the screen's left edge to see all their open apps. Well, you can still slide your finger inward, but you'll only see a monthly calendar and any waiting notifications.

Clicking the task view icon shows your currently running apps, making it easy to return to work. Clicking the task view icon also lets you create a *virtual desktop*, an odd concept that gives you more than one desktop. For details, see Chapter 4.

Finding Lost Windows on the Desktop

The Windows desktop works much like a regular desktop in that every time you open a new window or app, you toss another piece of information on top of what's already there. Just a sheets of paper can pile up on a real desktop, app windows can pile up on a computer desktop. The window on top is easy to spot, but how do you reach the windows lying beneath it?

If you can see any part of a buried window's edge or corner, a well-placed click fetches it, bringing it to the top.

When your window is completely buried, look at the desktop's *taskbar* — that strip along your screen's bottom edge. Spot your missing window's icon on the taskbar? Click it to dredge the window back to the top. (See Chapter 3 for details about the taskbar.)

Still can't get at that missing window? Press Alt+Tab. Windows shows thumbnails of all your open windows in a strip across the screen's center, as shown in Figure 7-2. While holding down the Alt key, repeatedly press Tab to cycle forward through thumbnails, and press Alt+Shift+Tab to cycle backward through thumbnails. When the thumbnail for the app you want is highlighted, let go of the Alt key, and that window will appear on your desktop.

FIGURE 7-2:
Hold down the Alt key and press Tab repeatedly to cycle through your open windows.

TIP

Clicking the task view icon, described in the preceding section, also lets you see miniature views of every open window. When you spot the window you want to bring back to the forefront, return to it with a click.

Locating a Missing App, Setting, or File

The preceding two sections explain how to find *currently running* apps. But what about finding things that you haven't looked at for a while?

That's the job of the Search box, which now lives on top of the Start menu. To jump immediately to the Search box, click the magnifying glass icon, which appears next to the start icon on the taskbar.

But whether you reach the Search box from the Start menu or from the magnifying glass icon, the Search box searches through *everything*, both on your PC and the internet. That helps you find wandering files, hidden settings, and informational tidbits, all with one search.

To search for missing things, follow these steps:

1. Click the taskbar's Search box to summon the Search window, and then type what you'd like to find.

As you type, Windows immediately begins searching for matches.

For example, here's what happens when searching for Jimi Hendrix: As I begin typing letters, Windows begins listing files with matching names, as shown in Figure 7-3. After typing **Jimi** on my computer, for example, Windows found several matches and organized them in the Search window in these categories:

- **Best Match:** The Search box lists all matching terms, with the best match at the top, in this case, a folder on my PC with the music of American guitarist Jimi Hendrix.

- **Search the Web:** Below the best match, the Search window shows internet links to other potential matches. Some may seem way off base (such as Jiminy Cricket), but you can simply ignore those.

- **Music:** This section shows individual songs on my computer by Jimi Hendrix.

As you begin typing, the Search box concentrates on speed, so it searches only for matching filenames stored on your computer and OneDrive, as well as doing a quick internet search. The search box might also suggest a next word. For example, I got *Hendrix* as a suggested second word. When you see that sort of thing, press Tab to accept the suggested word. Otherwise, just keep typing to replace the suggested word.

If you spot your missing item, jump ahead to Step 3.

If you finish typing your complete search term but don't see your sought-after item on the Search list, move on to Step 2. You need to define your search more thoroughly.

2. **Limit your search to a specific category.**

   To route your search to a specific area, click one of the words near the top of the search results. Choosing Web, for example, lists links to websites about Jimi Hendrix, as shown in Figure 7-4.

   No matter which category you choose, Windows immediately shows any available matches. Changed your mind about a search category? Click a different word to route your search to that category, instead.

3. **Select a matching item to open it, bringing it to the screen.**

   Back in the original search (refer to Figure 7-3) clicking a song on my computer plays that song. In the Web results (refer to Figure 7-4), clicking Songs takes me to websites containing songs by Jimi Hendrix.

TIP

These tips can help you wring the most out of the Search feature:

>> In its emphasis on speed, the Search window lists only files with names that match your search term. While this strategy sometimes helps you find quick matches, it might not find, say, your shopping list if you search for **oranges**. When you don't spot a sure match, finish typing your search term and click one of the icons along the top of the pane to route your search to the appropriate spot.

FIGURE 7-4:
Narrow your
search further by
limiting it to
certain areas.

>> Don't press the Enter key after typing your search term. If you do that, Windows calls up the first match, which may not be what you want. Wait to see what matches turn up and then click the desired match.

>> The Search box scours every file in your Documents, Music, Pictures, and Videos folders. This feature makes storing your files in those folders more important than ever.

>> The Search box also scours every file you store on your OneDrive space, even if those files aren't also stored on your PC.

>> Windows doesn't search for files stored in removable devices, such as flash drives or portable hard drives.

>> If you're searching for a common word and the Search box finds too many files, limit your search by typing a short phrase from your sought-after file: **Shortly after the cat nibbled the bamboo**, for example. The more words you type, the better your chances of pinpointing a particular file.

>> The Search box ignores capital letters. It considers **Bee** and **bee** to be the same insect.

NEW

>> If you forget all of what I just told you, tell Copilot, "Help me find a missing file." Or if you remember part of the filename, ask Copilot, "Where are my files with *aimee* in the name?" (replacing *aimee* with your own search word).

Finding a Missing File inside a Folder

The Start menu's Search box can be overkill when you're poking around in a single desktop folder, looking for a missing file. To solve the "sea of files in a folder" problem, File Explorer (the app that shows you the contents of any folder you open), includes a Search box in its upper-right corner. That Search box limits your search to files in that particular folder.

To find a missing file in a specific folder, open the folder and then click the Search box. Start typing a word or short phrase from your missing file. As you type letters and words, Windows begins filtering out files that are missing your sought-after word or phrase. It keeps narrowing the candidates until the folder displays only a few files, including, I hope, your runaway file.

When the Search box locates too many possible matches, bring in some other helping hands. Click the View icon on File Explorer's toolbar (near the top) and choose Details from the drop-down menu. That lines up your filenames in one column, as shown in Figure 7-5. The first column, Name, lists the name of each file, and the adjacent columns list details about each file.

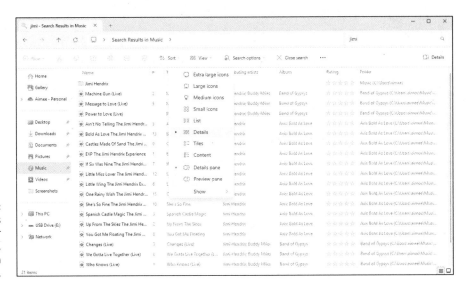

FIGURE 7-5: Details view lets you sort your files by name, making them easier to find.

TIP

See the column headers, such as Name, Album, and Rating, at the top of each column? Click any of those headers to sort your files by that term. Here's how to sort by some of the column headers you may see in your Documents folder:

>> **Name:** Know the first letter of the filename? Then click here to sort your files alphabetically. You can then pluck your file from the list. (Click Name again to reverse the sort order.)

>> **Date Modified:** If you remember the approximate date you last changed a document, click the Date Modified header. If you don't see that column heading, right-click any column heading and choose Date Modified to add that column. Your newest files will be at the top of the list, making them easy to locate. (Clicking Date Modified again reverses the order, a handy way to weed out old files you may no longer need.)

>> **Type:** This header sorts files by their contents. Again, if you don't see this column heading, right-click any column heading and choose Type. If there are many different kinds of files in the folder, this choice will group them by type, separating pictures from Word documents from other file types. It's a handy way to find, say, a few stray photos swimming in a sea of text files.

>> **Tags:** Windows often lets you assign tags to your documents and photos, a task I describe later in this chapter. Adding a Moldy Cheese tag to that pungent photo session lets you retrieve those pictures by either typing the tag or sorting a folder's files by their tags.

TIP

The column headings that appear in the Details view vary depending on the folder's contents. But don't worry, you can view any columns you like, in any order you like, with these awesome techniques:

>> To add a column to your view, right-click any column heading and then click the name of the column you want to add.

>> To hide a column, right-click any column heading and then click the column you want to hide. (The column name will have a check mark, indicating that it's currently displayed.)

>> Widen or narrow any column by dragging the bar at the right side of the column heading right or left.

>> Rearrange columns by dragging a column heading left or right.

>> To sort by a column, click its column heading.

>> To switch between ascending and descending orders, click the arrow at the right side of the sorted column.

DEEP SORT

A folder's Details view (refer to Figure 7-5) arranges your filenames into a single column, with oodles of detail columns flowing off to the right. You can sort a folder's contents by clicking the word above any column: Name, Date Modified, Author, and so on. But the sort features in Windows go much deeper, as you'll notice when clicking the downward-pointing arrow that appears as you hover your mouse pointer over each column's name.

Click the arrow to the right of the Date Modified, for example, and a calendar drops down. Click a date, and the folder displays files modified on that particular date, filtering out all the rest. Below the calendar, check boxes let you view files created Today, Yesterday, Last Week, Earlier This Month, Earlier This Year, or simply A Long Time Ago. (The available check boxes change depending on the age of the files inside your currently viewed folder.) You can also check the Select a Date or Date Range check box above the calendar, click the start date in the calendar, and then Shift-click the end date in the calendar.

Similarly, click the arrow next to the Authors column header, and a drop-down menu lists the authors of every document in the folder. Select the check boxes next to the author names you'd like to see, and Windows immediately filters out files created by other people, leaving only the matches. (This feature works best with Microsoft Office documents.)

These hidden filters can be dangerous, however, because you can easily forget that you've turned them on. If you spot a check mark next to any column header, you've left a filter turned on, and the folder is hiding some of its files. To turn off the filter and see *all* that folder's files, click the check box next to the column heading and then clear any check boxes that are filtering the search results.

NEW

For more tips on using the Details view, tell Copilot, "Give me some tips on using File Explorer's Details view."

Finding Lost Photos

Windows indexes your files down to the last word, but it can't tell the difference between photos of your cat and photos of your office party. That's because computers don't have eyes (or a brain), so they can't see what's in a photo. When it comes to photos, the ID work lies in *your* hands, and these tips make the chore as easy as possible:

>> **Store shooting sessions in separate folders.** The Windows Photos importing feature automatically creates a folder to store each session, named after the current date. But if you're using some other app to dump photos, be sure to create a folder for each session. Then name the folder with a short description of your session, such as *Dog Walk, Kite Surfing,* or *Truffle Hunt.* (Windows indexes the folder names, making them easier to find down the road.)

>> **Sort by date.** Have you stumbled onto a massive folder that's a mishmash of digital photos? Try this quick sorting trick: Click the View icon along the folder's upper edge, and choose Large Icons to make the photos morph into identifiable thumbnails. Then, from the adjacent Sort menu, choose More from the drop-down menu. From there, choose Date Taken. Windows sorts the photos by the date you snapped them, turning chaos into organization.

>> **Tag your photos.** Tags let you assign keywords to photos that you can search for later. In File Explorer, right-click any photo's icon and choose Properties. Click the Details tab, and then click Tags. Type your tag word. If you want multiple tags, separate them with semicolons. For example, **Hawaii; beach; luau.** When you search for any one of those tag words, the photo will appear in the search results.

TIP

If you want to tag multiple photos with the same word or words, select the photos first, right-click any selected photo, and choose Properties.

>> **Rename your photos.** Instead of leaving your Tunisian vacation photos with their boring camera-given names such as DSC_2421 and DSC_2422, give them meaningful names. Select all the files in your Tunisia folder by clicking the Home tab on the ribbon and then clicking the Select All button. Then right-click the first picture, choose Rename, and type **Tunisia**. Windows names them Tunisia, Tunisia (2), Tunisia (3), and so on. (If you mess up, immediately press Ctrl+Z to undo the renaming.)

Following these simple rules helps keep your photo collection from becoming a jumble of files.

REMEMBER

Be *sure* to back up your digital photos to OneDrive, a USB drive, or another backup method I describe in Chapter 13. If they're not backed up, you'll lose your family history should your computer get lost, stolen, or damaged.

Chapter **8**

Printing and Scanning Your Work

O ccasionally you'll want to take text or an image away from your PC's whirling electrons and place it onto something more permanent: a piece of paper. This chapter tackles that job by explaining all you need to know about printing.

I explain how to print just the relevant portions of a website — without other pages, ads, menus, and printer-ink-wasting images. You also discover how to print from apps, print Copilot output, and make your own PDFs. (For details on setting up a printer, see Chapter 12.)

And should you find yourself near a printer spitting out 17 pages of the wrong thing, flip ahead to this chapter's coverage of the mysterious *print queue.* It's a little-known area that lets you cancel documents before they waste all your paper.

When you need to turn a piece of paper or printed photo into a file on your PC, check out the last section of this chapter. It provides a rundown on the Windows Scan app. When combined with a scanner, this app transforms maps, receipts, photos, and any other paper items into digital files that you can store on your PC.

Printing from an App

If a working printer is already available, printing a document usually starts with opening it in an appropriate app:

>> Get to the document's file in File Explorer, and then double-click the file's icon or filename to open it.

>> Open the app from which you want to print, choose File ➪ Open from that app's menu, and then open the document you want to print.

Most apps that allow you to work with text and pictures have a Print command. So the following steps should work for most apps:

1. Choose File ➪ Print in the app's menu bar, as shown in Figure 8-1.

Usually the File command is near the top-left corner. If you can't find a menu bar, the File command might be available by clicking a hamburger menu (three horizontal lines) or a more icon (three dots) near the top-right or top-left corner. Or press Ctrl+P.

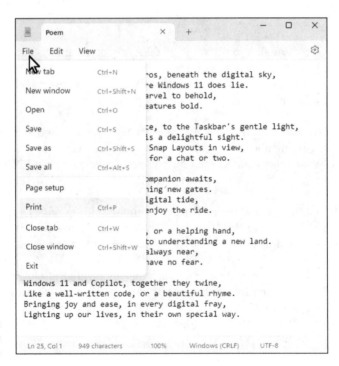

FIGURE 8-1:
File menu in the
Notepad app.

2. **Click the Printer drop-down menu to see which printers are available to you.**

   Some printers might have weird names, as shown in Figure 8-2. If you're at work and don't recognize any of the printer names, ask a colleague which printer you should use. If you don't have an installed printer, you'll see only an option to print to PDF (discussed later in this chapter). Click Cancel at this point if you need to bow out gracefully.

Notepad - Print

Printer

Microsoft Print to PDF

HPF27D1D (HP Officejet Pro 6230)

NPI90A09E (HP LaserJet CP1525nw)

OneNote (Desktop)

HP20161E (HP ENVY 110 series)

HP LaserJet CP1525nw (90A09E)

HP Officejet Pro 6230 [F27D1D]

FIGURE 8-2:
List of available printers.

3. **When you spot your printer from the list that appears, click its name.**

   New options related to your chosen printer appear.

4. **Make any final adjustments.**

   Depending on your printer, you may be able to adjust other settings, such as page orientation, the number of copies to print, which page (or pages) you want to print, and so on.

5. **Click the Print button.**

   Windows shuffles your work to the printer of your choice, using the settings you chose in Step 4.

Windows might need a few seconds to get its act together, so be patient. Take a minute or so to refresh your coffee. If the printer is turned on (and has paper and ink), Windows handles everything automatically, printing in the background while you do other things.

If the printed pages don't look quite right — perhaps the information doesn't fit on the paper correctly or it looks faded —you need to fiddle around with the print settings or perhaps change the paper quality, as described in the next sections.

>> To print a bunch of documents quickly, select all their icons. Then right-click the selected icons and choose Print. Windows shuttles all of them to the printer, where they emerge on paper, one after the other.

>> When printing with an inkjet printer, faded colors usually indicate that you need to replace your printer's color inkjet cartridges. You can buy replacement cartridges both online and at most office supply stores.

>> Still haven't installed a printer? Flip to Chapter 12, where I explain how to plug one into your computer and make Windows notice it.

Adjusting how your work fits on the page

In many apps, when you click File, you'll see a Page Setup command (refer to Figure 8-1). Click Page Setup to see commands similar to those shown in Figure 8-3.

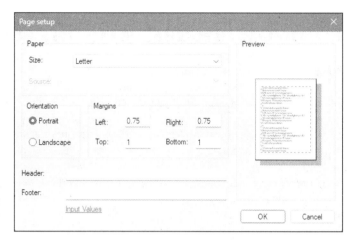

The exact commands available vary depending on the app, but the following list describes the options that you'll find most often and the settings that usually work best:

» **Paper size:** This option lets your program know the size of paper inside your printer. Leave this option set to Letter for printing on standard, 8.5-x-11-inch sheets of paper. Change this setting only if you're using legal-size paper (8.5 x 14), envelopes, or other paper sizes. (The nearby sidebar, "Printing envelopes without fuss," contains more information about printing envelopes.)

» **Source:** Choose Automatically Select or Sheet Feeder unless you're using a fancy printer that accepts paper from more than one printer tray. People who have printers with two or more printer trays can select the tray containing the correct paper size. Some printers offer a manual paper feed, where the printer waits until you slide in that single sheet of paper.

» **Header/footer:** Type codes in these boxes to customize what the printer places along the top and bottom of your pages, such as page numbers, titles, and dates, as well as their spacing. Unfortunately, different programs use different codes for the header and footer. If you spot a question mark in the Page Setup window's upper-right corner, click it and then click in the Header or Footer box for clues to the codes. In Figure 8-3, clicking the Input Value link provides useful information.

» **Orientation:** Leave this option set to Portrait to print normal pages that read vertically, like a letter. Choose Landscape only when you want to print sideways, which is a handy way to print large photos and wide spreadsheets. (If you choose Landscape, the printer automatically prints the page sideways; you don't need to slide the paper sideways into your printer.)

PRINTING ENVELOPES WITHOUT FUSS

Although clicking Envelopes in an app's Page Setup area is fairly easy, printing addresses in the correct spot on the envelope is extraordinarily difficult. Some printer models want you to insert envelopes upside down, but others prefer right side up. Your best bet is to run several tests, placing the envelope into your printer's tray in different ways until you finally stumble on the magic method. (Or you can pull out your printer's manual, if you still have it, and pore over the "proper envelope insertion" pictures.)

After you figure out the correct method for your particular printer, tape a successfully printed envelope above your printer and add an arrow pointing to the correct way to insert it.

Should you eventually give up on printing envelopes, try using Avery's free downloadable templates from Avery's website (www.avery.com). Compatible with Microsoft Word, the templates place boxes on your screen that precisely match the size of your particular Avery labels. Type the addresses in the boxes, insert the label sheet into your printer, and Word prints everything onto the stickers. You don't even need to lick them.

Or do as I did: Buy a rubber stamp with your return address. It's much faster than stickers or printers.

>> **Margins:** Feel free to reduce the margins to fit everything on a single sheet of paper. Or enlarge the margins to turn your six-page term paper into the required seven pages. Note that most printers don't allow you to set the margins to zero.

When you've finished adjusting settings, click OK to save your changes. Then choose File⇨ Print to print using the options you've selected.

TIP

To find the Page Setup box in some apps, click the arrow next to the app's Printer icon and choose Page Setup from the menu that drops down.

Canceling a print job

Just realized you sent the wrong 26-page document to the printer? Did you panic and hit the printer's Off button? Unfortunately, many printers automatically pick up where they left off when you turn them back on, leaving you or your co-workers to deal with the mess.

To purge the mistake from your printer's memory, follow these steps:

1. **In the lower-right corner of your screen, right-click your printer's icon and choose your printer's name from the pop-up menu.**

   To see your printer's icon, you may need to click the upward-pointing arrow to the left of the taskbar's icons next to the clock.

   When you choose your printer's name, the handy *print queue* window appears, as shown in Figure 8-4.

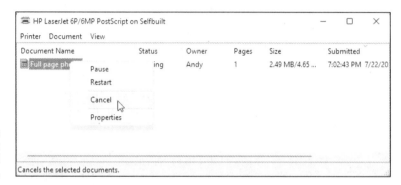

FIGURE 8-4:
Use the print queue to cancel a print job.

2. **Right-click your mistaken document, and choose Cancel to end the job. If asked to confirm, click Yes. Repeat with any other listed unwanted documents.**

The print queue can take a minute or two to clear itself. When the print queue is clear, turn your printer back on. Here are some more general tips when printing:

>> The print queue, also known as the *print spooler,* lists every document waiting patiently to reach your printer. Feel free to change the printing order by dragging and dropping documents up or down the list. (However, you can't move anything in front of the currently printing document.)

>> Sharing your printer on the network? Print jobs sent from other PCs sometimes end up in your computer's print queue, so you'll need to cancel the botched ones. (And networked folks who share their printer may need to delete your botched print jobs as well.)

>> If your printer runs out of paper during a job and stubbornly halts, add more paper. Then to start things flowing again, open the print queue, right-click your document, and choose Restart. (Some printers have an Online button that you push to begin printing again.)

» You can send items to the printer even when you're working in the coffee shop with your laptop. Later, when you connect the laptop to your printer, the print queue notices and begins sending your files. (Beware: When documents are in the print queue, they're formatted for your specific printer model. If you subsequently connect your laptop to a different printer model, the print queue's waiting documents might not print correctly.)

Printing a web page

Although information-stuffed web pages look awfully tempting, printing those web pages is rarely satisfying because they look so awful on paper. When sent to the printer, web pages often run off the page's right side, consume zillions of additional pages, or appear much too small to read.

To make matters worse, all those colorful advertisements can suck your printer's color cartridges dry fairly quickly. Only four things make for successfully printed web pages, and I rank them in order of their probable success:

» **Use the web page's built-in Print option.** Some websites offer a menu option called Print This Page, Text Version, Printer-Friendly Version, or something similar. This option, which tells the website to strip its garbage and reformat the page so that it fits neatly onto a sheet of paper, is the most reliable way to print a web page.

» **Choose Print Preview from your browser's File or Print menu.** After 20 years, some web page designers noticed that people want to print their pages, so they tweaked the settings, making their pages automatically reformat themselves when printed. If you're lucky, a clean look in the Print Preview window confirms that you've stumbled onto one of these printer-friendly sites.

» **Copy the portion you want, and paste it into a word processor.** Try selecting the desired text from the web page, copying it, and pasting it into Notepad or a word processor. Be aware that Notepad can accept only text, not pictures. Delete any unwanted remnants, adjust the margins, and print the portion you want. I explain how to select, copy, and paste in Chapter 6.

» **Copy the entire page, and paste it into a word processor.** This option is a lot of work. Right-click a blank portion of the web page and choose Select All. Right-click again and choose Copy. Next, open Microsoft Word or another full-featured word processor, and paste the web page inside a new document. By hacking away at the unwanted portions, you can sometimes end up with something printable.

These tips may also come in handy for moving a web page from screen to paper:

>> The Microsoft Edge web browser can print. To print what you're viewing in Edge, click the browser's three dots in the upper-right corner and choose Print from the drop-down menu.

>> If you spot an Email option but no Print option, email the page to yourself. Depending on your email app, you may have better success printing the page as an email message.

>> If a web page's table or photo insists on vanishing off the paper's right edge, try printing the page in landscape mode rather than portrait. See the "Adjusting how your work fits on the page" section, previously in this chapter, for details on landscape mode.

Troubleshooting your printer

When you can't print something, start with the basics: Are you *sure* that the printer is turned on, plugged into the wall, full of paper, and connected securely to your computer with a cable or via your network?

If not, try plugging the printer into different outlets, turning it on, and seeing whether its power light comes on. If the light stays off, your printer's power supply is probably blown.

Printers are almost always cheaper to replace than repair. Printer companies make their money on ink cartridges, so they often sell printers at a loss.

If the printer's power light beams brightly, check the following before giving up:

>> Make sure that a sheet of paper isn't jammed inside the printer. (A slow, steady pull usually extricates jammed paper. Sometimes opening and closing the printer's lid starts things moving again.)

>> Does your inkjet printer still have ink in its cartridges? Does your laser printer have toner? Try printing a test page: In the Search box next to the start icon, type **print**. Click Printers & Scanners on the Start menu, click your printer's name, and then click the Print Test Page button to see whether the computer and printer can talk to each other.

>> If you're using a wireless printer, try connecting it to your PC with a cable. That helps you see whether the problem is your wireless connection or the printer itself.

>> Try updating the printer's *driver,* the file that helps it talk with Windows. Visit the printer manufacturer's website, download the newest Windows driver for your particular printer model, and run its installation app. (I cover drivers in Chapter 13.)

Finally, here are a couple of tips to help you protect your printer and cartridges:

>> Turn off your printer when you're not using it. Older inkjet printers, especially, should be turned off when they're not in use. The heat tends to dry the cartridges, shortening their life.

WARNING

>> Don't unplug your inkjet printer to turn it off. Always use the on/off switch. The switch ensures that the cartridges slide back to their home positions, keeping them from drying out or clogging.

CHOOSING THE RIGHT PAPER FOR YOUR PRINTER

If you've strolled the aisles at an office-supply store lately, you've noticed a bewildering array of paper choices. Sometimes the paper's packaging lists its application, such as premium inkjet paper. Here's a list of different print jobs and the types of paper they require. Before printing, be sure to click the Printer's Preferences section to select the grade of paper you're using for that job.

- **Junk:** Keep some cheap or scrap paper around for testing the printer, printing quick drafts, leaving desktop notes, and printing other on-the-fly jobs. Botched print jobs work great here; just use the paper's other side.

- **Letter quality:** Bearing the words Premium or Bright White, this paper works fine for letters, reports, memos, and other documents you want to show to others.

- **Photos:** You can print photos on any type of paper, but they look like photos only on actual photo-quality paper — the expensive stuff. Slide the paper carefully into your printer tray so that the picture prints on the glossy, shiny side. Some photo paper requires placing a cardboard sheet beneath it, which helps glide the paper smoothly through the printer.

- **Labels:** Avery, the paper company, offers templates that let Microsoft Word mesh with Avery's preformatted mailing labels, greeting cards, business cards, CD labels, and other items. You might also try the company's free Avery Design & Print app, available at their website (www.avery.com).

- **Transparencies:** For powerful PowerPoint presentations, buy special transparent plastic sheets designed to be used with your type of printer.

Before plunking down your money, make sure that your paper is designed for your printer type, be it laser or inkjet. Laser printers heat the pages, and some paper and transparencies can't take the heat.

Printing Copilot output

Copilot can type up virtually any document you request — at hundreds of words per minute, with zero mistakes. But how do you get all the content off the screen, and onto paper, into a PDF, or saved as a file? The short answer is simple: copy and paste. There's always a copy icon (two identical rectangles) near the end of the output. Content embedded in long output might have its own copy icon near the top-right corner, as shown in Figure 8-5.

FIGURE 8-5:
Copy icons in
Copilot output.

To print the Copilot output, you need to copy and paste it into an appropriate app. You can use Notepad, which comes with Windows, or more advanced word processors, such as Microsoft Word or Google Docs. In the following steps, I use Notepad:

1. **In your Copilot output, click the copy icon.**

2. **Open Notepad from the Start menu or the All Apps menu.**

   If Notepad already has content, choose File ➪ New to start with a blank page.

3. **Click anywhere in the blank Notepad document, and then press Ctrl+V.**

   You can instead choose Edit ➪ Paste or right-click anywhere in the empty document and choose Paste. The text you copied is pasted into the document.

4. **In Notepad, choose File ➪ Print.**

   Choose your printer and any other options, as described previously in this chapter, and then click Print.

If you'd like to save the output to re-use it later, choose File ➪ Save from Notepad's menu. Put the document in your Documents folder or wherever you like. Type a file name, and then click Save.

If you'd like to make a PDF file to share with others, print the document to a PDF file, as described in the next sections.

Making a PDF

Portable Document Format (PDF) is a file format for sharing electronic documents. People often attach PDF documents to email messages to share information. Like any document, each PDF is stored in its own file. The filename extension is (not surprisingly) .pdf. If you have an electronic document you want to share with others, you can save it as a PDF file. You don't need to own a printer for this to work. Just go through the steps of printing the document, as described at the beginning of the "Printing from an App" section. But in the Print window, choose Microsoft Print to PDF as your printer (see Figure 8-6).

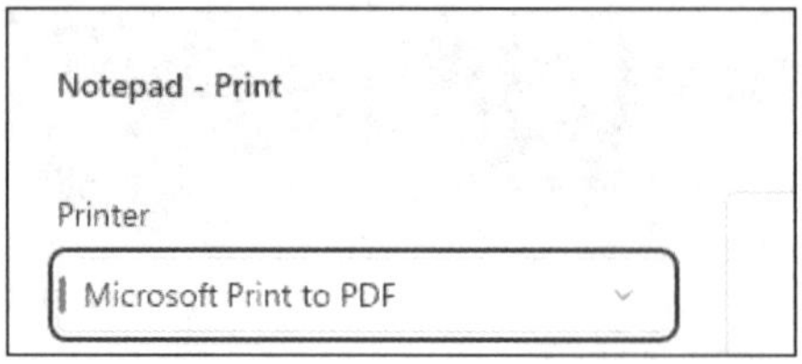

Notepad - Print

Printer

| Microsoft Print to PDF   ⌄ |

FIGURE 8-6:
To make a PDF, choose Microsoft Print to PDF.

When you click the Print button, Windows asks where you want to put the PDF file and what you want to name it, as shown in Figure 8-7. You can put the file on your desktop, or in your Documents folder. Name the file whatever you want; the .pdf extension is added automatically. Then click Save.

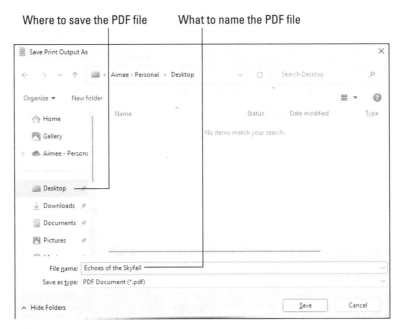

FIGURE 8-7:
Choose a location, and name your PDF file.

The PDF file will be created and placed where you specified. Double-click the PDF file's icon to open it and take a look. To share the file with others via email, just attach it to an email message.

Scanning from the Start Menu

Scanning converts paper documents to electronic documents. You need a scanner for that to work. Some printers have a built-in scanner. If you have a scanner, it probably came with an app you can use to scan documents. If have a scanner but no app for it, you might be able to use the free Scan app, available from the Microsoft Store. Look for the app by its new name, Windows Scan. (I explain how to get apps from the Microsoft Store in Chapter 6.) Note that the Windows Scan app doesn't work with some older scanners.

I can't give you step-by-step directions for your particular scanner because they all work slightly differently. But if your scanner is relatively new, you may find

Windows Scan a refreshing change from the complicated software bundled with most scanners.

NEW

If Windows Scan can't find your scanner, ask Copilot for help. If possible, include the scanner model information in your prompt. For example, you might ask, "How do I connect my HP OfficeJet scanner in Windows 11?"

After installing the Windows Scan app from the Microsoft Store and connecting your scanner, follow these steps to scan something into your computer:

1. **From the Start menu, open the Windows Scan app.**

   If you don't spot the Windows Scan app on the Start menu, click All Apps in the Start menu's upper-right corner. The Start menu lists all its apps alphabetically.

   Although the Microsoft Store calls the app Windows Scan, the app renames itself to simply *Scan* when it installs on your PC. Thanks, Microsoft.

    Click the icon for the Scan app (shown in the margin), and the Scan app appears on the screen. If it complains that your scanner isn't connected, make sure your scanner is connected via a cable or your network.

   If your scanner is plugged in and turned on, the Scan app lists your scanner's name, as shown in Figure 8-8, and the file type used for saving your files. (The PNG file type is widely accepted by most apps.)

   If the app doesn't recognize your scanner, your scanner is too old. You're stuck with using your scanner's bundled software — if it works — or, unfortunately, buying a new scanner.

2. **(Optional) To change the Scan app's settings, click the Show More link.**

   The app's default settings work fine for most jobs. The Show More link offers these options for specific types of scans:

   - **File Type:** Choose a file type from the drop-down menu. PDF is a good choice for most scans. If you're scanning a photo or a picture (no text), you could choose PNG or JPEG.

   - **Color Mode:** Choose Color for color items, including photos and glossy magazine pages. Choose Grayscale for nearly everything else, and choose Black and White *only* for line drawings or black-and-white clip art.

   - **Resolution (DPI):** For most work, the default 300 works fine. Higher resolution scans (larger numbers) bring more detail but consume more space, making them difficult to email. Lower resolution scans show less detail but create smaller file sizes. You may need to experiment to find the settings that meet your needs.

- **Save File To:** The Scan app creates a Scan folder in your PC's Pictures folder, where it stores your newly scanned images. If you want, you can change the Scan folder's name or create a different folder for each scanning session.

3. **Click the Preview icon to make sure your scan appears correctly.**

The Scan app makes a first pass, letting you preview a scan made with your chosen settings.

If the preview doesn't look right, make sure you've made the right choice for the Color Mode option, which is described in the preceding step. If the preview shows a blank white page, make sure you've unlocked the scanner as described in the scanner's bundled instruction sheets.

If you're scanning a smaller item that doesn't fill the entire scanner bed, look for the circle markers in each corner of the preview scan. Drag each circle inward to surround the area you want to copy.

4. **Click the Scan icon. When the scan finishes, click the View button to see your scan.**

The Scan app scans your image and then saves it in your Pictures folder's Scan folder.

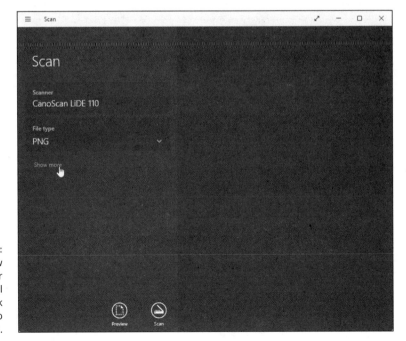

FIGURE 8-8:
Click the Show More link for additional options, or click Preview to test a scan.

The Scan app works well for fast, easy scans. But because it relies on simple, built-in Windows software, your scanner's built-in control buttons won't work.

If you want your scanner's buttons to work or you need finer control over your scans, skip the Scan app and install your scanner's bundled software. (For some scanner models, Windows Update installs the scanner's bundled software automatically as soon as you plug in the scanner.)

TIP

For quick-and-dirty scans, just take a picture of the document with the camera built into your phone or tablet. It's an easy way to keep track of receipts and invoices. If you photograph documents a lot, consider using Microsoft Lens, which you can download for free from Apple's App Store (for iPhone) or Google Play (for Android). Microsoft Lens is a handy app that can capture (photograph) text from written documents, whiteboards, and business cards and convert it into editable text.

3

Doing Things on the Internet

Find an internet service provider and connect to the internet.

Stay connected with email, chat, and video calls.

Stay safe on the internet.

IN THIS CHAPTER

» **Finding out about internet service providers**

» **Connecting to the internet**

» **Navigating the web with Microsoft Edge**

» **Finding information on the web**

» **Summarizing pages and magnifying pictures**

» **Saving information from the internet**

Chapter **9**

Cruising the Web

E ven while being installed, Windows reaches for the Internet, hungry for any hint of a connection. After connecting, Windows quickly downloads updates to make your PC run more smoothly. Other motives are less pure: Windows also checks in with Microsoft to make sure that you're not installing a pirated copy.

To help you visit the internet, Windows 11 includes a web browser named Microsoft Edge. Fast and sleek, Microsoft Edge helps you move in and out of today's internet-dependent world. This chapter explains how to find and fire up Microsoft Edge, connect to the internet, visit websites, and find what you're seeking online.

For ways to keep out the bad stuff, be sure to flip ahead to Chapter 11. This primer on safe computing explains how to avoid the web's bad neighborhoods, which harbor viruses, spyware, hijackers, and other internet parasites.

What's an ISP, and Why Do I Need One?

Everybody needs three things to connect with the internet and visit websites: a computer, web browser software, and an Internet Service Provider (ISP).

You already have the computer, be it a tablet, laptop, or desktop PC. And the newly enhanced browser, Microsoft Edge, handles the software side.

This means you probably need to find only an ISP. Most coffee shops, airports, and hotels let you connect wirelessly, often for free. For the privilege of surfing the web at home, though, you must pay an ISP. When your computer connects to your ISP's computers, Windows automatically finds the internet, and you're ready to surf the web.

Choosing an ISP is easy because you're often stuck with whichever ISPs serve your particular geographic area. Ask your friends and neighbors how they connect and whether they recommend their ISP. Call several ISPs serving your area for a quote and then compare rates. Most bill on a monthly basis, so if you're not happy, you can always switch. Here are some additional helpful tips about ISPs:

>> Although ISPs charge for internet access, you don't always have to pay. More and more public businesses share their internet access for free, usually through a wireless connection.

>> Although a handful of ISPs charge for each minute you're connected, most charge from $30 to $100 a month for service. (Some also offer faster connection speeds for more money.) Make sure you know your rate before hopping aboard, or you may be unpleasantly surprised at the month's end. Some ISPs offer bundled plans that include not only internet access, but television channels and telephone service.

TIP

>> You need to pay an ISP for only *one* internet connection. You can share that single connection with any other computers, cellphones, smart TVs, refrigerators, thermostats, lightbulbs, personal assistants such as Amazon's Alexa, and other internet-aware gadgetry in your home, office, and kitchen. (I explain how to share an internet connection by creating your own wired or wireless network in Chapter 15.)

Connecting to the Internet

Windows constantly searches for a working internet connection, whether your computer connects through a cable or scans the airwaves for a wireless (Wi-Fi) connection. If your computer finds a Wi-Fi connection that you've previously connected with, you're set: Windows connects to it, and you're online.

When you're traveling, however, the wireless networks are often new, forcing you to find and authorize these new connections.

To connect to a nearby wireless network for the first time (whether it's in your own home or in a public place), follow these steps:

1. **Click the taskbar's Wi-Fi icon (shown in the margin), which is near the clock.**

   Don't see the Wi-Fi icon? If you're not connected to the internet, you see the sad-looking no internet access icon (shown in the margin). Click that icon, instead. A menu pops, as shown in Figure 9-1.

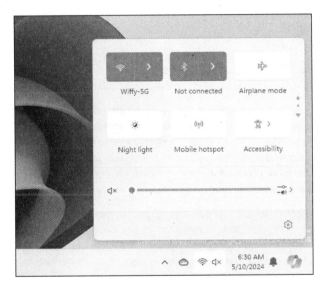

FIGURE 9-1:
Click the Wi-Fi (or no internet access) icon to see the pop-up menu.

2. **Click the right arrow next to the pop-up menu's Wi-Fi icon.**

   If that Wi-Fi icon appears dim, click it to enable Wi-Fi. Then click the arrow. Windows lists all nearby wireless networks, as shown in Figure 9-2. The networks are ranked by signal strength, with the strongest network at the top.

3. **Connect to a network by clicking its name and then clicking the Connect button that appears.**

   If you're connecting to an *unsecured network* — a network that doesn't require a password — you're finished. Windows warns you about connecting to an unsecured network, but a click or tap of the Connect button lets you connect anyway. (Don't do anything involving money or entering passwords on an unsecured connection.)

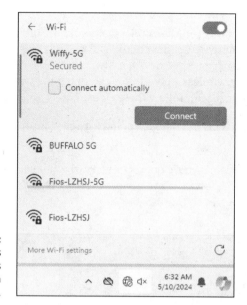

FIGURE 9-2:
Windows displays
the wireless
networks within
your range.

WARNING

There's always a security risk to using public, unsecured Wi-Fi networks. If you have no choice, you can enable the free VPN (virtual private network) in Edge, and use Edge as your browser on that internet connection. The VPN will encrypt your traffic so it can't be stolen by someone on the unsecured network. For more information, just ask Copilot, "How to I enable free VPN in Microsoft Edge?"

TIP

Unless you don't want to connect to that network automatically, leave the adjacent Connect Automatically check box selected. This tells Windows to connect automatically to that network whenever you're within range, sparing you from following these steps each time.

4. **Enter a password if needed.**

   If you try to connect to a security-enabled wireless connection, Windows asks you to enter a *network security key* — technospeak for a password. If you're at home, here's where you type the same password you entered for your router when setting up your wireless network.

   If you're connecting to someone else's password-protected wireless network, ask the network's owner for the password. Note that some hotels and coffee shops charge for access.

5. **If connecting for the first time, choose whether you want to share your files with other people on the network.**

   If you're connecting on your own home or office network, choose Yes, Turn on Sharing and Connect to Devices. Windows makes your network *private*, meaning you may safely share files with others on your private network, as well as connect to shared devices, such as printers.

If you're connecting in a public area, by contrast, always choose No, Don't Turn on Sharing or Connect to Devices. Windows makes your network *public,* meaning you can connect with the internet but other networked computers can't connect to your computer to view or access your files. This feature helps keep out snoops.

TIP

If you're still having problems connecting, try the following tips:

» When Windows says that it can't connect to your wireless network, it offers to bring up Network Troubleshooter. Network Troubleshooter mulls over the problem and usually says something about the signal being weak. It's really telling you this: "Move your computer closer to the wireless transmitter."

» At some businesses, your browser will open to a terms of services agreement. There, you must agree to the company's terms before being allowed to browse further.

» If you're in a hotel room, moving your computer closer to a window may help you find a stronger wireless signal. (The computer might even pick up a variety of available wireless networks.) If you don't mind moving outside your room, wander down to the lobby or hotel coffee shop to find a better connection.

» If you can't connect to the secured network you want, try connecting to one of the unsecured networks. Unsecured networks are fine for casual browsing on the internet.

Browsing the Web with Microsoft Edge

To open Microsoft Edge, click its icon (shown in the margin) on the taskbar along the bottom of your screen. If you've removed this taskbar icon, click Start and open Edge from the menu. The browser opens with either your last-viewed site or a launch screen that displays the top news, weather, and links to popular sites. Near the top of Edge's window (shown in Figure 9-3) are some key components I explain as you go through the chapter.

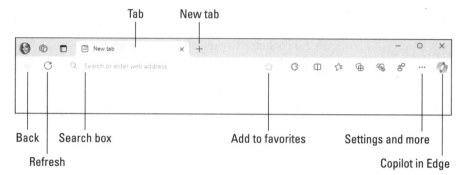

Tab   New tab

FIGURE 9-3:
The title bar and
address bar in
Microsoft Edge.

Back   Search box   Add to favorites   Settings and more

Refresh   Copilot in Edge

Navigating with the address bar

Microsoft Edge is a web browser. You may be familiar with similar products such as Google Chrome, Apple Safari, or Firefox. Like all *web browsers,* Edge lets you visit websites — basically everything available online. The address bar near the top of Edge's window is one of your main tools for visiting websites. Every web page has an address, just as most homes have a street address. On the web, that address is called a URL (Uniform Resource Locator). A URL looks something like this:

```
https://domain.tld
```

The https:// part is called the *protocol,* but you rarely see that and never have to type it. The *domain* is the name of the site. The *.tld* after the domain name is the *top-level domain,* which further identifies the type of the site. For example, .com (commercial), .net (network), .gov (government), and .edu (education) are common top-level domain names. When you combine a domain name, such as facebook, with a tld (such as .com), you end up with a *fully qualified domain name* (FQDN): facebook.com. People refer to a fully qualified domain name also as just a *domain* or a *domain name.*

Sometimes the domain part is preceded by www or something else. Typically, the www part doesn't matter, and you don't even need to type it. But in some situations, that prefix indicates a portion of a larger site, and so including it makes a difference. For example, google.com takes you to the Google search engine. But finance.google.com and news.google.com take you to specific areas on Google's website. You don't have to memorize any of these URLs; there are plenty of other ways to browse the web.

If you happen to know the URL of the site you want to visit, type it in the Search box and press Enter. As you type, a drop-down menu under the Search box tries to guess what you're going to type. If you see the URL you were intending to type, you can stop typing and then click its name. Otherwise, just type the entire URL. For example, if you type youtube.com in the Search box and press Enter, YouTube opens in the browser.

The Search box in Edge isn't fussy. If you don't know the URL of the site you want to visit, type the words that describe what you're looking for, such as *Target store in Telluride* or *puppies in Poughkeepsie* or *farm stands in Mercer county.*

You can also type Copilot prompts and questions in Edge's Search box. For example, ask Copilot, "When and how did dinosaurs go extinct?" or "Why is my Edge Back button not working?" If you can think it, you can ask it. No special commands or incantations needed.

Browsing by voice

Not everyone is a terrific typist. If you prefer to interact by voice, first make sure your computer microphone is turned on. Then follow these steps:

1. **In Edge's Search box, type** bing.com **and press Enter.**

2. **In the Ask Me Anything box, shown in Figure 9-4, click the microphone icon.**

3. **If you're asked to give permission, click Allow.**

4. **When you see the Listening prompt, say what you're looking for or ask your question.**

   Edge starts its search when it senses that you've finished talking.

Microphone icon

FIGURE 9-4:
Search by voice
using the
microphone
icon in Bing.

Browsing with links

Web pages, and many other electronic documents, often contains links. A *link* is a word, phrase, or picture that, when clicked, takes you to a specific web page. Some links appear as underlined text in blue (for a page you've never visited) or magenta (for a page you have visited). However, the link text or picture can look like anything. The only way to know for sure if something is a link it to touch it with the tip of the mouse pointer. If the mouse pointer turns to a pointing hand, as shown in Figure 9-5, that's a link, and you can click it to go to the linked web page.

FIGURE 9-5:
The hand
mouse pointer
indicates a link.

In many cases, as soon as you touch the mouse pointer to a link, the link's URL appears near the lower-left corner of the app's window. This feature is handy if you'd like to know where the link plans to take you. If you don't like the intended location, don't click the link.

Browsing with tabs and the back icon

When you click a link, the linked page opens. If the page opens in the same tab as the page you were viewing previously, you can get back to the previous page by clicking the back icon on the left side of the browser's address bar.

Sometimes, a page will open in a new tab. In that case, the back icon in the browser is disabled (dimmed), and clicking it does nothing. But the original page is still open in its own tab to the left of the page you opened, and you can switch between the two pages by clicking their tabs. See Figure 9-6. Click the close icon (X) on any tab to close that tab's page.

FIGURE 9-6:
You can open
multiple pages,
each in
its own tab.

You can also choose to open one or more linked pages in a new tab. Just right-click the link and choose Open in New Tab, as shown in Figure 9-7. Or Ctrl+click a link to open the linked page in a new tab. The new tab might not open automatically. If you don't see a change on your screen right away, note which tabs are currently open along the top of the browser window.

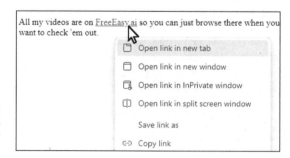

FIGURE 9-7:
Right-click a link
to open its page
in a new tab.

If you end up with a lot of open tabs and want to get back to one tab, you don't have to close the open tabs one at a time. Instead, click any tab to bring it to the forefront, and then right-click that tab and choose Close Other Tabs.

Making Microsoft Edge open to your favorite site

When you open Edge, you see its home page. However, the home page can be any website you want. To make Microsoft Edge open to your favorite site, you need to jump through these convoluted hoops:

1. **Visit your favorite website or websites.**

   For example, if you regularly visit Instagram or YouTube, browse to that site. Feel free to open more than one favorite site in other tabs.

2. **Click the three dots icon (settings and more) near the upper-right corner of Edge's window, and choose Settings from the drop-down menu.**

   The Settings pane appears, listing your settings.

   While you're in Settings, you can click Appearance in the left column to change the colors and overall appearance of the Edge browser.

   TIP

3. **Click the Start, Home, and New Tabs entry in the left column.**

   You'll see many settings for handling how Edge behaves when it opens.

4. Choose one of the following:

   - Open a New Tab Page: Open to a startup page that has a search box and items you saw the first time you opened Edge.

- Open Tabs from Previous Session: Open to whatever tabs and pages were displayed the last time you closed Edge.

- Open These Pages: Specify the page (or pages) you want to have open each time you open Edge.

After Microsoft Edge opens with your chosen home page or pages, you can browse the internet, searching for topics by typing them in the address bar or clicking different links.

TIP

Just as your browser's home page is the site you see when your browser opens, a website's home page is its cover, like the cover of a magazine. When you navigate to a website, you usually start at the site's home page and begin browsing from there.

Revisiting favorite places

Sooner or later, you'll stumble across a web page that's indescribably delicious. To make sure that you can find it again later, add it to your list of favorite pages.

To add the page you're currently viewing to your favorites list, follow these steps:

1. **Click the add to favorites icon (shown in the margin), which is at the end of the site's address along the top of the Microsoft Edge browser.**

   The Favorite Added dialog appears, listing the site's name.

2. **If you want, edit the name to make it more descriptive.**

3. **Click the Done button.**

   The name is added to your favorites list.

To return to a favorite page, click Microsoft Edge's favorites icon (shown in the margin). Your list of added sites appears, and you can return to one with a click on its name.

To keep favorites handy, you can display the favorites bar in Edge. Click the three dots near Edge's upper-right corner and choose Favorites. Near the top-right corner of the Favorites menu that drops down, click the three dots and choose Show Favorites Bar ⇨ Always. You see icons and names for your saved favorites in a bar below the browser's address bar. If you choose Open Favorites Page (in the Favorites menu), you can organize your favorites by creating folders and dragging favorites into those folders.

MICROSOFT EDGE'S HISTORY OF YOUR WEB VISITS

Microsoft Edge keeps a record of every website you visit. Although Microsoft Edge's History list provides a handy record of your computing activities, it's a spy's dream.

To see what Microsoft Edge has recorded, click its settings and more icon (three dots) and then click History from the drop-down menu. Microsoft Edge lists the last few websites you've visited, sorted by date. (Your latest visits appear at the top.) By presenting the sites in the order you viewed them, Microsoft Edge makes it easy to jump back to a site you found interesting this morning, last week, or even several months ago.

To remove items from your browsing history, click the more options icon (three dots at the top of the History drop-down), and then click Open History Page. The History page that opens lists every site you've visited. Click the X next to any site you want to remove from your history. To delete larger chunks of history or your entire history, click Delete Browsing Data from the top of the History page, choose a time range, choose Browsing History, and click Clear Now.

TIP

To remove a disappointing site from your list of favorites, right-click the site's name in Favorites and choose Delete from the drop-down menu.

Finding things on the internet

When looking for something in a text book, you might flip to the index and start searching. The same holds true for the internet when you need to find a piece of information. To help you out, you can consult a *search engine,* a service that contains a vast index of internet sites.

To search for something, head for the address bar — the space where you normally type the address of the website you want to visit. Instead, though, type your search term — **exotic orchids,** for example — directly in the address bar, and then press Enter. Microsoft Edge fires your search off to Bing, Microsoft's own search engine, and spits out names of websites dealing in exotic orchids. Click a website's name to drop by.

Don't like Bing handling your search needs? You can change the search engine to Google (https://google.com), DuckDuckGo (www.duckduckgo.com), or another search engine. Sometimes, just visiting another search engine triggers a pop-up message on your screen asking if you'd like to make it your default search engine.

Click the Yes or Okay button if it's your favorite search engine. Otherwise, follow these steps if you want to change Microsoft Edge's Bing to another search engine:

1. **Click the three dots icon (settings and more), located in Microsoft Edge's upper-right corner, and choose Settings from the drop-down menu that appears.**

   The Settings window appears as a new tab.

2. **From the Settings tab's left edge, click the Privacy, Search, and Services entry.**

   Another page full of settings appears.

3. **In the Services section of the new page, click the Address Bar and Search category.**

   The Address Bar and Search menu appears.

4. **Click the drop-down menu adjacent to the words Search Engine Used in Address Bar, and choose your preferred search engine.**

   Your change takes place immediately. To close the Settings tab, click the X on the tab.

Microsoft Edge replaces Bing with your newly selected search provider.

Finding More Information about Anything

Clicking a website's links lets you jump easily to other places online. But what if you want to know more about something that *doesn't* have a clickable link? For example, what if you spot an address for a paleo-diet-friendly donut shop and want to see it on a map? What if you see a term you don't understand, and you simply want more information about it?

Microsoft Edge helps you find extra information about things you find online. Here's how it works:

1. **When visiting a web page in Microsoft Edge, select the terms you want to explore.**

   To select a word, double-click it. To highlight a phrase, point at the beginning of the phrase, hold down the mouse button, point at the end of a phrase, and then release the mouse button. I provide details on selecting items in Chapter 6.

2. **Right-click the highlighted information, and choose Search the Web For from the pop-up menu.**

   Microsoft Edge sends your highlighted term to your chosen search engine, searches the internet for pertinent information, and then displays it, as shown in Figure 9-8.

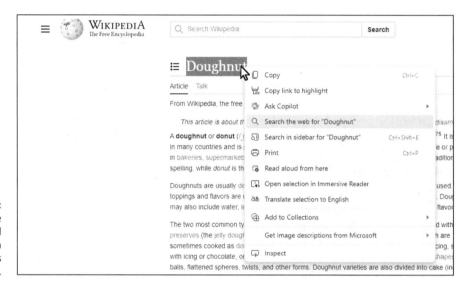

FIGURE 9-8:
Microsoft Edge
lets you find
information
about terms
found online.

Letting AI Summarize a Page

Sometimes when exploring a topic, you'll end up at a page that contains an enormous amount of information, such as a page on Wikipedia.org. When you just need a summary, not an exhaustive exegesis, you can tell Copilot in Edge to summarize the page. Unlike Copilot in Windows, Copilot in Edge knows what you're looking at right now in Edge. Start Copilot by clicking the Copilot icon near the top-right corner of the Edge browser. Then simply tell Copilot to "Summarize this page."

Copilot in Edge is a bit more attuned to the Edge browser and browsing the web. So you can ask it questions about Edge, the internet, the web, or whatever. You can use Copilot to help you find things online, particularly in your area. For example, if you ask Copilot, "Where can I get a good tamale in my area?" it will happily suggest some local restaurants.

Enlarging Pictures

The internet (and AI) basically put all the world's knowledge at your fingertips: not just text, but pictures too. Sometimes, however, a picture on a web page is so tiny you need a microscope to see it. Well, I have a great alternative to a microscope. Just touch the mouse pointer to the image you want to enlarge and then tap the Ctrl key twice, in rapid succession.

If the image still isn't big enough, move the mouse pointer down to the lower-left corner of the magnified image until you see some icons. Then click the zoom in icon (a magnifying glass with +) to zoom in some more. You can drag the enlarged image around in its window to look at different parts of the image. When you're finished, click X (close) in the upper-right corner of the enlarged image.

Saving Stuff from the Internet

Hankering for a handy Fahrenheit/Centigrade conversion chart? Need that sushi ID chart for dinner? Want to save the itinerary for next month's trip to Norway? When you find a web page with indispensable information, sometimes you can't resist saving a copy to your computer for further viewing, perusal, or even printing at a later date.

To save a web page, right-click a blank portion of the page, choose Save As from the pop-up menu, and then click the Save button.

 Microsoft Edge saves a copy of the coveted web page in the Downloads folder. To visit the Downloads folder, open File Explorer and then click Downloads from the left pane. (I explain how to navigate File Explorer in Chapter 5.)

Note that your saved page won't change if the page on the internet is updated. If you want consistently up-to-date information, add the site to your Favorites list, covered earlier in the "Revisiting favorite places" section.

Saving text

To save just a little of a web page's text, select the text you want to grab, right-click it, and choose Copy. (I explain how to select, copy, and paste text in Chapter 6.) Open your word processor, paste the text into a new document, and save it in the Documents folder with a descriptive name.

Saving a picture

As you browse through web pages, if you spot a picture that is too good to pass up, save it to your computer. Right-click the picture and choose Save Image As, as shown in Figure 9-9. The Save As dialog appears, letting you enter a new filename for the picture, if desired. Click Save to place your pilfered picture in the folder of your choice, usually Downloads or Pictures.

The crowded pop-up menu shown in Figure 9-9 offers other handy options, letting you choose to open just that image in a new tab, copy the image to the clipboard for pasting into another program, or search the web for other versions of the image.

FIGURE 9-9:
Right-click the coveted picture, and choose Save Image As from the pop-up menu.

TIP

Remember the picture by your name on the Windows Start menu? Feel free to replace it with any picture from the internet. Right-click the new picture, and save it to your Pictures folder. Then use the Settings app (see Chapter 2) to transform the picture into your new user account picture.

Downloading stuff from the internet

Many websites offer links to files you can *download*, which means to copy from some outside resource (in this case, the internet) to your own computer.

To download something from a website, click the item's link or its download icon (if one is available). Microsoft Edge downloads the item and places it in your Downloads folder for easy retrieval.

WARNING

When clicking the download icon, make sure you're clicking the correct icon. Many sites deliberately try to confuse you into downloading spyware, a virus, or something else that gives the website a payback.

You can find your downloaded item in either of two ways:

>> **Downloads folder:** Downloaded items move into your Downloads folder. To find them, click the File Explorer icon (shown in the margin) from the taskbar. When File Explorer opens, click the Downloads folder listed in the program's left pane. The Downloads folder appears, showing all your downloaded items.

>> **Microsoft Edge's download queue:** Click the settings and more icon (shown in the margin) in Microsoft Edge. When the Settings menu drops down, click Downloads. You see a list of all your downloads. You can click the folder icon at the top of the list to head straight for the Downloads folder mentioned in the preceding bullet.

Compressing and uncompressing files

Many downloaded files come packaged in a tidy folder with a zipper icon, known as a *zip file*. Windows treats them like normal folders, so you can just double-click them to see what's inside. (The files are compressed inside the folder to save download time.) To extract copies of the zipped files, right-click the zipped file and choose Extract All.

NEW

Zip files, which have the .zip filename extension, are a common way to compress one or more large files or folders into a smaller size to speed up the download process. But there are other compression algorithms, including 7zip and Tar (whose filename extensions are .7zip and .tar, respectively). If you receive either type, right-click the file's icon and choose Extract All to decompress the file's contents.

You can also compress files and folders into zip, 7zip, and tar files. In File Explorer, select the files or folders you want to compress. Right-click any selected item and choose Compress To, and then select the type of compression you want. If you forget all that and find yourself puzzling over a compressed file someone sent you via email, just ask Copilot in Windows, "How do I uncompress a file?"

Chapter **10**

Being Social: Email, Chat, and Video Calls

Windows 11 2024 Update contains apps for email and online meetings. For email, there's Outlook for Windows, a free version of Microsoft Outlook, which is widely used in the business world. For online meet-ups, there's Microsoft Teams for business world and Teams Chat for quick chats and video calls with family and friends.

That chapter focuses on Outlook for Windows and Teams Chat. However, every-thing you learn about these two apps will apply to their larger business-world browsers as well.

Getting Started with Email

Windows 11 2024 Update doesn't require you to do anything new or different when sending and receiving email. You can skip this section and just keep writing emails as you've been doing all along. However, if you don't have an email address yet, or you want to create a secondary email address for family and friends or for business, or you want to take Outlook for Windows for a spin, read on.

Getting a new email address

This section is for people who want a new email address and don't mind if it ends in @outlook.com or @hotmail.com. You need to come up with a name to precede the @outlook.com part. The name must start with a letter (a-z) and can be followed by any other letters, numbers, hyphens, underscores, or periods. The name must also be unique, so you might have to go through several names to find one that is available.

You'll need a password too. The password must be at least eight characters and should contain at least two of the following: uppercase letters, lowercase letters, numbers, and symbols. The password cannot include the name you chose (the part that comes before @ in your email address). Passwords are case-sensitive. Make sure you write down the password and put it someplace where you can easily find it if necessary.

NEW

Outlook for Windows is new in Windows 11 2024 Update, and the app can change at any time. If you hit a snag or get an error message, Copilot is your best resource. When asking your question, include the phrase "the new Outlook for Windows" in your prompt so Copilot doesn't assume you're asking about the older Outlook that's part of Microsoft 365.

To create a new email address, follow these steps:

1. **Click the start icon and then click Outlook (New). Or click the Outlook (New) icon if one appears on the taskbar.**

   If you already have Outlook that comes with Microsoft 365, the icon will look much like the original icon, but the name includes (New).

2. **If you've never set up an email account in Outlook:**

   a. *Click Create an* Outlook.com *email account.*

   b. *Click the settings icon (gear).*

   c. *Under Email Accounts, click Add Account.*

   d. *Click Create an* Outlook.com *Email Account.*

3. **Enter your preferred email address name, and then choose @**outlook.**com or @**hotmail.com **for the domain portion of the address. Click Next.**

   Figure 10-1 shows an example where the email address will be Aimee.AI@ hotmail.com, if that address is available. If your preferred email address isn't available, you'll see a message. Keep trying until you come up with a unique email address.

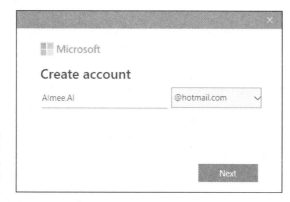

FIGURE 10-1: Creating an email address in Outlook for Windows.

4. **Type your password, and then click Next.**

   If your password is not acceptable, try another password that meets the requirements mentioned previously.

   You can deselect the check box if you're don't want to receive information about Microsoft products and services. If you're wondering what you're agreeing to, click the Privacy Statement and Microsoft Services Agreement before continuing.

5. **Enter your first and last name, and then click Next.**

6. **Choose your country or region, enter your birthdate, and click Next.**

   If you're a minor, your birthdate will have some effect on your account. But I assume that you're an adult.

7. **Click Next.**

   It might take a while for Windows to set everything up.

8. **Click Next or Accept in response to any prompts that appear.**

   When the process is complete, your new email address and new account will be set up and ready to go and you'll be logged into Outlook for Windows automatically.

You can skip the next section because your Outlook for Windows account will use the email and password you just created.

Configuring Outlook for an email account

An *email client* is an app that lets you send and receive email. If you're already happy with your current way of doing email, there's no need to set up Outlook for Windows as your email client.

If you want to try Outlook for Windows and are currently using Mail and Calendar in Windows as your email client, you don't have to go through the steps in this section. You'll be prompted to switch to the new Outlook when you start either app.

If you aren't using the Mail and Calendar app, do the following using an existing email address and password. You can use the same email address and password you use to sign into your Microsoft account:

1. **Click the start icon and then click the Outlook (New) icon.**

   If you have an Outlook (New) icon on your taskbar, you can click that instead. Be sure to use the icon with (New); the other one is for the original Outlook that comes with Microsoft 365.

2. **Choose an account from the options listed under Suggested Accounts, as shown in Figure 10-2.**

   If the account you want to use isn't an option, close the Outlook window, click the start icon, Settings, Accounts, and Email & Accounts, and then add an account with the appropriate email address. Then close the Accounts window.

3. **Click Continue.**

   Windows attempts to set up the account for the email address you provided.

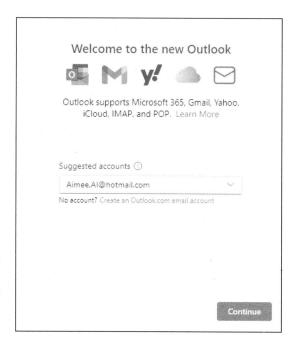

FIGURE 10-2:
Creating an
Outlook
for Windows
account for an
email address.

Welcome to the new Outlook

Outlook supports Microsoft 365, Gmail, Yahoo,
iCloud, IMAP, and POP. Learn More

Suggested accounts ⓘ

Aimee.AI@hotmail.com

No account? Create an Outlook.com email account

Continue

4. **If Windows needs more information, follow the on-screen instructions.**

5. **Click Next and Accept, as prompted.**

    The opening page for Outlook for Windows appears.

Using Outlook for Windows

This section explains how to use Outlook for Windows for an email address you've already configured, as described in the previous sections. I assume you're no longer logged into your account and are starting from the Windows desktop. First, you need to open Outlook for Windows and sign into your account:

1. **Click the start icon and choose Outlook (New).**

    If you have an Outlook (New) icon on your taskbar, you can click that rather than going through the Start menu.

2. **If prompted for an email address, choose one from the list.**

    If you've only set up one account in Outlook for Windows, chances are you won't have to enter an email address or password. Windows will just open Outlook for Windows, all ready to go, as shown in Figure 10-3.

FIGURE 10-3:
Outlook
for Windows.

Like other files, email messages can be categorized into folders, such as those listed on the left side of Figure 10-3. Here's a summary of the email folders you're most likely to use:

» **Inbox:** Contains all incoming emails.

» **Sent Items:** Stores a copy of all the emails you've sent.

» **Drafts:** Stores emails that you've start to write but haven't sent.

» **Junk Email:** Contains spam, which are junk email messages. Outlook decides which messages are likely spam.

» **Deleted Items:** Contains email messages that you've deleted.

» **Archive:** Stores email messages you want to keep for future reference but don't want cluttering up your inbox.

Additional folders may be visible, depending on what other apps you've installed. But these folders aren't directly related to email, so you can ignore them if you like. The Notes folder is used for notes in OneNote, a note-taking app. Windows 10 came with a free version of OneNote, but the version of OneNote included with the Microsoft 365 suite isn't free. The Conversation History folder stores conversations you've had in Microsoft Teams. The Groups folder provides a workspace for Microsoft 365 groups, which are used in business.

To see what's in any folder, just click the folder's name. In Figure 10-3, the Inbox folder is selected. To the right you see previews of three messages in that folder: two from Outlook Team and one from Microsoft Teams. Below the sender's name is the subject of the message and the time it arrived. Below that you see the first few words of the message. To read a message, click anywhere in the preview. The entire message opens in the pane to the right.

Sending email

To send someone an email, make sure you're in Outlook for Windows first. Then follow these steps:

1. **In Outlook, click Mail in the upper-left corner, click Home, and then click New Mail.**

    You see a blank email message, ready for you to fill out, as shown in Figure 10-4.

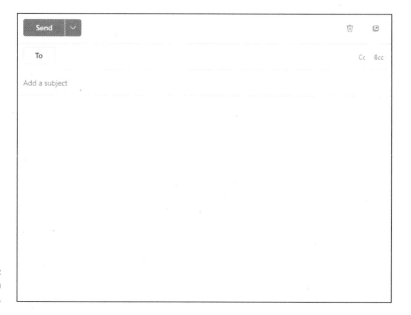

Send

To   Cc   Bcc

Add a subject

FIGURE 10-4:
Starting an
email message.

2. **In the To box, type the recipient's email address.**

    Feel free to address the email to yourself if you just want to test the waters. If you have a list of contacts with email addresses, you can click the To button, click + next to the recipient's name, and then click Save to add that person's email address to the recipients list.

3. **If you want to enter another email address, press Tab and type the address, or click To and add the recipient. Repeat as many times as necessary.**

4. **Click Add a Subject and type your subject.**

   The subject should be a brief description about the message. If you're sending a message to yourself as a test, you can just put Test as the subject.

5. **Press Tab or Enter, or click in the main body of the email message.**

   The cursor moves down in the main body of the email message.

6. **Type the main body of the email message.**

   When writing business or formal messages, feel free to ask Copilot for help, as discussed in the "Let Copilot Write Your Email Messages" sidebar.

7. **Click Send.**

   The message is sent and disappears from your screen. A copy of the message is stored in your Sent Items folder.

If you sent the message to yourself, you should see it in your inbox in a minute or two.

LET COPILOT WRITE YOUR EMAIL MESSAGES

When writing formal business email messages, you want to make a good impression by making sure the spelling and grammar are correct. Consider asking Copilot for help. Do the following:

1. Click the Copilot icon in the lower-right corner of your screen, click New Topic, and choose a conversation style (Creative, Balanced, Precise).

2. When typing your prompt, start with the words "Write an email" to give Copilot guidance on the message's length and style. Then state what your message should be about, such as, "Write an email about the benefits of organic food."

3. Click the copy icon.

4. Click in the main body area of your email message, and press Ctrl+V to paste Copilot's text.

   Or right-click inside the body of the message and choose Paste.

5. Review what you just pasted and adjust it as needed before clicking Send.

Reading your email

New email messages (excluding junk mail) arrive in your inbox. To check your new messages, open Outlook for Windows and click the Inbox folder (if you're not already in that folder). Newer messages are always listed first, so you shouldn't have to go digging around for them. You'll see a preview of each message, with the sender, subject, and maybe a few words from the body of the message.

To read a message, click its preview. The entire message opens in the content pane to the right. After you read the message, it will be marked as read, which means the sender and subject in the preview message won't be darkened. But the message remains in your inbox if you take no further action.

Once you open an email message, several icons appear near the top-right corner of the message, as shown in Figure 10-5. Use them to choose what to do with the message after you read the message contents. Here are your choices:

>> **Reply:** Opens a new message, already addressed to the sender. Type your reply above the sender's message, and click Send.

>> **Reply all:** Opens a new message, already addressed to the initial sender and all other recipients of the original message.

>> **Forward:** Passes the message on to someone else. You need to enter the email address of the person to whom you're forwarding the message.

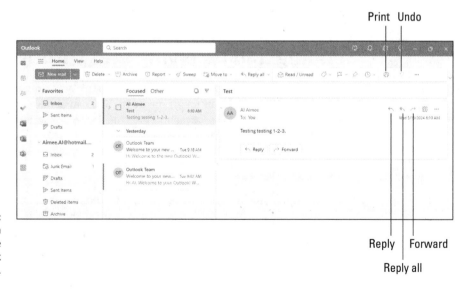

FIGURE 10-5:
Responding to an email message in Outlook for Windows.

The toolbar above the message has icons that let you do still more with the message you're viewing. Here are the ones used most often:

>> **Delete:** Delete the message from your inbox and puts it in your Deleted Items folder.

>> **Archive:** Move the message from your inbox and into your Archive folder.

>> **Move To:** Move the message to your choice of folder. If you don't see your desired folder when the menu first drops down, click Move to a Different Folder and then choose the folder from the extended list that opens.

>> **Read/Unread:** Mark an unread folder as read, or vice versa.

>> **Flag/Unflag**: Mark the message with a flag to remind yourself to deal with the message later, or remove the flag.

>> **Undo:** Undo your last action. For example, if you mistakenly delete a message, click the undo icon to put the deleted message back in your inbox.

To print the email message, click the ellipses (. . .) to the right side of the toolbar and choose Print.

If you receive an unexpected email from a bank, Social Security, your credit card company, or any other money-related website, don't click any links in the email. A criminal industry called *phishing* sends emails that try to trick you into entering your name and password on a phony website. You end up giving coveted information to people who promptly steal your money. I write more about phishing schemes and how to avoid them in Chapter 11.

Sending and receiving files through email

Like a gift card slipped into the envelope of a thank-you note, an attachment is a file that piggybacks onto an email message. You can send or receive any type of file, including photos, as an attachment. This section describes how to send and receive a file through the Outlook app.

Saving a received attachment

When you open an email that includes an attachment, you'll see a small box with the filename or a thumbnail image of a picture if the attachment is a photo. To download the attached file or photo to your own hard drive, follow these simple steps:

1. **Do one of the following:**

   - If the attachment is a file, click the down arrow near the filename and choose Download.

   - If the attachment is a photo, rest the mouse pointer on the thumbnail image, and then click the down arrow that appears and choose Download.

   A Save As window opens, so you can specify where you want to put the attached file (lower half of Figure 10-6).

2. **In the Save As window, navigate to the folder where you want to put the attached file or photo and click Save.**

   You're done! The file or photo is saved, and the Save As window closes. To open the file later, just navigate to the folder containing the file.

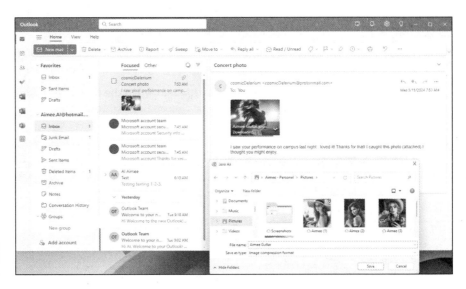

FIGURE 10-6: Saving an email attachment.

NEW

If the downloaded file is compressed, you should decompress it into a regular folder before trying to access its contents. The icon for a compressed file typically looks like a folder with a zipper on it, and has a .zip, .7z,.tar, .tar.gz, or .tar.tgz extension. To decompress, right-click the compressed file's icon and choose Extract All, and then click Extract. Files in the compressed file open into a folder that has the same name as the compressed file but without a filename extension. The icon looks like a regular folder.

Once you have the decompressed folder, there's no need to keep the compressed file around, so feel free to delete it.

Sending a file as an attachment

You can attach photos and other files to your email messages. If you want to send multiple files, it might be easier to compress them first. In File Explorer, select the files you want to send. Then right-click any selected file, and choose Compress To and then a format. (The .zip format is the most widely recognized, so go with that if you don't have a preference.)

You can then send that compressed file like any other by following these steps:

1. **Open Outlook for Windows (if it isn't already open) and click the New Mail button to start a new message.**

   As an alternative to creating a message, you can reply to a message from the intended recipient, and then attach the file to that reply.

2. **Type the recipient's email address, the subject, and any text you want to include in your message.**

   Again, this part is just business-as-usual for sending an email. You don't have to type the email address or subject if you're replying to an email.

3. **Click the attach file icon (paper clip) in the menu bar near the top, as shown in Figure 10-7, and choose Browse Computer.**

FIGURE 10-7:
Click the attach file icon to attach files to an email.

4. **In the Open window that appears, navigate to the folder that contains the file you want to attach, click the file, and then click Open.**

   An icon for the attached file (or a thumbnail of the attached photo) appears in the email message.

5. **Click the Send button near the top of the email message you're writing.**

   Outlook for Windows whisks off your mail and its attachment to the recipient.

REMEMBER

When you send an attached file, you're sending only a copy. Your original stays safely on your computer. Note that many ISPs limit how large a file you can attach, in the range of 10MB to 25MB. That's enough to send a few photos, but rarely enough for videos. (Share those on YouTube or Facebook.)

TIP

Here's a shortcut you can use when emailing a file. In File Explorer, right-click the file you want to send, and then choose Show More Options, Send To, Email Recipient, and then click Attach. Then just address the email as usual.

That should be enough to get you started sending and receiving email with Windows 11 2024 Update. Remember that if you have a question while you're composing an email, you can always ask Copilot.

Meeting Online

Microsoft Teams, a free app that comes with Windows 11, has been widely used for years for online meetings, interviews, teleconferences, and more. There are two versions of Teams, but they are both called Teams on their icons and inside the app window.

If you have a personal Microsoft account with a personal email address, the version of Teams you're using is Teams Chat. It's simple and ideally suited to chatting online with friends and family. The version of Microsoft Teams that comes free with Windows 11 2024 Update replaces Teams Chat from the original Windows 11 version.

Some people who use Windows were given an email address (and user account) through work or school. They don't use their personal email address for that account. This account is Microsoft Teams for Work or School, which is more complex than the version covered in this chapter.

This section explains how to start the free version of Teams that comes with Windows 11 2024 Update. Use the app to connect with your friends, family, or coworkers, and begin chatting, either through text messages or video.

Starting Teams

The Teams icon (shown in the margin) is on the taskbar. Yours might also display the word New. You can also start Teams from the Start menu if you don't have a Teams icon in your taskbar.

The first time you open Teams, you'll likely be asked to sign in. You need to use a Microsoft account for the free version of Microsoft Teams, so make sure you sign in with a Microsoft account. Here are a couple caveats to be aware of when signing in:

>> If you sign in with a school or work account (an account provided by your school or workplace), you'll be logged into Teams for Work or School. For more on that version of Teams, check out *Microsoft Teams For Dummies, Second Edition,* by Rosemarie Withee.

>> If you sign in with a local account, you won't be able to initiate chats. But you can join any meeting by entering the meeting ID sent by the person who organized the meeting.

The rest of this chapter assumes you'll sign in with your personal Microsoft account.

Here are the easy steps for starting Teams:

1. **Click the Teams icon on the taskbar, or click the start icon and then click Teams.**

2. **If this is the first time you're using Teams, follow the onscreen instructions to sign in with your personal Microsoft account.**

   The first time you sign into Teams, the app will look like Figure 10-8.

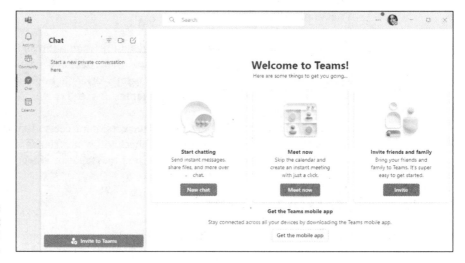

FIGURE 10-8:
Teams Chat
for personal
accounts.

Sending text messages

Sending text messages in Teams works much like sending text messages on your phone and most other places on the internet. All such messaging apps use a technology called SMS (Short Message Service), so you can contact people for a chat using their email address or cellphone number. Here's how:

1. **In the Teams app (refer to Figure 10-8), click New Chat.**

   A panel opens on the right. You can use the back icon (<) if you want to get back to a previous screen.

2. **In the To: box, type the email address or phone number of the person you're trying to contact, and press Enter.**

3. **If this is the first time you've contacted this person, type their name and click Add Name.**

4. **In the Type a Message box, type a brief message.**

5. **Click the send icon (paper airplane) or press Ctrl+Enter.**

   If you entered a phone number, the recipient sees your message on their cellphone (or watch). If you entered an email address, the recipient receives an email inviting them to join the conversation.

What happens next depends on whether or not the recipient is available. If the recipient sees the message and responds right away, you'll see their reply, and you can carry on your conversation from there. If nothing happens, the recipient may not be available, so you'll have to wait.

When you make contact, carry on your conversation as you normally would. To end the chat session, just close the Teams app.

Holding video and voice chats

If you and the person you're chatting with have microphones and video cameras, you can easily switch to a voice chat or video chat, respectively, during your conversation. Simply do the following:

1. **Open Teams and start a chat session by following the steps in the preceding section.**

2. **Near the upper-right corner of the Chat window, click the video icon to switch to a video call, or click the phone icon to switch to a voice-only call.**

   If either icon is disabled (dimmed), that usually means that a video camera or microphone is not available.

That should be enough to get you going. If you have a problem, remember that Copilot knows all about Teams in Windows 11 2024 update. Just be sure to start your Copilot prompt with, "In Windows 11 2024 Update Teams."

Chapter **11**

Safe Computing

Most of us learn through the school of hard knocks that appearances can be deceiving, and this is true in the online world as well. What appears to be a great offer, a fun game or app, an easy way to make money, a good-looking flirtatious stranger, or a warning from a bank telling you to take action immediately might be masking something insidious.

This chapter helps you recognize the warning signs and explains the steps you can take to protect yourself from harm and minimize damage. Along the way, I introduce you to the Windows Security section and its suite of tools that help identify and avert threats.

Understanding Those Annoying Permission Messages

When you download and install an app, Windows can't be entirely sure whether you are intentionally doing the installing or the procedure started behind your back when you thought you were doing something else. Therefore, when you try to install an app that has the potential to change a system setting that increases your vulnerability, Windows might ask your permission first, as shown in Figure 11-1.

User Account Control

×

Do you want to allow this app to make changes to your device?

KeyFinder Setup

Verified publisher: ONE UP LTD.
File origin: Hard drive on this computer

Show more details

Yes

No

FIGURE 11-1:
Click No if a
message similar
to this one
appears
unexpectedly.

Most of the time, you can just click Yes and go on about your business. But if a permission message appears out of the blue or when you're trying to install something you downloaded from a suspicious site or received unexpectedly through email, you can slam on the brakes and stop the procedure by clicking No.

If you don't hold an Administrator account, however, you can't simply approve the deed. You must track down an Administrator account holder (usually the PC's owner) and ask them to grant permission.

Staying Safe with Windows Security

In the past, people would subscribe to antivirus apps to keep their computers safe from computer viruses. These days, Windows has built-in security to protect you from viruses and other *malware* (apps that look innocent on the outside but harbor ill intent). Windows Security is automatically on the job 24/7. And if you inadvertently change something that might weaken the security, the app quickly notifies you and shows you which toggle switch needs to be flipped to the safer position.

You can verify that the built-in security is working behind the scenes by opening the Windows Security app, shown in Figure 11-2. Click the start icon, click All Apps, and scroll to and click the Windows Security app's icon.

A check mark in a green circle next to an icon means that security feature is turned on. If you spot an X in a red circle or an exclamation point in a yellow triangle next to an icon, click the icon. Windows guides you to the switch that needs to be flipped.

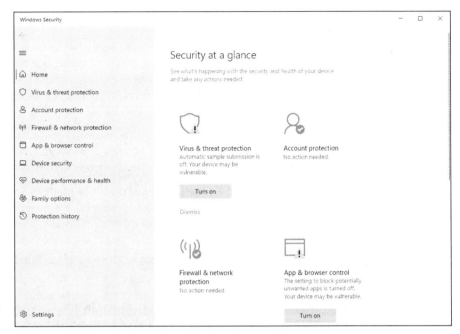

FIGURE 11-2:
The Windows
Security suite of
apps helps to
keep your
computer safe.

Windows Security offers the following types of protection:

>> **Virus & Threat Protection:** Covered in the next section, this area lets you access settings for Microsoft Defender Antivirus. The app runs automatically, constantly scanning your PC for threats. But you may want to visit here to run a quick, unscheduled scan if you suspect foul play.

>> **Account Protection:** Go here to check on the security of your user account. You can also set up a fingerprint reader, so that a swipe of your fingertip lets you into your PC, without typing a password.

>> **Firewall & Network Protection:** This section has settings for the built-in firewall, which helps stop hackers from breaking into your computer through the internet. This feature is turned on automatically, so you'll probably never need to visit this section.

>> **App & Browser Control:** These settings tell Microsoft Defender to warn you if you try to download an unsafe app or file or if the Microsoft Edge browser visits an unsafe website. I cover this subject in the "Avoiding Phishing Scams" section, later in this chapter.

>> **Device Security:** This category enables you to check on the security measures built directly into your PC's hardware, including its memory chips and central processing unit (CPU).

>> **Device Performance & Health:** If Windows doesn't seem to be running correctly, visit this section, which lets you know whether your PC is running low on storage room and notifies you of any problems with *drivers* (software that lets your PC talk with devices such as the mouse and keyboard). This section also alerts you to trouble with any of your apps. (I devote Chapter 19 to troubleshooting Windows 11.)

>> **Family Options:** This section takes you online to set up ways to control and monitor how your children use their PCs and other Windows devices. (For more on this subject, see the "Setting Up Controls for Children" section.)

>> **Protection History:** This section lists all the times Windows Security has found and thwarted something unsafe on your PC. It also recommends actions you should take to make your PC more secure.

If you've installed third-party antivirus or firewall apps, Windows Security provides updates on those as well.

REMEMBER

When everything is running smoothly, the icons in Windows Security bear a check mark circled in green. An X circled in red or an exclamation point in a yellow triangle indicate something is amiss, alerting you that you should visit that category and take the recommended action.

Avoiding and Removing Viruses

When it comes to viruses, *everything* is suspect. Viruses travel not only through email messages, websites, apps, files, networks, and flash drives, but also in screen savers, themes, toolbars, and other Windows add-ons. To combat the problem, Windows Security includes the free Microsoft Defender Antivirus app.

Microsoft Defender Antivirus scans everything that enters your computer, whether through downloads, email, networks, messaging apps, USB drives, or whatever. Unless you tell it not to, the app casts a watchful eye on your OneDrive files as well.

When Microsoft Defender Antivirus notices something evil trying to enter your computer, it lets you know with a message in your screen's lower-right corner, as shown in Figure 11-3. Then the antivirus app quickly quarantines the virus before it has a chance to infect your computer. Whew!

Microsoft Defender Antivirus automatically updates to recognize new viruses and constantly scans your PC for threats in the background.

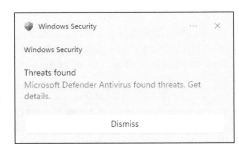

FIGURE 11-3:
Microsoft
Defender
Antivirus detects
and removes
an intruder.

Even with Windows Security's suite of apps watching your back, follow these rules to reduce your computer's risk of infection:

REMEMBER

>> Open only attachments that you're expecting. If you receive something unexpected from a friend, don't open it. Instead, email, message, or phone that person to ask whether they really sent you something. Your friend's computer might be infected and trying to infect your computer as well.

>> Be wary of an item arriving in an email that asks for a click. For example, if you receive a message saying somebody wants to be a Facebook friend, don't click it. Instead, visit Facebook from your browser and look to see whether the person is listed in your Friend Request list. The more emailed links you can avoid, the safer you'll be.

>> If you receive an important-looking email from a financial institution that asks you to click a link and type your name and password, don't do it. Instead, visit your financial institution's website through your web browser and log in there. Chances are good that there's nothing wrong with your account — the email was trying to steal your username and password. (This type of scam is often called *phishing,* and I describe it further in the next section.)

NEW

Copilot knows a lot about the Windows Security app and computer security in general. If you're not comfortable with a setting or not sure about some terminology, just ask Copilot for help. If you don't get a great answer from Copilot right off the bat, continue the conversation until Copilot zeros in on the information you seek. Refer to Chapter 3 if you need reminders on asking Copilot questions.

Avoiding Phishing Scams

You might receive an email from a bank, eBay, PayPal, or a similar website announcing a problem with your account. Invariably, the email offers a handy link to click, saying that you must enter your username and password to set things in order.

Don't do it, no matter how realistic the email and website appear. You're seeing an ugly industry called *phishing:* Fraudsters send millions of these messages world-wide, hoping to convince a few frightened souls into typing their precious account name and password.

How do you tell the real emails from the fake ones? It's easy because *all* these emails are fake. Finance-related sites may send you legitimate history state-ments, receipts, or confirmation notices, but they will never, ever email you an unexpected link for you to click and enter your password.

TIP

If you're suspicious, visit the company's *real* website by typing the web address in your browser's address bar. Or if you regularly interact with the company through a phone app, sign in with that app and see if you can verify the message there.

Microsoft Edge uses Microsoft SmartScreen Filter technology, which compares a website's address with a list of known phishing sites. If it finds a match, the SmartScreen filter keeps you from entering, as shown in Figure 11-4. Should you ever spot this screen, close the web page by clicking the Go Back button in the warning message.

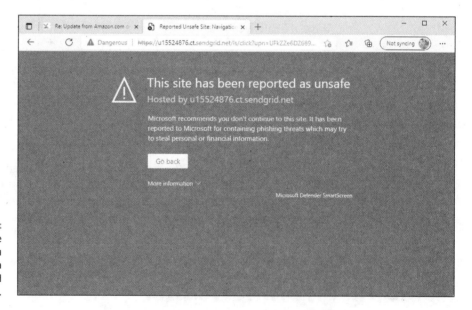

FIGURE 11-4:
Microsoft Edge warns you when you visit a suspected phishing site.

So why can't the authorities simply arrest the people responsible? Because inter-net thieves are notoriously difficult to track down and prosecute. The reach of the internet lets them work from anyplace in the world, hidden in a global maze of networks.

If you mistakenly enter information and then realize you shouldn't have, take these actions:

>> If you've already entered your name and password into a phishing site, act immediately: Visit the real website through your browser or a phone app, and change your password. Then contact the company involved and ask for help. They may be able to stop the thieves before they wrap their electronic fingers around your account.

>> If you've entered credit card information, call the card's issuer immediately. Check for a toll-free 24-hour phone number on the back of your credit card.

Setting Up Controls for Children

A feature much-welcomed by parents and much-booed by their children, the family options area in Windows Security offers several ways to monitor how children can access the computer as well as the internet.

Rather than running as an app on your computer, Microsoft's family options now work online through a Microsoft website called Family Safety. By tracking your children's activity through their Microsoft account usage, you can monitor their online activity wherever they log in to a Windows PC. The password-protected records stay online, where you can access them from any PC, tablet, or smartphone.

REMEMBER

Microsoft's family options work only if both you and your children have Microsoft accounts.

Microsoft's Family Safety website offers a variety of categories for monitoring or controlling different areas of behavior:

>> **Activity Reporting:** A haven for time-stressed parents, the Activity Reporting area offers a quick rundown of your child's computer activity, along with an option to have the information emailed to you each week.

>> **Screen Time:** Set time and day-of-the-week limits on when your child may access their PC or Xbox game system. If you click the Turn Limits On button, a grid appears for you to choose the hours your child is allowed to access the device.

>> **Content Filters:** Control whether your child needs adult approval for spending money, and block access to inappropriate apps, games, media, and websites.

>> **Screen Time:** Set time and day-of-the-week limits on when your child may open apps and games.

>> **Spending:** Want your child to be able to purchase items from the Microsoft Store app? Head here and click the button corresponding to the amount. It's withdrawn from the credit card attached to your Microsoft account and added to your child's account.

>> **Find Your Family:** If your child has an Android smartphone with the Microsoft Family Safety app installed, you can locate the device — and, I hope, your child — on a map. (You can download the Microsoft Family Safety app from Google's App Store.)

When you visit any of these categories, a new page opens with a toggle control at the top. You can turn on and off an entire category or fine-tune a category's settings.

To set up Microsoft's family options, follow these steps:

1. **Add your children and any adults who want to monitor the children as family members when creating their user accounts.**

   I describe how to add family members when creating user accounts in Chapter 14. When you add family members to your PC's list of user accounts, each member receives an email inviting them to join your family network; when they accept, their accounts automatically appear on your computer.

2. **Visit Microsoft's Family Safety website.**

   Open any browser and visit the website at https://account.microsoft.com/family.

   You can visit the online settings also by visiting Windows Security, covered earlier in this chapter, clicking Family Options, and then clicking the View Family Settings link.

3. **Log in with your Microsoft account, if asked.**

   The site displays the list of family members who have accepted their invitations.

4. **Click the name of a family member.**

   You can now set limits on that child's computer behavior, as well as monitor their activity, as shown in Figure 11-5.

5. **Turn on the categories you'd like to enforce, and set the limits.**

6. **When you're done, close the window in your browser.**

   Your changes take place immediately.

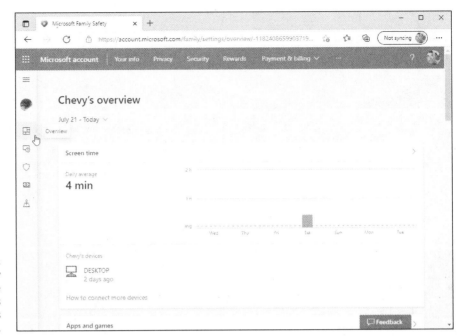

FIGURE 11-5:
Microsoft's Family
Safety website
lets you set limits
on your children's
computer activity.

Although Microsoft's family options work well, few things in the computer world are foolproof. If you're worried about your children's computer use, cast an occasional eye their way. Also, some of these options monitor your children only when they log in with their Microsoft account and use Microsoft Edge. If you spot an unfamiliar account (or a different browser) on the PC, it's time to ask some questions.

4

Customizing and Upgrading Windows 11

IN THIS CHAPTER

» **Finding the correct setting**

» **Altering the appearance of Windows**

» **Changing video modes**

» **Installing or removing apps**

» **Installing a printer or scanner**

» **Adding a Bluetooth gadget**

» **Setting the computer's time and date automatically**

» **Adjusting AutoPlay settings**

Chapter **12**

Customizing Settings in Windows

M any people dread changing settings in Windows, and for good reason: They're too complicated. How do you know which setting works best? How can you even *find* the right setting? And if you flip the wrong switch, how do you undo any peripheral damage?

Windows doesn't make this easy, unfortunately. Each app includes its own batch of settings. Windows, too, contains another set of master settings known as the Settings app. Finally, Windows occasionally kicks you to that old switch-filled circuit box known as Control Panel, a remnant from earlier Windows versions.

No matter which bank of switches you face, you can use them to customize the look, feel, behavior, and vibe of Windows and its apps. This chapter explains how to find the settings you need, what to do with them once discovered, and how to undo their handiwork if they make things worse.

A word of caution: Some settings can be changed only by the person holding the almighty Administrator account — usually the computer's owner. If Windows refuses to flip a switch, call the PC's owner for help.

Finding the Right Setting

Windows 11 2024 Update sports hundreds if not thousands of settings. To find the setting, let Windows help you. Follow these steps to find the setting you need:

1. **Click in the Search box next to the start icon, and type a word describing the setting you want to find.**

   When you type the first letter, every setting containing that letter appears in a list above the Search box. If you don't know the exact name of your setting, begin typing a keyword: *display, troubleshoot, mouse, user, privacy,* or something that describes your need.

   TIP

   Don't see the right setting? Press the Backspace key to delete the letters you've typed and try again with a different word.

   The Search box lists other matches for your keyword: files on your computer, apps from Microsoft Store, and even items found on websites. If you see too much clutter, filter the results: Type **settings:** in the Search box, followed by a space and your search term. For example, to search for camera settings, type this in the Search box and press Enter:

   ```
   settings: camera
   ```

2. **Click your desired setting in the list.**

   Windows takes you directly to that setting.

NEW

Copilot knows all about Windows 11 2024 Update and its many settings. Feel free to ask Copilot technical question anytime. It never hurts to start your prompt with "In Windows 11 2024 Update" to ensure that Copilot answers your question for your version of Windows. If you're looking for help related to a specific app, replace *Windows 11 2024 Update* with the name of the app. See Chapter 3 if you need reminders on using Copilot.

Looking for the settings inside a particular app, rather than inside Windows itself? Look in the app's upper-right corner for an icon containing either three stacked lines or three dots in a row. Click that icon, and a drop-down menu appears, almost always listing an entry for Settings.

Most Windows settings live in the Settings app, shown in Figure 12-1, which opens when you press Windows+I or click Start and choose Settings.

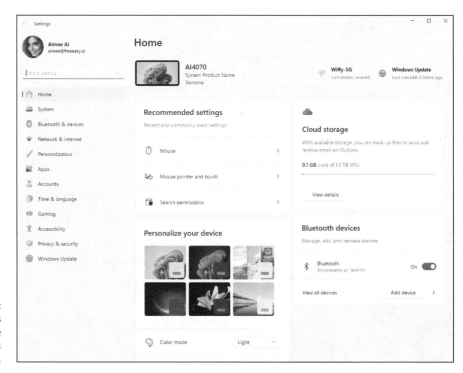

FIGURE 12-1:
Use the Settings app to change your computer's behavior.

The Settings app breaks its settings down into categories in the left column. Click a category name to access the settings within that category. The rest of the chapter describes the available settings.

Adjusting System Settings

The System category is a huge catch-all category for settings that don't fit neatly anywhere else. For instance, you can find ways to adjust your monitor's *resolution* — the amount of information it can pack onto a screen without making everything too tiny to read. You head to the System category also to control all the notifications that pop up in your screen's lower-right corner.

The rest of this section covers the most important settings you'll eventually need to tweak in the System category.

Changing the resolution and text size

One of the many change-it-once-and-forget-about-it options in Windows, your screen resolution determines how many pixels, and therefore how much information, Windows can cram onto your computer screen. Although you can't tell with the naked eye, thousands of tiny lighted dots, called *pixels*, display what's on your screen. The more pixels, the higher the *resolution* of the monitor. A screen's *native resolution* is often expressed in the format *width* x *height*, where *width* is the number of pixels across and *height* is the number of pixels up.

When adjusting settings for a display monitor, you'll usually see a setting marked (Recommended). That's the screen's native resolution, which provides a clear, crisp image. But sometimes, a high resolution on a small monitor can make text on the screen tiny and difficult to see.

If it's hard to see things on your screen, adjusting the screen resolution or text size can help. Here is how you can get to those settings:

1. **Right-click the desktop and choose Display Settings. Or click the start icon, click Settings, and then choose System ⇨ Display.**

The Display settings appear, as shown in Figure 12-2.

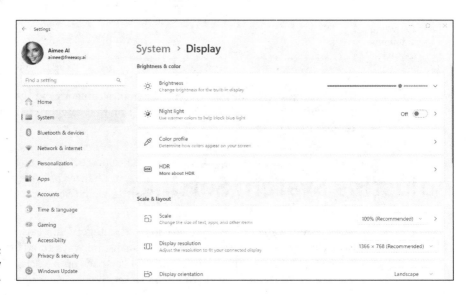

FIGURE 12-2:
The Display settings.

2. **To change the screen resolution, click the Display Resolution drop-down list and select your desired resolution.**

   The recommended setting matches the screen's native resolution and will likely give you the clearest image. But if you want to choose a lower resolution to make things larger on the screen, try a different resolution. Windows immediately changes to the new resolution.

3. If you like the change, click the Keep Changes button. If you don't like the new resolution, just wait for the screen to return to its previous setting.

When Windows makes changes your display's resolution, it gives you 15 seconds to approve the change. If a technical glitch renders your screen unreadable, you won't be able to see or click the onscreen button. However, Windows will note that you didn't approve the changes and will revert to your original, viewable display settings. Whew!

If you end up with a screen that's blurry and hard to see, you can repeat the preceding steps and return to the Recommended resolution. Then, go back to Display Settings and click the Scale option. You'll see a warning about possibly getting into trouble if you get too carried away with custom scaling. However, if you click the Text option and then use the slider to make the text a little larger, you can probably increase the text size without losing clarity. Click Apply after setting a text size to apply it to the entire screen.

It may take some experimenting to get things just right. If you think the best solution might be a bigger screen, you can always add one to your current laptop or desktop computer, as described next.

Adding a second monitor or projector

If you have a hard time seeing what's on a laptop's screen and messing with the text size and resolution (as described in the preceding section) didn't help, you might want to add a larger external monitor. Chances are that the laptop already has an HDMI, DisplayPort, or USB-C port to which you can connect an external monitor. But you'll need to check the laptop's documentation.

Some desktop PCs already have two or more connections for monitors, so you can add a second screen at any time. But again, check your computer's specs. If you connect a second monitor to your computer, and it doesn't react right away, make sure the monitor is plugged into the wall socket, turned on, and properly connected to the computer. Then follow these steps to tell Windows you've added a second monitor:

1. **Right-click the desktop and choose Display Settings. Or click the start icon, click Settings, and then choose System ⇨ Display.**

   You see the Display settings, with two monitors side-by-side, as shown in Figure 12-3.

FIGURE 12-3: The Display settings page opens to show that your display is duplicated on each monitor.

2. **Choose how Windows should display itself on the two monitors.**

   At first, Windows assumes you want to duplicate your display on both monitors. However, you can choose how Windows should behave on the second monitor by clicking the drop-down menu showing Extend These Displays in Figure 12-3. The menu offers the following options, each handy for different scenarios:

   - *Duplicate These Displays:* This option duplicates your desktop on both screens, which is helpful when you want to project an image of your desktop onto a wall or screen for a presentation.

- *Extend These Displays:* This setting stretches Windows to fit across both screens, giving you an extra-wide desktop. This works best when you like to view *lots* of open windows simultaneously.

- *Show Only on 1:* Choose this before you're ready to show off your presentation; it blanks the screen on the second monitor. When you're ready for action, switch to Duplicate These Displays so that your second screen duplicates your first.

- *Show Only on 2:* Choose this option to show only the second display, which is useful when hooking up a PC to a TV for watching movies in a dark room.

Each time you choose one of the preceding options, a window appears onscreen. Click the Keep Changes button to change to your new display settings, or click the Revert button if you don't like the change. If changing the display makes the screen illegible, just wait a few seconds: If you don't click Keep Changes, Windows assumes something is wrong and reverts to your earlier setting.

3. **Click the Multiple Displays section to choose the presentation mode for your monitors.**

This section, useful for both troubleshooters and people who frequently plug in a second monitor, holds some extra settings, each described in the following list:

- *Remember Window Locations Based on Monitor Connection:* Selecting this check box tells Windows to remember all the work you did setting up your extra monitors. Keep this setting selected unless you constantly connect your PC to different monitors in different situations.

- *Minimize Windows When a Monitor Is Disconnected:* This check box normally remains deselected, which automatically minimizes any open windows when you unplug the second monitor.

NEW

- *Ease cursor movement between displays:* If you find that things don't line up when trying to move the cursor or a window from one monitor to another, selecting this option will help smooth the transition from one screen to the other.

- *Detect Other Display:* Handy when troubleshooting, this option lets you know whether Windows recognizes the second monitor, projector, or TV that you've plugged in.

- *Identify:* Windows identifies its monitors by numbers, but sometimes you can't tell which monitor is assigned which number. Click this option, located below the picture representing your two monitors, and each monitor displays its assigned number in the center of its screen.

- *Connect to a Wireless Display:* Useful for connecting without a cable. Click this button to open a pop-up that lets you connect to any wireless monitors that Windows finds.

4. **If necessary, change your monitor's orientation in the Display Orientation area, and choose which monitor should have the start icon on its taskbar.**

   Windows assumes your monitor is in *landscape* mode, where the monitor's display is wider than it is tall. (Most monitors and all TV sets are set up this way.) If you have a swiveling monitor or tablet that's set up vertically, visit the Display Orientation section to tell Windows how you've rotated your monitors.

   The Display Orientation section lets you choose the default landscape mode or portrait mode if you've turned a monitor or tablet sideways, perhaps to better display a full page of reading material.

   Finally, decide which of the two monitors listed onscreen should reveal the Start menu when you press the Windows key. Click the desired onscreen monitor, and then select the Make This My Main Display check box.

5. **If necessary, drag and drop the onscreen computer screens to the right or left until they match the physical placement of the real computer screens on your desk. Then choose your main display.**

6. **When everything is set up the way you want, click the Keep Changes button.**

TIP

These same steps also let you connect your computer to most widescreen TVs for viewing photos and watching movies.

Running Windows with two (or more) monitors may require a few other settings tweaks, as well:

» To change the resolution or text size of one monitor, right-click the desktop and choose Display Settings. Click the thumbnail for the screen you want to change. Any selections you make below the thumbnails will be applied to the selected monitor.

» If you move the physical position of either of your two monitors, return to the first step and start over. You need to tell Windows about their new positions so that it places the correct display on the correct monitor.

» Windows normally displays the taskbar along the bottom of your second monitor, which looks odd when connecting to TVs or during presentations. To hide that taskbar, open the Personalization category in the Settings app and choose Taskbar Behaviors from the right column. To hide the taskbar on the secondary monitor, clear the check mark next to Show My Taskbar on All Displays.

Cutting back on notifications and ads

Notifications are the informational blurbs that appear for a few seconds in your screen's bottom corner and then hunker down in the Notifications pane for later reading. Some people like to stay constantly up to date, glancing at notifications to see the latest headline, for example, or the subject line of an incoming email. Others find the messages an intrusion.

To control these messages, visit the Notifications settings in the Systems category by following these steps:

1. **Click the start icon and then click the Settings icon.**

2. **Click the System icon (shown in the margin).**

3. **Click Notifications in the right pane.**

   The Settings app displays the Notifications settings, as shown in Figure 12-4. All the settings apply to the Notifications pane — the information-filled strip that appears when you click the time and date area, located on the taskbar's right edge.

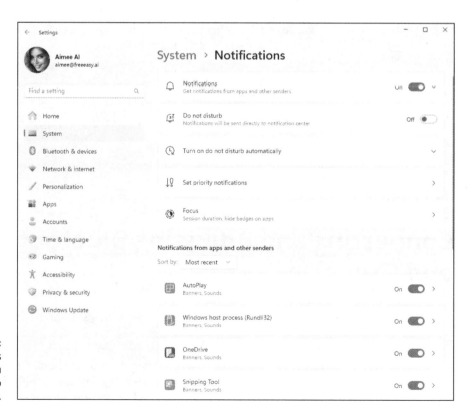

FIGURE 12-4:
The Notifications settings let you turn off pop-up announcements.

4. **Adjust the following settings as needed:**

- *Notifications:* Click this single toggle switch to stop all your apps from bugging you with notifications. (Click the toggle switch back on if you miss your apps' notifications.)

- *Do Not Disturb:* Set this option on to prevent notifications from popping up and making a sound.

- *Turn On Do Not Disturb Automatically:* Set this on to choose when do not disturb mode kicks in automatically, based on the time of day or specific activities.

- *Set Priority Notifications:* Choose which kinds of notifications (if any) are allowed to come through, even when your PC is in do not disturb mode.

- *Focus:* Focus is similar to do not disturb mode, in that it hides and silences notifications. However, you can set a duration for how long the focus session lasts so you don't have to remember to turn off do not disturb manually.

- *Notifications from Apps and Other Senders:* Choose which apps may send notifications. This setting offers a great way to stop the obnoxious ones and preserve the important ones. Use the Sort By drop-down menu to sort the list of apps alphabetically by name or by time (with the last app to notify you appearing at the top of the list).

- *Additional Settings:* Control what kinds of tips and suggestions pop up automatically while you use your PC. Although helpful at first, these notifications may turn into a nuisance after you've used Windows for a few months. At that point, toggle them off.

By carefully flipping these toggle switches, you can remove most of the nags from the Notifications pane. Miss the notifications? Reverse your decision by clicking the missed setting's toggle.

Connecting and Adjusting Bluetooth and Other Devices

In Windows, *devices* are physical things such as a mouse, keyboard, printer, memory cards, and scanner. Accordingly, the Devices category of the Settings app contains settings to adjust your mouse's scroll wheel, as well as how your computer reacts when you insert a memory card. In short, device settings are a hodgepodge that you can locate most easily by searching from the Start menu's Search box, as described in this chapter's first section, "Finding the Right Switch."

After you find the Devices category in the Settings app, you can use it to make all the adjustments covered in the next few sections.

Adding a Bluetooth gadget

Bluetooth technology lets you connect nearby gadgets wirelessly to your computer, removing clutter from your desktop. On a tablet, Bluetooth lets you add a wireless mouse and keyboard, an external speaker, and other devices without hogging your computer's coveted USB ports — those rectangular or oval holes where you plug in flash drives and other gadgetry.

Most tablets, laptops, and new desktop PCs come with built-in Bluetooth; you can add it to an older PC by plugging a Bluetooth module into a vacant USB port.

Bluetooth can also connect your computer, laptop, or tablet with some smart-phones for wireless internet access — if your wireless provider allows it — in a process known as *tethering*.

Connecting a Bluetooth device starts with *pairing*, where you're simply establish-ing a connection between the computer and the device. Typically, you need to pair only once. After that, you can connect to and disconnect from the device as needed without pairing. Here are the steps to follow to pair a device for the first time:

1. **Make sure that your Bluetooth device is turned on and ready to pair.**

    Most Bluetooth devices have a simple on/off switch. Telling the device to begin pairing is a little more difficult. Sometimes you simply flip a switch. Other devices make you hold down a button until its light begins flashing. When you spot the flashing light, the device is ready to pair with another Bluetooth device including, you hope, your computer.

2. **Click the start icon, click the Settings icon, and in the Settings app, click the Bluetooth & Devices icon (shown in the margin).**

    The Bluetooth & Devices screen appears, as shown in Figure 12-5.

3. **If your computer's Bluetooth toggle is set off, click it to turn it on.**

4. **Click the large + Add Device option, and then click the Bluetooth option from the Add a Device window.**

    Your computer quickly begins searching for any nearby Bluetooth devices that want to connect, or *pair* in Bluetooth parlance.

    If your device doesn't appear, head back to Step 1 and make sure that your Bluetooth device is still turned on and ready to pair. (Many impatient gadgets give up and turn off after 30 seconds of waiting for a connection.)

FIGURE 12-5:
To add a
Bluetooth
wireless gadget,
click Add Device.

5. **When your device's name appears below the words Add a Device, click the device's name.**

6. **Type your device's code if necessary. If asked, click the Pair button.**

   Here's where things get tricky. For security reasons, some devices make you prove that you're sitting in front of your computer, not a stranger trying to break in. Unfortunately, devices employ slightly different tactics when making you prove your innocence.

   Sometimes you need to type a string of numbers called a *passcode* in both the device and your computer. (The code is usually hidden somewhere in your device's manual.) But you need to type quickly before the other gadget stops waiting.

   On some gadgets, particularly Bluetooth mice, you hold down a push button on the mouse's belly at this step. Cellphones sometimes make you click a Pair button if you see matching passcodes on both your computer and phone.

TIP

   When in doubt, type **0000** on your keyboard or press the Enter key. That's often recognized as a universal passcode for frustrated Bluetooth device owners who are trying to connect their gadgets.

Make sure your computer's Bluetooth isn't turned off: The toggle switch below the word Bluetooth (refer to Figure 12-5) should be turned on. Turning it off extends the battery life on tablets and laptops; on desktop PCs, always leave it turned on. Don't see the Bluetooth toggle? Then your computer doesn't have built-in Bluetooth and you'll need to buy a Bluetooth adapter, an inexpensive device that plugs into your computer's USB port.

After a gadget successfully pairs with your computer, its name and icon appear when you click View More Devices (refer to the right side of Figure 12-5).

You can turn Bluetooth on and off, as needed, right from the system tray. Click the Wi-Fi or speaker icon near the date and time in the lower-right corner of the screen, and then click the Bluetooth icon (the letter B) to turn Bluetooth on or off. (The icon appears dimmed when Bluetooth is turned off.) When Bluetooth is on, you can click the > to the right of the Bluetooth icon to see a list of connected and available devices. Click a listed device to connect to it or disconnect from it.

If you don't think you'll be using a specific Bluetooth device in the future, you can make the computer "forget" the device and its connection. Click the start icon, click the Settings icon, and then click Bluetooth & Devices. Make sure Bluetooth is on. You see thumbnails of the devices you've paired in the past. To unpair a device, click the three dots in the upper-right corner of the device's thumbnail and then click Remove Device.

Adding a printer or scanner

Quarrelling printer manufacturers couldn't agree on how printers and scanners should be installed. As a result, you install your printer in one of two ways:

» Some manufacturers simply require you to plug in your printer or scanner with a USB cable. Windows automatically notices, recognizes, and embraces your new device.

» Other manufacturers take an uglier approach, saying you must install their bundled software *before* plugging in your device. And if you don't install the software first, the printer or scanner may not work correctly.

Unfortunately, the only way to know how your printer or scanner should be installed is to check the manual. (Usually, this information appears on a colorful, one-page Quick Installation sheet packed in the printer's box.) No manual? Most manufacturers now offer them online on their website.

If your printer lacks installation software, install the cartridges, add paper to the tray, and follow these instructions to put it to work:

1. **With Windows up and running, plug your printer into your PC and turn on the printer.**

   Windows may send a message saying that your printer is installed successfully, but follow the next step to test it.

2. **Click the start icon, click the Settings icon, and in the Settings app, click the Bluetooth and devices icon (shown in the margin).**

   The Bluetooth & Devices category appears (refer to Figure 12-5).

3. **From the right side of the Settings app, choose Printers and Scanners.**

   The Settings app displays any printers and scanners attached to your PC. If you spot your printer listed by its model or brand name, click its name, click the Manage button, and then click Print a Test Page when the Managing Your Device window appears. If the test page prints correctly, you're finished. Congratulations.

   The test page *didn't* work? Check that all the packaging is removed from inside your printer and that it has ink cartridges. If it still doesn't print, your printer may be defective. Contact the store where you bought it, and ask who to contact for assistance.

   The Managing Your Device window for your printer often contains a Printer Properties button as well. A click on that button lets you access and change the settings for your printer or scanner.

That's it. If you're like most people, your printer works like a charm. If it doesn't, see the tips and fix–it tricks in the printing section of Chapter 8. Here are some additional things to know about working with printers:

» To remove a printer you no longer use, click its name in Step 3 and then click Remove in the upper-right corner. The printer's name will no longer appears as an option when you try to print from an app. If Windows asks to uninstall the printer's drivers and software, click Yes — unless you think you might install that printer again sometime.

» You don't need to go into Settings to change things for just one print job. Typically, after you choose File ➪ Print from an app's menu bar, you can adjust the page orientation and such for that one print job. If the app doesn't have a File menu, look for a print icon in the toolbar or three dots near the right side of the app, or just press Ctrl+P.

» When you create a network, which I describe how to do in Chapter 15, you can share your printer with other computers and devices on your network. Your printer will be listed as available to all the computers on the network.

TIP

» If your printer's software confuses you, try clicking the Help button in its menus. Many buttons are customized for your particular printer model and offer advice not found in Windows.

» To print from your tablet and phone, buy and install a Wi-Fi printer. After it's hooked up to your network and shared, it should appear as a print option in most popular Wi-Fi devices.

» I cover printers and scanners in Chapter 8.

Connecting your phone

Windows 11 2024 Update includes a new Phone Link app that allows you to connect your iPhone or Android phone to your computer. Once connected, you can make calls, reply to text, access photos, and share files between your computer and phone easily. To use the Phone Link app, do the following:

1. **In the Search box next to the start icon, type *phone link*.**

2. **Click the Phone Link icon on the Start menu.**

   The first time you use the app, you are invited to pair a phone, as shown in Figure 12-6.

FIGURE 12-6: The Phone Link app for connecting a phone to your computer.

3. **Make sure your phone is turned on and ready to use, and then click Android or iPhone, depending on the type of phone you're connecting.**

4. **As instructed on the screen, scan the QR code with your phone.**

5. **On your phone, open the link the QR code sent, and download the Link to Windows app.**

6. **When the phone download is complete, open the Link to Windows app that you just downloaded.**

7. **Follow the instructions on your phone to complete the setup. Click the Done button on the last setup page.**

   Back on your computer screen, the Phone Link app displays You Are All Set.

8. **Click the Continue button.**

That's it for the steps you take on the phone. Next, on your computer screen, you see options for pinning Phone Link to the taskbar and automatically opening Phone Link each time you start the computer. Regardless of which options you choose, you can always start Phone Link as you would any other app, by clicking the **start icon** (or the All Apps button) and then clicking Phone Link.

From now on, every time you open the Phone Link app, it should automatically show you what's on your phone. Use the Messages, Calls, and Photos tabs near the top to access messages, phone calls, and photos, respectively. If you need help, ask Copilot, specifying the Phone Link app and your phone type. For example, you might ask, "How do I use Windows 11 Phone Link with my iPhone?"

Connecting to nearby Wi-Fi networks and internet

For most people, the Wi-Fi settings in the Network & Internet category contain only one useful item: a way to find and connect with nearby Wi-Fi networks.

 To bypass the Settings app and leapfrog directly to those settings, click the Wi-Fi icon in the system tray, which is just to the left of the date and time near the lower-right corner of the screen. A panel pops up. Click the right-pointing arrow next to the Wi-Fi icon in the menu's upper-left corner. Finally, when the list of nearby Wi-Fi networks appears, click the name of your desired network. (The strongest network always appears at the top of the list.) Flip back to Chapter 9 for more details.

The other items in the Settings app's Network & Internet category apply mostly to techies and can be safely ignored. Here, geeks can tweak their VPN (Virtual Private Network), and old-schoolers can create dial-up internet connections.

I devote Chapter 15 to networking, and the internet gets its due in Chapter 9.

Personalizing Your PC

One of the most popular categories in the Settings app is the Personalization category, which lets you change the look, feel, and behavior of Windows in a wide variety of ways. You may have already encountered some of these settings when personalizing your computer back in Chapter 3. On the Personalization page await these nine icons:

>> **Background:** Paydirt for budding interior designers, the Background settings let you choose a particular color or photo (sometimes called *wallpaper*) for your desktop. I cover changing wallpaper in the next section.

>> **Colors:** When you're satisfied with your background, choose Colors from the left pane to choose the color of the frames around your Start menu, windows, apps, and taskbar. Click a color from the presented grid, and you're through. (To mix your own favorite color, click the View Colors button below the color grid.)

>> **Themes:** After you've chosen your favorite background, colors, and lock screen, visit here to save them as a *theme* — a collection of your embellishments that can be easily slipped on or removed. The Get More Themes in Microsoft Store link takes you to the Microsoft Store, where you can download dozens of free themes that change the look of Windows.

NEW

>> **Dynamic Lighting:** Some computers and devices (such as keyboards and mice) include RGB (red green blue) lighting. But the devices that offer this feature display a wide range of colors. In Settings, Dynamic Lighting lets you extend your Windows desktop accent colors to those devices, change the brightness of that lighting, and more.

>> **Lock Screen:** Normally, Windows chooses from its own bundled photos to place on the *lock screen* — the image that appears when you first turn on your PC. Under Related Settings, you can use the Screen Timeout settings to determine how long your computer remains turned on while unattended before the screen turns off, the computer goes to sleep, or the computer goes into hibernate mode.

>> **Text Input:** Handy only for touchscreen owners, this setting lets you splash different colors across the onscreen keyboard. More importantly, it lets you change the onscreen keyboard's size, handy mostly for thumb typers and owners of wide-screen tablets and laptops.

>> **Start:** Visit here to control the look and feel of the Start menu itself. (I describe these settings in Chapter 2, which covers the Start menu in detail.)

>> **Taskbar:** Head here to customize the behavior of your *taskbar,* the icon-filled strip living along your desktop's bottom edge. I cover the taskbar in Chapter 3. (To jump quickly to the taskbar's Settings window, right-click the taskbar and choose Properties. The window that appears also lets you change your Start menu's settings.)

>> **Fonts:** Open the Fonts app, where you can review the fonts that come free with Windows. You can add more fonts from the Microsoft Store, Google Fonts, or any other online source. When given a choice of font file formats, stick with .ttf or .otf for best results in Windows 11.

>> **Device Usage:** Confused about Windows 11? Click here and toggle on all the ways you plan on using your computer: Gaming, Family, Creativity, School, Entertainment, or Business. Windows then tosses up suggestions about how to manage those tasks more easily.

In the next few sections, I explain the Personalization tasks that you'll reach for most often and how to handle the settings that appear.

Changing the desktop background

A *background*, also known as wallpaper, is simply the picture covering your desktop. To change it, follow these steps:

1. **Click the start icon, click the Settings icon, and open the Personalization category.**

   Windows quickly kicks you over to the Settings app's Personalization category, open to the Theme setting.

TIP

   You can visit the Personalization category more quickly by right-clicking the desktop and choosing Personalize from the pop-up menu. The Personalization category opens directly to the Theme setting.

2. **Click the Background category in the right pane, and choose Picture from the Personalize Your Background drop-down menu shown in Figure 12-7.**

   The Background menu lets you create a background from a picture, a solid color, or a *slideshow* — a combination of photos that automatically changes at preset intervals.

FIGURE 12-7:
Use the
Personalization
category to
control how
Windows looks
on your PC.

3. **Click a new picture for the background.**

   Microsoft lists a few pictures to choose from. If you don't like Microsoft's offerings, click the Browse Photos button, listed in the Choose a Photo section, to search your computer's Pictures folder for potential backgrounds.

   When you click a new picture, Windows places it across your desktop and shows you a preview at the top of the Personalization page. If you're pleased, move on to Step 4; otherwise, keep browsing the available photos.

4. **Decide whether to fill, fit, stretch, tile, center, or span the picture.**

   Although Windows tries to choose the best-looking setting, few pictures fit perfectly across the desktop. Small pictures, for example, need to be stretched to fit the space or spread across the screen in rows like tiles on a floor. When tiling and stretching make your background look odd or distorted, visit the Choose a Fit drop-down menu. There, you can try the Fill or Fit option to keep the perspective. Or try centering the image and leaving blank space around its edges. Choose the Span option only if you've connected your PC to two monitors and want the image to fill both screens.

As you choose different options, Windows changes the background to show your new choice. Like what you see? Close the Settings window, and you're done. Windows automatically saves your new background across your screen.

Changing the computer's theme

Themes are collections of settings to spruce up your computer's appearance: You can save your favorite screen saver and desktop background as a theme, for example. Then, by switching between themes, you can change your computer's clothes more quickly.

To try one of the built-in themes in Windows, follow these steps:

1. **Click the start icon, click the Settings icon, and open the Personalization category.**

2. **Choose Themes from the Settings app's right side.**

   The Settings app opens to display themes bundled with Windows, as shown in Figure 12-8.

3. **Click any theme, and Windows tries it on immediately.**

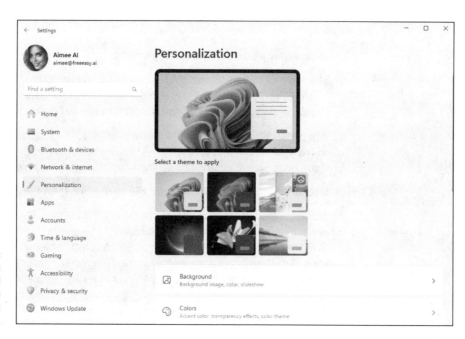

FIGURE 12-8:
Choose a
preconfigured
theme to change
how Windows
looks and sounds.

Instead of choosing from the built-in themes, feel free to make your own by clicking Save Theme to save your currently assigned desktop background, window color, sounds, screen saver, and mouse cursor. Type a name for your theme, and it appears as a choice in this section.

You can also download themes from the Microsoft Store.

Fixing and Removing Apps

The App category lets you uninstall unwanted apps and reset malfunctioning ones. You can also choose *default* apps — the apps that open automatically when you double-click a document file's icon. You can also choose which apps open automatically as soon as you start Windows.

If you want to remove an app from your system, follow these steps:

1. **Click the start icon, click the Settings icon, and then click the Apps icon in the left pane (and shown in the margin).**

   You'll see many options for managing apps, as shown in Figure 12-9.

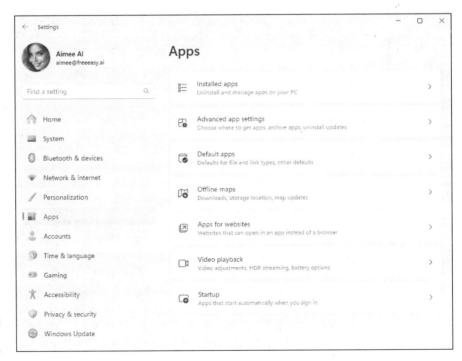

FIGURE 12-9: Windows 11 settings for Apps.

2. **Click Installed apps.**

   An alphabetical list of your installed apps appears.

3. **Click the three dots to the right of the app you want to remove and then choose Uninstall.**

4. **Follow the onscreen instructions to complete the process.**

After you delete an app, it's gone for good. You won't see its icon on the Start menu, and you won't be able to restore the app from the recycle bin.

WARNING

Always use the Settings app to uninstall unwanted apps. Simply deleting their files or folders doesn't do the trick. In fact, doing so often confuses your computer into sending bothersome error messages.

Microsoft doesn't let you delete many of the apps bundled with Windows 11 because they're built into the operating system. But you can still remove them from the Start menu by right-clicking their icons and choosing Unpin from Start from the pop-up menu.

INSTALLING NEW APPS

Today, most apps install automatically as soon as you download them from the Microsoft Store or double-click their downloaded installation file.

If you're not sure whether an app has been installed, go to the Start menu and look for its name. If it appears in the All Apps alphabetical list, you're all set.

But if the app doesn't automatically leap into your computer, try these tips:

- You need an Administrator account to install apps. (Most computer owners automatically have an Administrator account.) This requirement keeps the kids, with their Standard or Child accounts, from installing apps and messing up the computer. I explain user accounts in Chapter 14.

- Downloaded an app? Windows saves downloaded files in your Downloads folder. To find the Downloads folder, open any folder and click Downloads in the folder's Quick Access area, located at the top of its left pane. When the Downloads folder appears, double-click the downloaded app's name to install it.

- Many eager, newly installed apps want to add a desktop shortcut, a start menu icon, and a Quick Launch toolbar shortcut. Say "yes" to all. That way, you can start the app from the desktop, avoiding a trip to the Start menu. (Changed your mind? Right-click any unwanted shortcuts and choose either Delete or Unpin to remove them.)

Creating and Changing Accounts for Others

Head to the Accounts category to create or change accounts for people who can use your computer, a chore I cover in Chapter 14, as well as to delete accounts for those no longer welcome. This category also lets you change your password or account picture.

Changing Date, Time, and Language Settings Quickly

Visited mostly by frequent fliers, the Time & Language category lets you change your time zone, adjust the time and date formats to match your region, and tweak other settings relating to your language and geographic location.

Laptop and tablet owners will want to drop by here when visiting different time zones. Bilingual computer owners will also appreciate settings that allow characters from different languages.

To start, click the start icon, click the Settings icon, and then click Time & Language category. Four entries appear in the right pane:

>> **Date and Time:** These settings are self-explanatory. (Right-clicking your taskbar's date and time area and choosing Adjust Date and Time lets you visit here as well.)

>> **Language and Region:** Moved to a new country? Update your location here. Your computer passes on the name of the new country to any apps that require that information. If you're bilingual or multilingual, go here when you're working on documents that require entering characters from different languages.

>> **Typing:** A plethora of options await to control how Windows interprets your typing. Toggles let you decide whether Windows should automatically correct or highlight misspelled words. You can also visit your corrections history to change mistakes Windows has made.

>> **Speech:** These settings let you adjust speech recognition as well as voices used by Windows to read aloud. Set the Speech Language to the language you speak when using the computer. If Windows has a hard time understanding you, select the Recognize Non-Native Accents for this Language. You can also choose different voices for the built-in text-to-speech services.

Setting Up for Video Games

The Gaming category lets you control how you record video games on Windows. It also lets you check your PC's connection to Microsoft's Xbox gaming consoles and activate the Xbox Game Bar.

Adapting Windows to Your Special Needs

Nearly everybody finds Windows to be challenging, but some people face physical challenges as well. To assist them, the Accessibility category offers a variety of welcome changes.

NEW

If you need help with a specific impairment or disability and aren't sure how to proceed, talk it over with Copilot. If you start your question with "In Windows 11 2024 Update," Copilot will tailor its answer to features available in this current version of Windows. See Chapter 3 if you need reminders on chatting with Copilot.

Follow these steps to modify the settings in Windows:

1. **Open Settings from the Start menu or by pressing Windows + I.**

2. **Select the Accessibility icon.**

   The Accessibility area appears, as shown in Figure 12-10.

3. **Change the settings according to your needs.**

   To make your computer easier to control, the Accessibility window offers three groups of settings: Vision, Hearing, and Interaction. Each offers ways to help you see, hear, or control your PC, respectively. To turn a feature on or off, click its toggle button in these categories:

   - **Text Size:** Enlarges text in Windows and its apps.

   - **Visual Effects:** Always Show Scrollbars, the first toggle switch, makes the scroll bars more visible. It's my first stop after installing Windows 11.

   - **Mouse Pointer and Touch:** Changes the size, color, and shape of the mouse pointer, making it easier to spot in a sea of text.

   - **Text Cursor:** Changes the cursor, the bar that appears when you type.

   - **Magnifier:** Enlarges the area around the mouse pointer when it moves, making it easier to point and click in the right locations.

- **Color Filters:** Adjusts the colors to make them easier to distinguish, a help for color-blind PC owners.

- **Contrast Themes:** Adjusts or eliminates most onscreen color, a change that helps vision-impaired people view the screen more clearly.

- **Narrator:** Activates a computerized voice that describes the words, buttons, and bars displayed onscreen, making them easier for people with visual challenges to find and click.

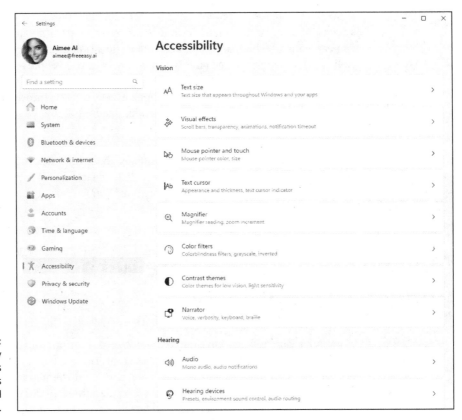

FIGURE 12-10:
The Accessibility window provides help for users with physical limitations.

The Hearing section offers additional settings for those with hearing difficulties. The Interaction section adds settings for those with limited mobility.

Choose any option's toggle switch to turn on the feature immediately. If it makes matters worse, choose the switch again to toggle it off.

Some centers that assist physically challenged people may offer assistance in making these changes.

If you're not sure how to begin, feel free to experiment with the settings. Most of the settings are toggle switches that immediately turn a setting on or off. If you don't care for what the setting does, click the toggle switch again to turn it off.

Managing Privacy and Security

Little privacy is left today when it comes to the internet. Nonetheless, the Privacy & Security category lets you see the controls that Windows offers to limit the amount of information that apps and websites can gather about you. For example, you can control which apps can access your location and control your camera, as well as which apps can see your list of contacts in the People app.

Remember, though, that if you deny apps access to your information, they won't be as helpful. The Maps app, for example, needs to know your physical location before it can give you directions.

If you see constant messages from Windows about not knowing your location and don't mind if apps know where you are, click Location, and then turn on Location Services and Let Apps Access Your Location. You can also choose which apps are allowed to us Location services.

Staying Current and Safe with Windows Update

TIP

When Microsoft releases an update, you receive it automatically via the internet. But if you want to make sure your PC is current, control when (or if) updates happen, or see what updates you already have, check out the Windows Update section in Settings. Most of these options are self-explanatory. In Chapter 13, I talk about the most important updates related to keeping your PC running in tip-top shape.

Changing AutoPlay Settings

When you connect a USB drive or memory card to your computer, Windows asks if you want to set a default action for that device. The *default action* defines what happens automatically every time you connect that device. If you realize you made a bad choice in the past, you're not stuck with that choice. You can change Auto-Play settings for any device at any time. The steps for doing so are similar to those for all other settings:

1. **Click the start icon and then click Settings, or press Windows+I.**

2. **In the left column, click Bluetooth & Devices.**

3. **Scroll down, if necessary, and click AutoPlay.**

   You'll see a drop-down menu for removable drives (USB drives) and for memory cards.

4. **Use the menu below either option to change the default.**

   Perhaps the easiest choice is Ask Me Every Time, so that you can decide what you want to do with the external device each time you connect that device.

If you're trying to prevent an app from opening on your desktop every time you log in, that's something different. I show you how to do that next, but first an important warning.

WARNING

Turn off auto-start only for apps that you no longer want to appear on your desktop at startup when you log. Some auto-start apps run in the *background*, meaning they have no visible presence on the desktop, but they still do important tasks. Windows Security and Microsoft OneDrive are two such apps that should auto-start. If you're unsure about an app, ask Copilot "In Windows 11, what would be the effect of preventing *app* from auto-starting?" Replace *app* with the name of the app you're considering.

To stop an app from auto-starting when you log in, do the following:

1. **Click the start icon and choose Settings.**

2. **Click Apps in the left column.**

3. **Click Startup in the main pane to the right.**

   Toggles appear for various apps.

4. Toggle off any app that you no longer want to auto-start.

   Of course, you can also toggle on any app you do want to have open automatically each time you start your computer.

Chapter **13**

Keeping Windows from Breaking

This chapter is a checklist of sorts, with each section explaining a simple and necessary task to keep Windows running at its best. You also learn how to create a recovery drive, which can save you if a disaster prevents your computer from starting up normally.

Backing Up Your Computer with File History

If your computer's hard drive dies, it will take everything down with it: years of digital photos, music, letters, financial records, scanned memorabilia, and anything else you've created or stored on your PC. That's why you should back up your files regularly. When it comes to computers, creating at least two copies of everything, and saving the copies in different locations, is the safest bet.

OneDrive is a quick, easy way to maintain backups, because they happen automatically and behind the scenes. Chapter 5 tells you how to turn on backup with OneDrive. Note that space on OneDrive is limited to 5GB if you don't subscribe to Microsoft 365. You can get anywhere from 100GB to 6TB of OneDrive space by subscribing to Microsoft 365.

If you prefer a physical drive for backup, rather than or in addition to something out in the nebulous cloud, read on.

Using the cloud for backups protects your data from loss to due fire or theft because the data is stored outside your property. Backing up solely to a physical device on your property doesn't offer the same level of protection.

Like earlier versions, Windows 11 includes an app called File History, which backs up the files in your main folders every hour to a second hard drive connected to your computer. Before File History can go to work, however, you need a portable hard drive, which is relatively inexpensive. A cord connects from the drive to one of your computer's USB ports, and when you plug in the drive, Windows recognizes it immediately.

It's difficult to keep a portable hard drive constantly plugged into laptops or tablets because you move them around so often. A safer but slightly more expensive option is to buy a Wi-Fi hard drive that stays at home. When you walk in the front door, Windows will find the wireless drive and automatically back up your files.

Follow these steps to tell your computer to start backing up your work automatically every hour:

1. **Plug your portable drive's cable into your USB port.**

The rectangular-shaped plug on the end of the drive or its cable plugs into the rectangular-shaped USB port on your computer. (If the plug doesn't fit the first time, flip it over.) Some newer computers also include smaller USB-C ports, which are oval. These push into the computer's matching oval slot in either direction. Somebody finally made computers simpler!

Using a wireless drive? Install it according to its instructions so that Windows will recognize it. (Unfortunately, I can't give you instructions because the steps differ depending on the brand and model.) Some models plug into a USB port on your router, that box that turns your internet connection into a Wi-Fi hotspot in your home.

2. **Click the taskbar's Search box (to the right of the start icon), type** File History, **and press Enter.**

The File History settings area jumps to the screen, as shown in Figure 13-1, and begins searching for a plugged-in hard drive or memory card.

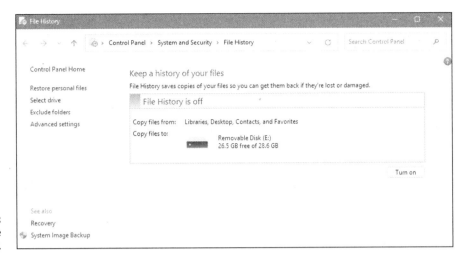

FIGURE 13-1:
The File
History window.

3. **If File History doesn't find and select your plugged-in portable drive automatically, click Select Drive in the left column, and then click the drive you want to use in the list of available drives.**

   If your drive isn't listed, Windows isn't recognizing it. Try unplugging the drive, restarting your computer, and then plugging the drive back into a different USB port. If you've never formatted the drive, you may need to format it. Note that formatting a drive will permanently remove all the files on the drive.

   TECHNICAL STUFF

   If you have network drives in your local network and want to use one of them to store your File History backups, click the Select a Network Drive link in File History's opening window. Networked drives work well as backup locations for portable PCs, such as tablets and laptops. (I explain how to create a home network in Chapter 15.) If you try to save to a networked drive on another PC, Windows asks you to enter a username and password from an Administrator account on the other PC.

4. **Click OK.**

5. **Click the Turn On button.**

   The backup process starts rolling.

When you turn on File History, Windows immediately starts its backup — even if one isn't scheduled. That's because the ever-vigilant Windows wants to make sure it grabs everything right now, before something goes wrong. The first backup can take a *long* time.

After backing up everything, though, Windows backs up only the changed files every hour, which takes much less time. It keeps the first batch of backed-up files in case you want to retrieve those down the road.

Although File History does a remarkable job at keeping everything easy to use and automatic, it comes with a few bits of fine print:

» File History backs up everything in your main user account folders: Documents, Music, Pictures, Videos, Desktop, Favorites, and Downloads folders, as well as a few other folders. (The dialog uses the older term Libraries.) To exclude some folders (perhaps your Videos folder if you already store backup copies of your videos elsewhere), click the Exclude Folders link in the File History window's left pane. There, you can remove some folders and even add others.

» Windows normally backs up changed files every hour automatically. To change that schedule, click the Advanced Settings link in File History's left pane. Then choose the backup frequency. (You can choose between every 10 minutes to once a day.) You can also tell File History how long to keep backups. (I chose Until Space Is Needed.)

» When you turn on File History, it backs up only *your* files and settings. Other people with accounts on your PC must turn on File History while logged into their accounts, too.

TIP

» File History provides a handy way to move your files from an old Windows 10 PC to a new Windows 11 PC, a tiresome chore I describe in Chapter 21.

» Not only does File History work in emergencies, but it enables you to compare current files with versions you created hours or days earlier. I describe how to restore files from the File History backup in Chapter 19. That section is worth looking at now, though.

WARNING

» Windows saves your backup in a folder named FileHistory on your chosen drive. Don't move or delete that folder. Otherwise, Windows may not be able to find it again if you choose to restore it.

Finding Technical Information about Your Computer

If you ever need to look under the Windows hood, heaven forbid, head for the Settings app by clicking the start icon and choosing the Settings icon (shown in the margin).

When the Settings app appears, select the System category and choose About from the bottom of the right column. Shown in Figure 13-2, the screen offers a technical briefing about your PC's viscera:

- >> **Device Specifications:** This area lists your PC's processor (its brains, so to speak) along with its amount of memory, known as RAM.

- >> **Windows Specifications:** Windows comes in several editions and versions. In this section, Windows lists the edition that's running on your computer, as well as the version of that edition. Chances are, you'll see Windows 11 Home or Pro listed here under Edition. Windows 11 2024 Update is version 24H2. (When asking Copilot questions, you can start with, "In Windows 24H2" instead of "In Windows 11 2024 Update.")

TECHNICAL
STUFF

- >> **Related Links:** This section offers a few links to little-used settings that are mainly useful to techies and network administrators.

FIGURE 13-2:
Clicking the System category provides technical information about your PC.

WARNING

Most of the stuff listed in the Settings app's System window is complicated, so don't mess with it unless you're sure of what you're doing or a technical support person tells you to change a specific setting.

TECHNICAL
STUFF

If you're an advanced user who is looking for information about GPU or NPU, the Task Manager or System Information app will likely be your best bet. Just ask Copilot for help, such as, "In Windows 11, where can I get GPU usage stats?" or "In Windows 11, where can I check my NPU chip?"

DRIVES, RAM, AND MEMORY

When techies talk about computer memory, they're usually talking about RAM (random access memory). *RAM* holds a bit of Windows and only the apps and documents you have open at the moment. When you start an app or open a document, Windows grabs a copy of that app or document from your hard drive and loads it into RAM. RAM is much faster than any hard drive, so working with a copy of the app in RAM lets you interact with the app smoothly and without long delays between actions. The thing that does the actual work is the *CPU* (central processing unit), often referred to simply as the *processor* in nerd land.

The downside to RAM is that it's volatile. When you turn off your computer or lose power, everything in RAM disappears. If everything in your computer were stored in RAM, then Windows and all your apps and documents would disappear every time the computer lost power or you shut down your PC. Not convenient.

Computers generally have a lot more hard drive storage space than RAM because people generally work with only a few open apps at a time. If you tried to open every app and every document on your computer, you would eventually get an error message that reads "Not enuf memory" (yes, it's spelled *enuf* in the error message). But you may never see that because most computers have enough RAM to hold quite a few open apps and documents at the same time.

Freeing Up Space on Your Hard Drive

If Windows begins whining about running out of storage space, you can tell it to fix the problem itself. You just need to turn on *Storage Sense*, which tells Windows to take out its trash.

To turn on Storage Sense, which makes Windows automatically empty its recycle bin and delete temporary files left behind by your apps, follow these steps:

1. **Click the start icon and then click the Settings icon (shown in the margin).**

   The Settings app appears.

2. **Click the System category, and then click Storage in the right column.**

   The Storage section appears, as shown in Figure 13-3.

3. **Click the Storage Sense toggle switch on.**

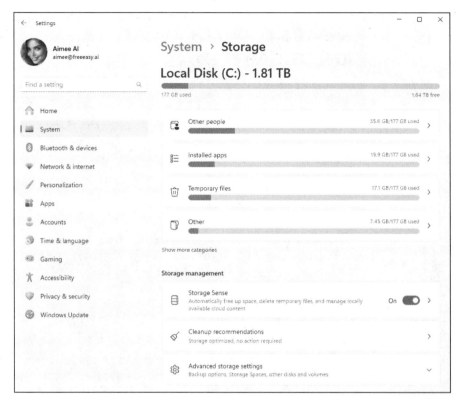

FIGURE 13-3:
The Storage section offers many ways to increase storage space on your PC.

After you complete the preceding steps, Windows begins taking care of its own housekeeping automatically. To fine-tune how Windows manages its storage space, click Storage Sense or the arrow to the right. The Settings app's Storage Sense section offers several other options:

>> **Cleanup of Temporary Files:** Choose how often Windows deletes temporary files that it created in the background for its own housekeeping tasks. You never see these files because they're all created without your knowledge. Chances are good that you'll never miss them.

>> **Automatic User Content Cleanup:** Make Windows free up storage space every day, every week, every month, or only when your disk space runs low. You can also tell it how often to empty your recycle bin. Don't tell it when to delete the contents of your Downloads folder unless you're diligent about moving downloaded files to another folder.

>> **Locally Available Cloud Content:** When you access files stored on OneDrive, Windows saves copies on your PC. Here, you can tell Windows to delete those downloaded copies if you haven't opened them for a certain amount of time.

>> **OneDrive:** When you access a file stored on OneDrive, Windows downloads a copy to your PC for you to open. If you haven't touched that copy for a while, Storage Sense will delete it, leaving an identical copy safely stored on OneDrive. To free up space by deleting these extraneous files, open File Explorer. Right-click the icon for OneDrive in the navigation pane (typically the icon shows a cloud, your username, and Personal). Then choose choose Free Up Space from the pop-up menu.

>> **Run Storage Sense Now:** Free up disk space immediately by having Storage Space delete temporary files and old deleted files in your recycle bin.

These options should help you free up enough space to continue working.

Fiddling with Drivers

Windows comes with an arsenal of *drivers* — software that lets Windows commu-nicate with the gadgets you plug into your PC. Normally, Windows automatically recognizes your new device and it simply works. Other times, Windows heads to the internet and fetches some instructions before finishing the job.

Luckily, you need to install drivers only in these two cases:

>> You've just bought and installed a new piece of hardware, and it's not working correctly. Drivers packaged with computer gadgets are usually old. Visit the manufacturer's website, download the latest driver, and install it.

>> You've plugged in a new gadget that Windows doesn't recognize. Tracking down and installing the latest driver can often fix the problem.

If you're not having trouble with a piece of hardware, don't bother updating its driver, even if you find a newer one online. Chances are good that the newer driver adds support only for newer models. And that new driver might throw a wrench into something that was working fine.

Finally, don't bother signing up for a service that claims to keep your computer up to date with the latest drivers. They can do more harm than good.

Local computer repair shops deal are usually a good resource for solving device and driver problems. If you're not feeling confident about your skills in this arena, consider taking the computer to a nearby tech repair shop.

Windows Update can update some drivers, so make sure you're up to date with Windows Updates before you go digging around. Type **update** in the Search box next to the start icon and then click Check for Updates.

If your device still doesn't work after updating Windows, follow these steps:

1. **Right-click the start icon and choose Device Manager.**

   A list of device categories opens, each with > to the left, which you can click to see what's in the category.

2. **Click the device name that needs updating.**

   Often the device name will have a yellow warning sign next to it.

3. **When you're confident that you've clicked the correct device name, do one of the following:**

   - *If you haven't already downloaded an updated driver: Right-click the device name and choose Update Driver.*

   - If you have downloaded an updated driver: Choose Browse My Computer, navigate to the driver, and then double-click the driver's icon. Or choose Search Automatically and let Windows scour the internet for an updated driver.

4. **Follow the onscreen instructions to update the driver.**

   The rest of the process is automatic.

5. **When you've completed the steps, close Device Manager.**

If none of these steps work, the device itself might be bad, and updating the driver won't have any effect. You may need to take the computer to a repair shop for further diagnosis.

TIP

If your newly installed driver makes things even worse, head back to Device Manager, double-click the troublesome part's name, and click the Driver tab in the Properties window. Keep your breathing steady. Then click the Roll Back Driver button. Windows ditches the newly installed driver and returns to the previous one.

Making a Recovery Drive

Making a recovery drive gives you a way to recover when your hard drive fails and you can't even get into your computer. A *recovery drive* contains all the files that make up Windows, plus all system files. The system files are specific to your computer and contain information that Windows uses to operate the computer on your behalf.

The recovery drive won't contain personal files or apps you downloaded. You should still back up your personal files separately using OneDrive (discussed in Chapter 5) or File History, covered earlier in this chapter.

For the recovery drive, you need a USB drive with at least 16GB of space. Don't use a drive that already contains important files because all those files will be erased when you create the recovery drive.

Follow these steps to make a recovery drive:

1. **Insert the USB drive into a USB port.**

2. **In the Search box next to the start icon, type** Create a recovery drive, **and then click Create a Recovery Drive (Control Panel) in the Start menu.**

3. **Click Yes when prompted.**

4. **Make sure the check box about backing up system files is selected, and then click Next.**

5. **If more than one external drive is connected, make sure the USB drive for recovery is selected under Available Drive(s).**

6. **Click Next.**

    You're reminded that everything on that drive will be deleted.

7. **To proceed, click Create.**

    Follow the onscreen instructions. The process may take a few minutes, so be patient.

Store the USB drive in a safe place. Don't use the drive for any other purpose, other than to restore Windows when no other repair option works. The drive will be *bootable*, meaning you can start your computer from the drive. For more on using a bootable drive, see Chapter 19.

IN THIS CHAPTER

» Figuring out user accounts

» Adding, deleting, and changing user accounts

» Switching between users

» Changing your account pic

» Understanding passwords

» Using Windows Hello to sign in

Chapter **14**

Sharing Your Computer

Windows allows several people to share a computer, laptop, or tablet — but no one can peek into anyone else's personal files. The secret? Windows grants each person a *user account*, which neatly isolates that person's files. When a person types their user account name and password, the computer looks tailor-made just for them: It displays their personalized desktop background, menu choices, apps, and files but forbids them from seeing items belonging to other users.

This chapter explains how to set up a separate user account for everyone in your home. You also discover how to create accounts for children, which enable you to monitor their computer activity and set limits as necessary.

Understanding User Accounts

If you don't want to give access to all your files to everyone who shares your PC, you can set up user accounts. Then everyone who uses the computer will be able to run all the apps on that computer, but each person will have their own Documents, Pictures, Music, and Video folders.

Windows offers two types of user accounts: Administrator and Standard (as well as a special Standard account for children). Each type of account has permission to do different things on the computer:

>> **Administrator:** Administrator accounts have total control over the system. They can set up user accounts for others, install and remove apps, and more. There will always be at least one Administrator account on a computer, though there can be as many as you like.

>> **Standard:** Standard account holders can access most of the computer, but they can't make any big changes to it. They can use any app on the computer but can't install new apps.

>> **Child:** The Child account setting is just a Standard account with the Microsoft Family Safety settings automatically turned on. I cover Microsoft family controls in Chapter 11.

TIP

If someone is signed into their account but hasn't touched the keyboard for a while, the computer will go to sleep. When the computer wakes back up, only that person's user account and photo will appear onscreen. Windows lists the other account holders' names in the screen's lower-left corner, though, letting them sign in with a click.

TECHNICAL
STUFF

You may run across a reference to a *Local account,* which is simply an Administrator or Standard account that isn't a Microsoft account. Local accounts are tied to a specific computer. They don't require an email address, and they lack the perks of a Microsoft account.

Changing or Adding User Accounts

Windows offers two slightly different ways to add user accounts, depending on the two types of people you're most likely to add to your computer:

>> **Family members:** By choosing this type of account, you can automatically set up controls on your children's accounts. Any adults you add here can automatically monitor your children's computer usage. All family members must have Microsoft accounts; if they don't, the process helps you create them.

>> **Other users:** This type of account works best for roommates or other long-term guests who will use your computer but don't need monitoring or the ability to monitor children.

In this section, you discover how to create both types of accounts, as well as how to change existing accounts.

REMEMBER

Only Administrator accounts can add user accounts to a computer. If you don't have an Administrator account, ask the computer's Administrator to upgrade your account from Standard to Administrator.

Adding an account for a family member

Adding a family member adds an important distinction to the account. If you add a child, the child's activity is curtailed according to the limits you set. And if you add an adult, that person also has the ability to monitor the activity of any added children.

If you want to add an account that's not involved in these family matters, see the next section, Adding an account for a non-family member.

To add a family member, make sure you're logged into your computer as an Administrator and then follow these steps:

1. **Click the start icon, click Settings, and then click Accounts in the left column.**

   The Accounts page appears, as shown in Figure 14-1.

2. **Scroll down, if necessary, and click Family.**

   Under the Your Family heading, you should see your name and the name of anyone you've added to the family.

3. **To add a family member, click Add Someone.**

   The window shown in Figure 14-2 appears, asking you to enter the person's email address.

4. **Do one of the following:**

   - *If you're adding an account for a family member who is not a child, type that person's email address.*

   - *If you're adding an account for a child, click Create One for a Child and follow the on-screen instructions.* The page that appears lets you sign the child up for an email address that also serves as a Microsoft account.

   Your invited family member will receive an email saying that they've been invited to have a family account on your computer. After they accept the offer, they automatically appear as an account on your computer.

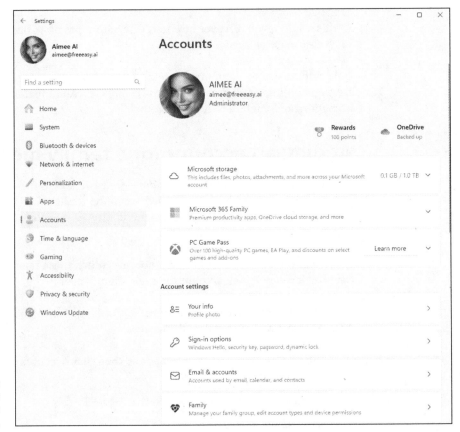

FIGURE 14-1:
Click Family
to create a
user account.

If the new user can't sign in through the normal login procedure, make sure they have permission to log in. See "Changing an existing user account," later in this chapter and make sure their account is set to "Can sign in."

TIP

Windows creates Standard accounts for all new users whether or not they've signed in with a Microsoft or Local account. If at a later time you want to change this, you can upgrade the Standard account to an Administrator account, as described in the upcoming "Changing an existing user account" section.

Adding an account for a non-family member

If you want to create a user account for a guest or other non-family member, you still use the Accounts page in Settings. Make sure you're logged into your computer as an Administrator, and then follow these steps:

Microsoft account

Add someone

Enter their email address

No Microsoft account? Create one for a child

Cancel   Next

FIGURE 14-2:
Choose whether you're adding a child or an adult family member.

1. **Click the start icon, click Settings, and then click Accounts in the left column.**

You're taken to the Accounts page.

2. **Scroll down and click Other Users.**

3. **Click Add Account.**

The screen shown in Figure 14-3 appears.

4. **Do one of the following:**

- *If the user you're adding has a Microsoft account for Windows, Microsoft 365, Outlook.com, or another Microsoft service, enter their email address or cell phone number, click Next, and then click Finish.*

- To create a Local account, which gives the user access to this one computer only, click I Don't Have This Person's Sign-In Information. Then click Add a User Without a Microsoft Account and give the person a username of your choosing. You can also give them a password or let the user make up a password later. Click Next to complete the process.

5. **Close the Settings page by clicking X in the upper-right corner.**

Adding a user
account for a
non-family
member.

At the login page, the user should be able to click their account to log in. Users with Microsoft accounts must enter their Microsoft account password. New users to whom you've not created a password will be prompted to create a password the first time they log in.

Changing an existing user account

You can change and delete user accounts at any time, using the Accounts page in Settings. You can also prevent users from logging into the computer, or allow them to log in if their account isn't appearing on the sign-in page.

Here are the steps:

1. **Click the start icon, click Settings, and then click Accounts on the left side.**

2. **To change settings for a family account, click Family. For a non-family account, click Other Users.**

3. **Click the account you want to change.**

CONVERTING A LOCAL ACCOUNT TO A MICROSOFT ACCOUNT

Are you ready to convert your lowly Local account into an upgraded Microsoft account? Just follow these steps:

1. **Sign in using your Local account.**

2. **From the Start menu, open the Settings app, and then click the Accounts section in the left pane.**

3. **In the Your Info section, select Sign In with a Microsoft Account Instead.**

4. **Enter the email and password for your existing Microsoft account, or choose the Create One! link and create a Microsoft account.**

Your Local account is transformed into your existing or new Microsoft account.

4. **Make the necessary changes to the account.**

You can change the account type to an Administrator or a Standard account. For users with Microsoft accounts, you can prevent them from logging in by choosing Block Sign In. Choose Allow Sign in to ensure that the user can log in from the sign-in page. To prevent Local account users from logging in, you can just delete their Local account.

5. **Close the Settings page by clicking the X in its upper-right corner.**

NEW

Managing user accounts can be daunting. Remember that Copilot knows all about managing user accounts. If you get lost in the process, ask Copilot any question about user accounts in Window 24H2 (version name) or Windows 11 2024 Update (product name).

Switching between Users

Windows enables an entire family, roommates, or employees in a small office to share a single computer or tablet. The computer keeps track of everyone's apps while different people use the computer. Mom can be playing chess and then let Jerry sign in to check his email. When Mom signs back in a few minutes later, her chess match is right where she left it, pondering the sacrifice of her rook.

Known as *fast user switching*, switching between users is quick and easy. When someone else wants to sign into their account for a moment, perhaps to check email, they should follow these steps:

1. **Click the start icon (or tap the Windows key).**

2. **Click the user account name or photo in the lower-left corner of the Start menu.**

3. **Click the three dots in the upper-right corner of the pop-up and choose Switch User.**

4. **Click the picture or name of the user account to which you want to sign in, and then enter the password or PIN for that user account.**

   The computer acts as though only that new user is signed in. However, both users are still signed in. If you use Switch User to go back to the account you were logged into originally, everything on the screen will be just as you left it.

Keep these tips in mind when juggling several people's accounts on a single PC:

>> With all this user switching, you may forget whose account you're using. To check, open the Start menu. The current account holder's picture and name appear in the Start menu's bottom-left corner.

>> To see other accounts currently signed in, press Ctrl+Alt+Del and choose Task Manager. In the left column, click the users icon (two tiny user account icons), You see icons and names for logged-in users. To close Task Manager, click the close icon (X) in the upper-right corner.

>> Don't restart the PC while another person is still signed in. Otherwise, that person will lose any work they haven't saved. (Windows warns you before restarting the PC, giving you a chance to ask the other person to sign back in and save their work.)

>> If a Standard account owner tries to change an important setting or install software, a window appears, asking for Administrator permission. If you want to approve the action, just step over to the PC and type your password in the approval window.

Changing a User Account's Picture

Okay, now the important stuff: changing the boring picture that Windows automatically assigns to your user account. For every newly created user account, Windows chooses a generic silhouette. You can change that picture to any picture you like, either a photo of yourself or an avatar.

To change your user account's picture, follow these steps:

1. **Click the start icon and then click Settings (or press Windows+I).**

2. **In the left column, click Accounts.**

3. **Under Account Settings, click Your Info.**

   You see two options for changing your account picture, as shown in Figure 14-4.

FIGURE 14-4:
Windows lets
each user
choose an
account picture.

4. **Do one of the following:**

   • *Take a Photo:* Click the adjacent Open Camera button, choose a camera (if you have one available), and take the picture right from your screen.

   • *Choose a File:* Click the Browse Files button, navigate to the folder that contains the picture you want to use, click that picture's icon, and then click Choose Picture. Windows quickly slaps that picture on your Start menu.

TIP

Here are a few more tips for choosing your all-important account photo:

>> After you've chosen an account photo, it attaches to your Microsoft account and anything you sign into with that account: Microsoft websites, apps, and other Windows computers that you sign into with your Microsoft account.

>> You can grab any picture off the internet and save it to your Pictures folder. Then click the Browse Files button in the Choose a File section to locate the picture and assign it as your account photo. (Right-click the internet picture and, depending on your web browser, choose Save Image As or a similar menu option.)

>> Don't worry about choosing a picture that's too large or too small. Windows automatically adjusts the size of the image to fit the circular space.

WHAT DOES MY MICROSOFT ACCOUNT KNOW ABOUT ME?

A Microsoft account is simply an email address and a password that lets Microsoft identify you. By logging in with a Microsoft account, you can access many Microsoft services. OneDrive, for example, gives you an online cubbyhole for storing and sharing files across your PC, tablet, and phone, even if it's from Apple or Android. You also need a Microsoft account to download and run many Windows apps.

Like just about every company these days, Microsoft collects information about you, which is made easier when you use a Microsoft account. Google, Facebook, Apple, and every website you visit gathers information about you. Most banks, internet service providers, credit card companies, and insurance companies also stockpile and sell information about their customers.

To help combat your erosion of privacy, visit the Microsoft Privacy Center at `https://account.microsoft.com/privacy` and sign in with your Microsoft account. You can view information about your billing and payments; renew, cancel, or subscribe to Microsoft services such as OneDrive, Office 365, and Xbox Live; find your lost Windows devices on a map; and clear your Bing search history. You can adjust your interests under Search and News Personalization and Personalize Ad Settings to eliminate communications about topics in which you have no interest. Plus, you can check your kids' computer activity, provided you've set them up with a Microsoft account.

To remove, enlarge, shrink, or rotate your account picture for a Microsoft account, browse to `https://account.microsoft.com/profile`, click Your info, and click Change Photo. In the Change Photo dialog that opens, make your changes to the photo. Then click Save.

Setting Up Passwords and Security

There's not much point to having a user account if you don't have a password. Without one, a snoop from the neighboring cubicle or another family member can click your account on the Sign In screen and peek through your files.

If your password becomes compromised, be sure to change it. Microsoft account holders can change their passwords online by visiting `https://account.microsoft.com`. Local account holders can create or change a password by following these steps:

1. **Click the start icon, click Settings, and then click the Accounts icon.**

   The familiar Accounts window appears (refer to Figure 14-1), where you can add other accounts, change your own, and perform other account-related chores.

2. **Choose the Sign-in Options button.**

   The Sign-In Options screen appears, listing all the ways you can log into your computer.

3. **Click the Password option on the window's right side. When the menu drops down, do one of the following:**

   - If you want to change an existing password, click Change. Type your existing password in the Current Password box.

   - If you haven't created a password yet, click Create a Password.

4. **In the New Password text box, type the password. If prompted to retype the new password a second time, retype the same password in the Retype Password text box below it. Then click Next.**

   Retyping the password eliminates the chance of typos.

You can find out more about passwords in Chapter 2.

Signing In with Windows Hello

Password-protected accounts help keep your account secure, from both seedy strangers on the internet and people nearby. But few people enjoy stopping their flow to type a password — if they can remember it.

Windows Hello lets you skip bothersome passwords and log in securely in less than a second. By attaching either a compatible camera or a fingerprint reader to your computer, you can log in with the swipe of a finger or a glance at the camera.

Many new laptops and PCs include built-in fingertip readers and cameras that are compatible with Windows Hello. If yours doesn't, you can buy one that plugs into your computer's USB port.

To set up Windows Hello, follow these steps:

1. **Click the start icon, click Settings, and then click Accounts.**

   The Accounts page appears.

2. **In the right pane, click Sign-In Options.**

   You see the options for signing into your account, as shown in Figure 14-5. If you don't see an option to set up Windows Hello, make sure your compatible fingerprint reader or camera is plugged into your computer and fully installed.

3. **Click Facial Recognition or Fingerprint Recognition.**

4. **Click the Set Up button for the option you chose and follow the instructions.**

   Windows walks you through scanning your fingerprint or enabling facial recognition. You may need to create a *PIN,* a four-digit number that adds an additional layer of security for special circumstances.

   If your computer has neither a camera for facial recognition nor a fingerprint reader, you're not out of luck. You can buy a fingerprint reader for under $30 online or at any store that sells tech gadgets.

   The need to constantly prove your identity by typing a password gets very old, very fast. Expect more advances in this area. As always, you can ask Copilot for help in understanding and using alternatives to passwords. Ask, "What are alternatives to passwords in Windows 11 2024 Update?" You should at least get a list of options, and you can then continue the conversation by zeroing in on any interesting alternatives.

Chapter **15**

Connecting Computers with a Network

I f you have Wi-Fi in your home or office, you already have a network. It may not be obvious because Windows doesn't automatically share printers and folders and computers among the devices sharing a network connection. But getting computers and devices to share resources is just a matter of tweaking some settings, as you learn in this chapter.

Setting Up a Network

Most home networks resemble a spider, as shown in Figure 15-1. The thing that lets the computers all share a single internet connection is called a *router*. If someone else set up the Wi-Fi in your home or office, you might not know that you have a router or where it's located. Mine is in my garage (I think). But if you have Wi-Fi, there is a router somewhere.

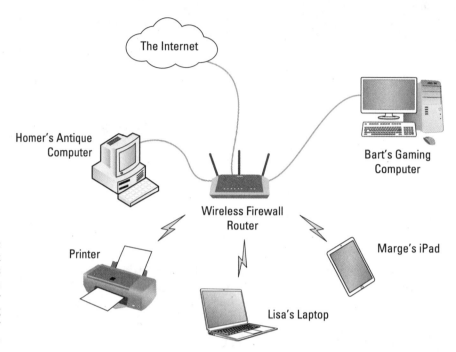

FIGURE 15-1:
A network
resembles
a spider, with
each computer
communicating
with a router near
the center.

The router divides its attention among networked computers efficiently, letting every computer simultaneously share a single internet connection. You might also have Wi-Fi extenders throughout the house. These electronic boxes ensure a strong Wi-Fi connection in every room and connect to the same central router. If you have a smart TV, Amazon Alexa devices, Fire TV, Roku, Chromecast, iPads, tablets, wireless gaming devices, and similar gadgets, those also connect to the router to share the same internet connection.

As soon as two or more computers connect to the same Wi-Fi connection, they're in a network. But it won't be obvious if the computers aren't *discoverable,* or visible on the network. The first and most important part of setting up a network is to make sure the computers are all on the same Wi-Fi network. This is especially important in homes and offices that have two or more possible Wi-Fi networks.

To see which Wi-Fi network (if any) a computer is currently using, click the Wi-Fi icon near the lower-right corner of your screen. You'll see the name of your current network in the pop-up that appears. My network is named Wiffy-5G, as shown in Figure 15-2.

WARNING

Assuming that two computers are on the same Wi-Fi network, without checking to make sure, is a leading cause of network failure, frustration, and cursing.

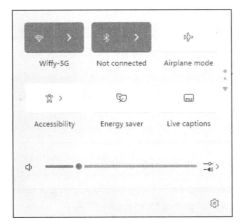

FIGURE 15-2:
Make sure
networked
computers are on
the same Wi-Fi
connection.

To make the computer at which you're currently sitting discoverable on the Wi-Fi network, you need to slog through some settings, which you do in the next section. You're also going to make sure that your network is secure in these steps.

Knowing your computer's name

Every computer in a network is identified by its name, preferably something that is easily recognized. You want to make sure that no two computers in the network have the same name. To see and optionally change a computer's name, follow these steps:

1. **Click the start icon, click System in the left column, and then click About.**

The name of the computer appears above System Product Name (AI-Machine in Figure 15-3).

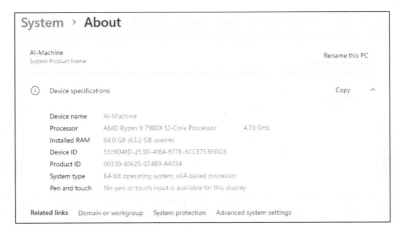

FIGURE 15-3:
Know your
computer's name,
or change it,
if you like.

2. **If you want to give the computer a better name, do the following:**

   a. *In the About window, click the Rename This PC button.*

   b. *Follow the onscreen instructions.* For the name, you can use letters, numbers, or hyphens, but no other punctuation marks, symbols, or spaces.

   c. *Restart the PC.*

   d. *Start again at Step 1.*

3. **Next to Related Links, click Domain or Workgroup.**

   A System Properties dialog opens. Optionally, you can give this computer a brief description, such as *Dad's office* in Figure 15-4.

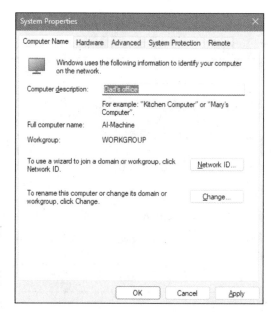

FIGURE 15-4:
In the System Properties dialog, type a short description of your computer.

4. **Make sure the workgroup name is WORKGROUP.**

   WORKGROUP is the default name. If someone changed it, you'll need to set it back to WORKGROUP.

5. **Close the System Properties dialog box by clicking OK.**

6. **Close the Systems settings page by clicking X.**

   You return to the Windows desktop, ready to forge ahead with the steps in the next section.

Turning on network discovery

To make your computer visible on your private network and capable of sharing resources, the next step is to turn on network discovery and sharing. Keep in mind that you want shared folders and resources to be visible only in your *private network*. In other words, the things you share should be visible when you're connected to your home or office Wi-Fi but not visible when you're connected to a public network in an airport or place of business.

Here are the steps for turning on network discovery:

1. **Click the start icon and then click Settings.**

2. **Click Network & Internet.**

3. **Scroll down, if necessary, and click Advanced Network Settings.**

4. **Click Advanced Sharing Settings.**

    The Advanced Sharing Settings page has three main sections titled Private Networks, Public Networks, and All Networks. Click any section to expand or and collapse it.

5. **Under Private Networks, make sure everything is on and selected as shown in Figure 15-5.**

    Everything else can be set off to minimize your computer's visibility on public networks. Use the recommended 128-bit encryption (which adds an extra layer of security).

    If you turn on the last option, Password Protected Sharing, only people who have a user account on the computer will be able to access its shared items. However, you'd have to set up a user account for everyone in the family (or office) so that they could access shared resources. If you want to be the only one who can access this computer's shared resources from the other computers in your network, turn on Password Protected Sharing. You don't need to turn on Password Protected Sharing to keep the public out.

6. **Close the Advanced Network Settings window.**

At this point, you're pretty much done. The computer will be visible in your private network, as you see shortly.

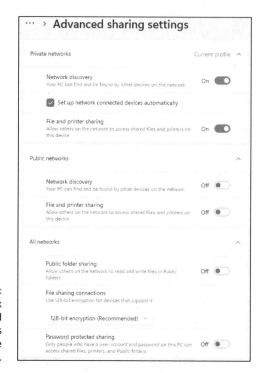

FIGURE 15-5:
Network discovery and sharing settings for a private network.

Sharing a Folder on Your Network

Sharing a folder on your network allows you to access the folder's contents from any computer in your private network. If you didn't turn on password-protected sharing, family members or office mates on the same Wi-Fi connection will also have access to those folders. This capability comes in handy, especially if you're currently using a sneaker network, where you copy files to and from USB drives and run from computer to computer trying to keep everything in sync.

So far, you haven't shared any folders. You've just set up a private network. To share a folder on the computer, follow these steps:

1. **Open File Explorer and navigate to the icon for the folder you want to share.**

   If you want to share your built-in Documents, Pictures, Music, or Videos folder, you can do so from the navigation pane in File Explorer. You can also share any OneDrive folder on your private network.

2. **Right-click the icon for the folder you want to share and choose Properties.**

The Properties dialog for the folder opens. On the General tab, the Location shows the exact location of the folder you're sharing. Typically it will be C:\ users\ followed by the username. If you have automatic backups turned on, you may see \OneDrive tacked onto the end.

If you want to share the Local folder, click Cancel to close the dialog. In the navigation pane click This PC, click Local Disk (C:), click Users, and then click the username.

3. **In the Properties dialog box, click the Sharing tab.**

Some folders will already be shared because that's the default setting. However, the folder won't be visible to others in the local network until you complete all the steps.

4. **Click Advanced Sharing.**

An Advanced Sharing dialog opens.

5. **Select the Share This Folder check box.**

6. **(Optional)** Change the share name to something more descriptive and add a comment, if you like, as shown in Figure 15-6.

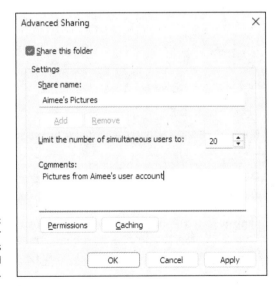

FIGURE 15-6:
Sharing a folder and changing its share name and description.

7. **Click Permissions and then set permissions for who can do what in the shared folder.**

The Everyone permission refers to people in the private network (not everyone in the world). If you want others to be able to only view and copy files in the shared folder (not change or delete files in the folder), leave the permission set at Read. If you want to give others free rein to do as they please in the folder, set the permission to Full Control, as shown in Figure 15-7.

Optionally, you can use the Add and Check Names buttons to add users by name, and then grant different permissions to different users.

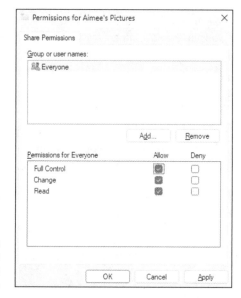

FIGURE 15-7:
Give other users
full access to a
shared folder.

8. **When you're finished, click OK in each open dialog box to save your changes.**

You haven't made any lifelong commitments here. To change any of these settings, simply repeat these steps.

NEW

You can share as many or as few folders as you like, from any user account on the current computer. You can repeat the process on other computers in the network to share resources from them.

NEW

If you need to add Windows 7/8/10 computers to your network, ask Copilot for instructions. For example, ask, "In Windows 10, how do I activate network discovery and sharing?" or "How do I share folders in Windows 8?"

Sharing a Printer

Sharing printers is one of the most common uses of a private network. If you've ever seen and chuckled at the internet meme titled "The myth of the printer that actually works," you probably know all too well how difficult it can be to get along with *one* printer. The thought of having multiple printers spread throughout the house might terrify you. Sharing one printer whittles the problem down to just one printer.

The first step to sharing a printer is to get it to work on just one computer in the network. If it's a wireless printer, it's probably already connected to your private network through your Wi-Fi connection, which helps. However, just because a computer is on a private network doesn't mean it can access the printer. You may still need to go to the computer from which you can access the printer, and share that access.

First, if you haven't already done so, turn on network discovery and sharing, as discussed previously. Make sure you log in to an Administrator account. Then follow these steps:

1. **Click the start icon and then click Settings.**

2. **Click Bluetooth & Devices.**

3. **Click Printers and Scanners, and then click the name of the printer you want to share.**

   If you don't see your printer listed, click Add Device. The printer should be listed on the next page that opens. If the printer doesn't appear, print something from your computer to make sure you can access the printer.

4. **Click Printer properties, and then click the Sharing tab.**

5. **Make sure that Share This Printer is selected and that the share name is the name of the printer.**

   Figure 15-8 shows an example, with my printer's name.

6. **Click OK.**

7. **Close the Settings page by clicking X.**

There's a good chance the printer was already shared, so you didn't have to change any settings. In the next section I explain how to access stuff you've shared on the network.

FIGURE 15-8:
Settings for a
shared printer.

Accessing Shared Network Resources

Sharing stuff on your network is one thing. Finding it on other computers in your network is another. In this section, you learn how to find the stuff you've shared.

Before you try to access shared resources on the current computer, make sure you log into that computer with your Microsoft password, rather than a PIN or other Windows Hello option.

Signing in with your Microsoft password

If you signed into the computer that contains the shared resources using a PIN or other Microsoft Hello option, other users in your network might have trouble accessing its resources. So before you go looking for shared resources from other computers, sign into this computer with your Microsoft password. You don't have to sign into the other computers with your Microsoft password.

Follow these steps on the PC from which you shared the resources:

1. **Click the start icon, click your user account picture at the bottom left of the Start menu.**

2. Click the three dots near the top-right corner of the pop-up that appears and then choose Sign Out.

3. On the lock screen, click the username or picture of an Administrator account that has a Microsoft account. If you normally sign in with a PIN or alternative option, click Sign In Options, and then click Microsoft Account password.

   Don't enter a PIN or use another Windows Hello method.

4. Type your Microsoft account password and then press Enter or click the arrow on the right side of the box.

   You won't notice anything different. Your PC will act as it always does. However, if you don't perform this step, you may have difficulty accessing shared resources from other computers in your network.

If the sharing computer shuts down or goes to sleep while you're trying to access its shared resources, you won't be able to get to those resources. To make sure the computer doesn't go to sleep or into hibernation too quickly when unattended, see the "Changing Sleep and Hibernation Timeouts" sidebar.

CHANGING SLEEP AND HIBERNATION TIMEOUTS

To prevent a computer that's sharing resources from becoming unavailable unexpectedly, you can adjust the sleep and hibernate timeouts. If you're sharing from a laptop, you may need to adjust settings for both Plugged In and Battery Power. Here are the steps:

1. Press Windows+I, or click the start icon and then click Settings.

2. In the left column, click System.

3. In the right column, click Power.

4. Click Screen, Sleep, & Hibernate Timeouts.

5. Next to Make My Device Sleep After, set a time that you think will be sufficient based on your usage.

   You can go up to 5 hours, or choose Never to prevent the computer from ever going to sleep.

(continued)

(continued)

6. Next to Make My Device Hibernate After, set an extended duration.

Or set it to Never to prevent the computer from ever going into hibernation.

7. On a battery-powered computer, if you think you'll be sharing resources from the laptop while it's on battery power, repeat Steps 5 and 6 for both Plugged In and Batter Powered.

8. Close the Settings page.

To learn more about sleep and hibernate, just ask Copilot, "What are sleep and hibernate in Windows 11?"

Finding shared resources

Thankfully, all the rigmarole you've just been through is over. You shouldn't have to go through any of that again. Now you can go to the other computers in your network and access your shared resources.

Here are the steps to access shared resources from any computer in your network:

1. On another computer, log in as you normally would.

Make sure that the computer uses the same Wi-Fi network as the computer that's sharing resources.

2. Open File Explorer by clicking its icon on the taskbar or on the Start menu.

See Chapter 5 if you're not familiar with File Explorer.

3. In the navigation pane on the left side of File Explorer, click Network.

If you don't see the navigation pane in File Explorer, click View in the File Explorer toolbar. Click Show and then click Navigation Pane. Finally, in the navigation pane, click Network.

4. If you see a message indicating that network discovery is turned off, as shown in Figure 15-9, click that message and choose the option to turn on network discovery and file sharing.

You won't see the message if network discovery is already turned on.

5. If you see a prompt asking if you want to turn on network discovery and file sharing for all public networks, choose the No, Make the Network That I Am Connected to a Private Network button.

FIGURE 15-9:
Turn on network
discovery to
access private
network
resources.

REMEMBER

If you turned off password-protected sharing but are still asked for network credentials or blocked from accessing the shared resource, go back to the PC from which you shared the resources and sign in with your Microsoft account and password (not a PIN), as described earlier.

Eventually, the main pane to the right shows everything in your local network, as shown in Figure 15-10. Don't be alarmed if it looks like your entire neighborhood is in there. You're seeing every internet-connected device in your home or office, including smart TVs, Wi-Fi extenders, Alexa devices, and other things you probably never think about. Most of them you can ignore. Your main concern is the other computers in the network, which are usually listed across the top of the pane.

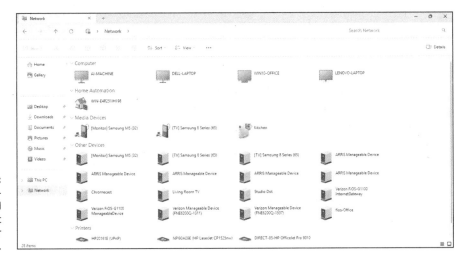

FIGURE 15-10:
Lots of internet-
connected
devices might
appear under
Network.

Accessing a shared folder

When you expand the Network category in File Explorer's navigation pane, all computers with shared resources should be listed (except for computers that are turned off or sleeping). To access shared folders on a computer, click the right arrow next to the computer's name. The shared folders will be listed below the computer's name.

When you click the name of a folder in the navigation pane, the contents of that folder open in the main pane to the right, just as when you view the contents of a local folder. To open a file, double-click the file's icon, as always.

If you have only read rights to the folder, you can open and view the contents of any file. But if you make changes to the file, you won't be able to save those changes back to the original folder. Instead, you can click Save As in whatever app you used to modify the file, and save your copy of the file to a local folder on your own computer. You can also copy a file from the shared folder just by dragging the file's icon into a local folder on your computer. You can then do as you please with that local copy of the file.

Accessing shared printers

When you click Network in File Explorer's navigation pane, the pane to the right shows all shared resources, including printers. However, to print to one of those printers, you don't use File Explorer. Rather, just print from any app as you normally would. For example, press Ctrl+P to open the Print dialog. Click the drop-down menu under Printer, and all your printers should be available, as shown in Figure 15-11. Then just click the name of the printer to which you want to print and continue normally, as you would with any local printer.

If you don't see the shared printer, click Add Printer at the bottom of the list. In the next window that opens, click the desired printer to add it to the drop-down menu for future use.

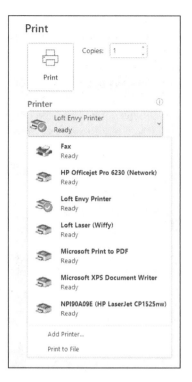

FIGURE 15-11:
Shared network
printers in
the Printer
drop-down
menu.

NEW

Remember, if you have problems while setting up and using a private network, Copilot can be your best friend. You can get help with specific error messages you encounter along the way. And you can ask more general questions about your Windows 11 private network.

Accessing Your PC from Laptops and Mac Computers

As an alternative to sharing specific folders on a Windows 11 PC, you can share the entire computer. Basically, you're working with your PC as you normally would but using the screen, keyboard, and mouse from another computer in your network. Doing so gives you unlimited access to that computer. Any apps you run this way run on the remote PC. If you access a high-end desktop for gaming or advanced AI, those apps will still run just fine even if you're using an older underpowered laptop.

There's one big catch. You must be using Windows 11 Pro. Windows Home Edition doesn't provide remote desktop access. To see which version of Windows you're using, click the start icon, Settings, System, and then About. Your Windows version appears next to Edition under Windows Specifications.

Enabling remote access involves two steps. First, you need to set up remote access on the Windows 11 Pro computer that you want to access from afar. I refer to that computer as the *main computer.* On other computers in your network, you *remote into* (that's the expression techies use) the main computer by using the Remote Desktop Connection app.

Setting up Remote Desktop

Remote Desktop is a Windows feature that's widely used in large corporations so that IT technicians can troubleshoot a user's computer remotely, without travelling to the PC.

In your home, you can use Remote Desktop to access your high-end gaming and AI desktop computers from your oldest, cheapest laptops, as well as from Macs, iPads, Android phones, and iPhones, as long as they're in the same Wi-Fi network. So, while you're reclining in front of your large-screen TV in the living room with your wimpiest laptop, you can still enjoy the mighty horsepower of your expensive desktop computer.

Your PC must be on your private network. In the following, I assume you've set up your network, following the steps provided earlier in this chapter. Then go to the Windows 11 Pro computer you want to access remotely and follow these steps:

1. **Click the start icon and then click Settings.**

2. **In the left column, click System.**

3. **Scroll down and click Remote Desktop.**

4. **Set the Remote Desktop toggle on.**

5. **When prompted, click Confirm to verify that you really want to do this.**

   The name of your computer appears next to *PC name.* This is the name you'll use to access the computer remotely.

6. **Click the down arrow next to the toggle and make sure that the Require Devices to Use Network Level Authentication to Connect (Recommended) option is selected, as shown in Figure 15-12.**

   You do not want to expose your PC to the internet. To stay safe, make sure you choose the recommended settings as you go through the Remote Desktop setup procedure.

FIGURE 15-12:
Setting up
Remote Desktop
on a Windows 11
Pro computer.

7. **Click Remote Desktop Users.**

    A Remote Desktop Users dialog opens. You should see that you have already been granted remote access, so you don't have to add yourself.

8. **If you're feeling magnanimous and trusting, grant remote access to other users of your network.**

    To add someone, click the Add button, start typing their username, and click Check Names to get the exact username needed by Remote Desktop.

9. **Click OK in the dialog after adding usernames, or click Cancel to grant access to only yourself.**

10. **Close the Settings window by clicking X.**

In the next section, I show you how to access the PC remotely.

WARNING

Before you can access this computer remotely, you need to sign into this computer (not the other computers) with your Microsoft password, rather than a PIN or other Windows Hello option. See the section "Signing in with your Microsoft password," earlier in the chapter, to ensure that other computers aren't blocked from gaining access remotely.

Accessing a PC remotely

After you've set up Remote Desktop on your PC and signed in with your Microsoft password, you can go to any other computer on your private network and access the PC remotely.

If you're connecting from another Windows computer, you shouldn't have to install any apps. If you're using an Apple device, download and install Remote Desktop Connection from Apple's App Store and use that app. If you're using an Android device, download and install Remote Desktop from Google's Play Store.

Then follow these steps:

1. **Open the Remote Desktop Connection app on the computer at which you're sitting.**

   To find the app in Windows, click the start icon, and start typing the word *remote* in the Search box. When Remote Desktop Connection appears in the search results, click it. If you're not using Windows, locate the app as you would any other app on your Apple or Android device.

2. **In the Remote Desktop Connection window that opens, type the name of the computer you want to access.**

   In my example, the name of the PC is AI-MACHINE.

3. **Click Connect.**

4. **Enter your user name and password, as shown in Figure 15-13.**

   This is the same Microsoft password you use to log into the PC you're trying to access remotely.

FIGURE 15-13: Accessing a PC with Remote Desktop Connection in Windows.

5. **(Optional) Choose Remember Me to streamline future access.**

6. **Click OK.**

7. **If you see a message indicating that the identity of the remote computer cannot be verified, you can select the Don't Ask Me Again check box to stop seeing that message in the future. Then click Yes.**

The desktop for the remote computer fills your screen. You can now use your screen, mouse, and keyboard to work with the remote computer, just as though you were sitting at that computer. You can run any app regardless of what operating system you're using on the remote computer.

Centered across the top of your screen is a small title bar. This is the only part of the screen that applies to the computer at which you're currently sitting. To end your remote access session, click X on the right side of that title bar. The remote session will terminate, and your screen, mouse, and keyboard will go back to operating the computer you're currently using, rather than the remote computer.

NEW

As usual, if you hit a snag or receive an error message, Copilot is your best tech support.

5

Working with Text, Sound, Photos, and Videos

Write like a pro, with help from AI.

Design professional-quality content with photos and AI images.

Create compelling movies with sound and video.

Chapter **16**

Working with Text

You've probably worked with words in the past, typing emails, homework assignments, and such. But not everyone has experience in creating and saving longer text documents. In this chapter, you learn the skills needed for working with longer text documents.

Getting Started with Notepad

Windows 11 comes with the Notepad text editor. Unlike some more complex word-processing apps, Notepad is simple to use. However, the skills you learn here can be applied to typing in any writing app, from other text editors to word-processing apps such as Microsoft Word and Google Docs.

Opening Notepad

To open Notepad, click the start icon. If you see Notepad on the Start menu, click its icon. Otherwise, click the All Apps button or type *notepad* in the Search box; when you see the Notepad app, click it.

The first time you open Notepad, you'll see a tab named Untitled and a blank sheet of paper on which you can type, as shown in Figure 16-1. If you've used Notepad in the past, you might see documents you've worked on instead.

Typing in Notepad

When you work with longer chunks of text, the text should *word wrap* inside the Notepad window so you don't have to scroll to see text that's off the screen. If you find you have to scroll left and right in a Notepad document, choose View ⇨ Word Wrap to turn on word wrap.

You can change text by first moving the cursor to where you want to make the change, either by clicking that spot or by using the arrow keys to move the cursor. With the cursor in place, you can then do any of the following:

>> To delete text to the left of the cursor, press Backspace.

>> To delete text to the right of the cursor, press Delete (Del).

>> To start a new line or insert a blank line, press Enter (or Return).

>> To undo whatever you just did, press Ctrl+Z. To redo (undo your undo), press Ctrl+Y.

Correcting spelling

As you type in Notepad, you might notice a word changing right after you type it. In most cases, Notepad decided that you misspelled the word, so it corrected the spelling automatically. If you're sure you had the word spelled correctly, right-click the corrected word and choose Undo to go back to your original spelling.

When Notepad doesn't recognize a word, it gets a wavy red underline. You can right-click the underlined word and choose Spelling to see Notepad's suggestions, as shown in Figure 16-2.

FIGURE 16-2: Right-click any word that has a wavy underline.

If you see the correctly spelled word, click it and you're done. Otherwise, you can choose from the other options:

>> **Ignore *Word*:** Leave the word spelled as-is, and remove the wavy underline from this instance of the word.

>> **Ignore All:** Leave the word as-is, and remove the underline from all other instances of the word.

>> **Add to Dictionary:** Leave the word as-is, and don't flag it as a misspelling in future documents.

>> **Turn Off Spell Check:** Stop checking your spelling.

TIP

If you have an Amazon Alexa device within earshot, you can also just say, "Alexa, how do you spell" and then state the word you want spelled.

Working with larger chunks of text

If you want to delete, copy, or move a large chunk of text, it's easiest if you select the text first. As you select text, its background color changes from white to a light blue. Here are some handy ways to select text using the mouse:

>> To select one word, double-click it.

>> To select one paragraph, triple-click it.

>> To select any other chunk of text, drag the mouse pointer through the text.

>> To select all the text in the document, choose Edit ⇨ Select All.

If you change your mind or need to start over, click anywhere in or outside the selected text.

You can also select text using the keyboard. First, move the cursor to where you want to start the selection. Here are a couple tricks for that:

>> To move to the start of a line, click the Home key.

>> To move to the end of the line, click the End key.

>> To move word-by-word, hold down the Ctrl key while pressing the left or right arrow key.

>> To move to the top of the document, press Ctrl+Home.

>> To move to the end of the document, press Ctrl+End.

>> To move by pages, use the Page Up (PgUp) and Page Down (PgDn) keys.

When you have the cursor placed where you want to start selecting, hold down the Shift key while using these same keys to extend the selection. For example:

>> To extend the selection in a particular direction, hold down the Shift key while pressing the up, down, left, or right arrow key, or the Page Up (PgUp) or Page Down (PgDn) key.

>> To select to the beginning of the line, press Shift+Ctrl+Home,

>> To select to the end of the line, press Shift+Ctrl+End.

>> To select one line, press Home to get to the start of the line, and then press Shift+down arrow.

>> To select from the cursor position to a specific place in the text, hold down the Shift key and click where you want to extend the selection.

>> To undo your selection, press any arrow key without holding down the Shift key.

And to select the entire document, simply press Ctrl+A (without pressing Shift).

Once you've selected text, here's what you can do with it:

>> To delete the selected text, press Delete or Backspace. (Press Ctrl+Z if you change your mind.)

>> To copy the text, press Ctrl+C, or choose Edit ➪ Copy, or right-click the selection and press Copy.

>> To move the text, press Ctrl+X, or choose Edit ➪ Cut, or right-click the selection and choose Cut.

>> To paste the text you copied or cut, move the cursor to where you want to place that text. Then press Ctrl+V, or choose Edit ➪ Paste, or right-click at the cursor and choose Paste.

NEW

If you forget any of these techniques, just ask Copilot, "What are all the ways I can select text?" or "How do I move or copy text?"

NEW

Letting AI write your text

As mentioned in Chapter 3, Copilot AI can write just about anything for you. You can get a little more control over the output using Copilot Compose in Microsoft Edge. Here's how:

1. **Open Microsoft Edge.**

2. **Click the Copilot icon in Edge's upper-right corner.**

3. **Click Compose at the top of Copilot's pane.**

   The options shown on the right in Figure 16-3 appear.

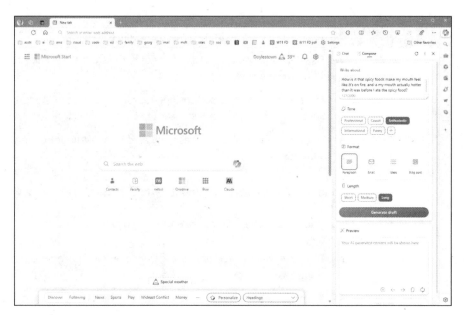

FIGURE 16-3:
Copilot Compose
in Microsoft Edge.

4. **Make your selections using the following guidelines:**

   a. *Write About: Type whatever you want Copilot to write about.*

   b. *Tone: Choose a tone of voice for the output (professional, casual, funny, or whatever).*

   c. *Format: Choose Paragraph for regular writing; choose Ideas for a bulleted list or outline; choose Email to format the output as an email message; or choose Blog Post to format the output as a blog or social media post.*

   d. *Length: Choose Short, Medium, or Long to specify the amount of text you want.*

5. **Click Generate Draft.**

   Copilot's text appears in the Preview section. You can widen or narrow the Copilot panel by dragging its inner border left or right, respectively, in the Edge browser window.

To edit the generated text, you can use the following icons, which are labeled in Figure 16-4:

>> **Stop icon:** While Copilot is writing your text, click this icon if you want to stop the output. Once the output stops, you can change your prompt or other choices, and then click Generate Draft to try again.

>> **Next draft and previous draft icons:** If you use the regenerate draft icon to generate multiple drafts, use these icons to scroll through the drafts.

>> **Copy icon:** Click this icon to copy the output. Then you can paste the text in Notepad (or another app).

>> **Regenerate draft icon:** If you're not thrilled with Copilot's output, click this icon to make AI generate another answer to your initial request.

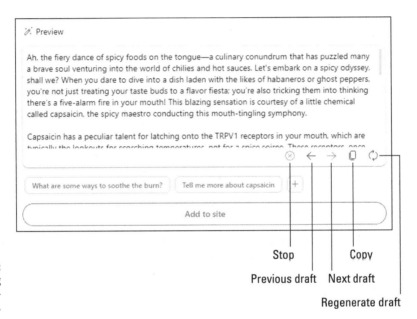

To keep the topic going and have Copilot provide additional output, click the suggested text under the icons. Or click the + button to add your own instructions.

If you're typing an electronic document such as an email or a blog post, you can position the cursor in that document, as if you were going to start typing. Then click Add to Site in the Copilot page to put the generated text in your document. Basically, it's a copy-and-paste operation.

Copilot isn't designed to compose an entire book or extensive documents. So don't expect to be an instant famous author of the Great American Novel. If you do need a long document, you can tell Copilot to "Write an outline for *topic*" and specify your topic. Copy and paste the outline into a document. Then ask Copilot to write an essay about each topic in your outline, one at a time, and copy and paste each essay under the appropriate heading in your outline.

If you need professional-grade writing support or academic papers with citations in APA or MLA format, consider asking Copilot in Windows, "What websites offer generative AI for professional writers (or academic writers)?" Then take a gander at some of the suggested resources (note that some of these resources may not be free).

Improving your own writing

Dyslexia is a common malady that prevents intelligent people from sticking to the countless rules of grammar, punctuation, and spelling that their language dictates. People afflicted with dyslexia are often insecure about showing others their writing. That problem is easily resolved, thanks to Copilot and modern AI. Here's how:

1. **In Notepad (or another app), type the text using your own words.**

2. **Select the text you want to improve, and press Ctrl+C to copy the selected text.**

3. **Click the Copilot icon in the taskbar.**

4. **If Copilot is already cluttered with previous dealings, click the new topic icon (shown in the margin).**

5. **Click your preferred writing style for Copilot's output (Creative, Balanced, Precise) from the drop-down menu near the top of the window.**

6. **In the Ask Me Anything box, type** Improve this: **and then press Ctrl+V to paste your copied text.**

7. **Press Enter or click the submit icon (paper airplane).**

   Copilot rewrites the text you pasted, making sure the spelling, grammar, and punctuation are perfect! Feel free to copy and paste the text into any document.

Saving Notepad documents

You can save and open Notepad documents just as you would any other document in any other app. To save a Notepad document, do one of the following:

» Choose File ⇨ Save from Notepad's menu bar.

» Press Ctrl+S.

>> Close the document's tab by clicking the X, and then click Save when asked if you want to save your work.

>> Close Notepad by clicking Notepad's X icon or by choosing File ⇨ Exit from Notepad's menu bar; then click Save when asked if you want to save your work.

If you've never saved the document before, a Save As dialog opens, as shown in Figure 16-5, so you can specify the name and location of the document. Most people use the Documents folder for written documents, but you can choose any folder you like. Keep the suggested file type, Text Documents (*.txt), and click Save.

Where to save the file   What to name the file

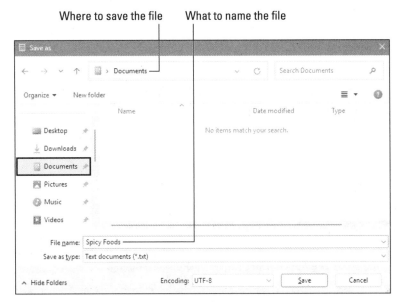

FIGURE 16-5:
The Save As
dialog for
saving a file.

Once you save the document, you won't have to specify its name or location the next time you save your changes.

Opening a Notepad document

If you close Notepad while you still have documents open, those documents will re-open the next time you open Notepad. To start a new document in Notepad, just choose File ⇨ New. To close a document, click X on the right side of the document's tab. If the document has unsaved changes you'll be prompted to save your changes.

You can open a Notepad document from within Notepad or from File Explorer. To open from Notepad, follow these steps:

1. **Open Notepad and choose File ⇨ Open.**

   An Open dialog appears, probably displaying the contents of your Documents folder, as shown in Figure 16-6.

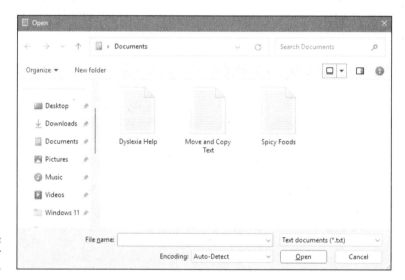

FIGURE 16-6:
The dialog for
opening a file.

2. **If you didn't save the document in your Documents folder, navigate to the appropriate folder in the Open dialog.**

   Use the navigation pane on the left side of the Open dialog, just as you'd use the navigation pane in File Explorer.

3. **Click the document's filename and choose Open, or simply double-click the filename.**

   The document opens in Notepad in its own tab.

As an alternative to opening Notepad first, open File Explorer and navigate to the folder in which you saved the document. Then double-click the name of the document you want to open. Provided the file has a .txt filename extension, it should open in Notepad automatically (unless you changed the default app for text files). If you don't see any filename extensions, you can reveal them by choosing View ⇨ Show ⇨ File Name Extensions in File Explorer.

If you want to open a file in another app rather than in the default app, right-click the filename, click Open With, and then click the name of the app you want to use. But be careful. Sometimes you may see gibberish because you opened a file type that's not supported by the current app. When that happens, just close the document but be sure to choose No when asked about saving the document.

Typing with Your Voice

Windows 11 2024 Update includes a feature called Voice Typing, where you can type with your voice rather than your fingers. (Oddly enough, you won't see an app named Voice Typing on the Start menu.) To use Voice Typing, you need a microphone, a text editor or word-processing app (such as Notepad), and an internet connection. Assuming you have all of that in place, here's how you can take Voice Typing for a spin:

1. **Open Notepad.**

   Or click in any text box on a form or any other place where you could type text.

2. **Press Windows+H.**

   A small window opens near the bottom of the screen, as shown in Figure 16-7.

When you're typing a document, I suggest that you click the settings icon (gear), to the left of the microphone icon, and turn on Automatic Punctuation. That way, you won't have to add punctuation while speaking. If you're filling in a form, you may want to leave Automatic Punctuation turned off, because fill-in-the-blank forms generally don't use punctuation the way regular text does. To close the Settings options, click the same gear icon.

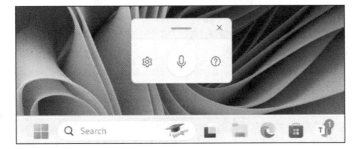

FIGURE 16-7:
The Voice
Typing window.

3. **Click the microphone icon in the Voice Typing window and speak slowly.**

   Words are typed as you speak. The process can take a little time, so speaking slowly helps.

4. **When you've finished speaking, click the microphone icon again.**

Voice Typing isn't perfect, so be sure to review the typed text and make any necessary corrections.

Technologies are available that can convert text documents you've already typed to spoken text. In fact, if you've ever watched a video where the narration sounds robotic, you're probably hearing a written script being read by text-to-speech technology.

NEW

In Windows 11 2024 Update, you can convert a written script to spoken narration, for free, by using the Clipchamp app. (See Chapter 18 for details.) Many other resources are available online. Just ask Copilot, "Where can I find free or inexpensive text-to-speech sites and apps?"

Speech to text (abbreviated STT) is the opposite of text to speech (TTS). STT converts spoken narration in a file to written text. To find free or inexpensive technologies for STT, ask Copilot, "Where can I find free or inexpensive speech-to-text sites and apps?"

Summarizing and Simplifying Websites

NEW

When browsing the web with Microsoft Edge, you can use Copilot in Edge to quickly summarize any lengthy page you encounter. While you're viewing a page, click the Copilot icon in the upper-right corner of Edge's window. The Copilot panel slides out from the right. Click the new topic icon (speech bubble next to Ask Me Anything) and choose a style for the summarized output: Creative, Balanced, or Precise.

In the Ask Me Anything box, type *summarize this* or *simplify this.* Copilot assumes that *this* refers to the page you're currently viewing in the browser.

You can both summarize and simplify if you like. Start with either *summarize this* or *simplify this.* When Copilot has finished that task, type *summarize that answer* or *simplify that answer,* which refers to the text Copilot just typed for you rather than the entire document.

Translating Text

If you receive some text in a language you don't understand, you can easily translate that text to English for free. Similarly, if you need to send text to a person who doesn't speak English, you can translate it to their language. Copilot in Windows doesn't have this capability, but Google Translate does. Follow these steps:

1. **Select the text you want to translate and press Ctrl+C to copy the text.**

    It doesn't matter where the text is displayed. If you want to translate your own words, feel free to type your text in English in Notepad. Then select and copy the text that you typed.

2. **Open Microsoft Edge (or another web browser, such as Chrome or Firefox) and browse to** `https://translate.google.com`.

    Google Translate opens, with two text boxes near the top, as shown in Figure 16-8.

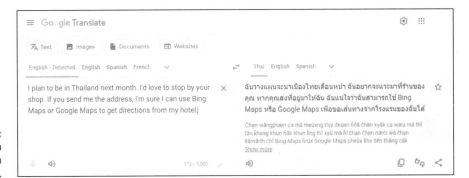

FIGURE 16-8:
Translating from English to Thai in Google Translate.

3. **Click in the left text box, and then press Ctrl+V to paste the text you copied.**

4. **Above the textbox on the right, click the V-shaped arrow and then click the name of the language to which you want to translate.**

    The text box on the right displays the translated text. As always, you can click the copy icon below the translated text and then paste the copied text.

IN THIS CHAPTER

» Asking AI to draw your pictures

» Removing objects (and people) from photos

» Modifying and annotating pictures

» Combing and layering pictures

Chapter **17**

Playing with Pictures

In the tech world, we commonly refer to pictures as *images*. That term encompasses all kinds of pictures, including, photographs, cartoons, drawings, diagrams, AI-generated art, whatever. The term *image file* refers to any file that contains a picture. In this chapter, you learn techniques for viewing your images, creating images, and modifying images.

Browsing through Your Pictures

NEW

Every picture in your computer is a file in some folder on your hard drive. The quickest, easiest way to see all the pictures you already have on your computer is to open File Explorer. If you haven't spent any time with File Explorer yet, now is a good time to flip back to Chapter 5, which covers File Explorer, folders, and files.

When you're in File Explorer, make sure the navigation pane is displayed on the left side of the window, as shown in Figure 17-1. If your navigation pane is missing, click the View button in File Explorer and choose Show ⇨ Navigation Pane. You can widen and narrow the navigation pane by dragging its inner border right and left.

At the top of the navigation pane, click Gallery. If you already have pictures in your computer, the main content pane to the right will display them, starting with the most recent photos at the top. Scroll down to go back in time.

FIGURE 17-1:
Gallery view in
File Explorer.

If you want to change how the photos look in File Explorer, click the View button in the toolbar. Then choose any view. For example, Extra Large displays each photo as a very large thumbnail. List displays just the filenames. Try out other views to discover what works best for you.

IMAGE FILE TYPES

Computers have two main types of image files: raster and vector. *Raster images* store information about the color of each *pixel* (each tiny colored dot that makes up the image) and are preferred for photorealistic images. *Vector images* are defined mathematically using shapes and curves and are more often used for logos and illustrations with clean lines and solid colors. Raster images are the most common but have one weakness: The more you enlarge a raster image, the more blurry it looks. Vector images maintain their quality no matter how much you enlarge them.

Each image category has many different file formats, or file types. A file's type is indicated by its filename extension. In Windows File Explorer, filename extensions are usually hidden. To display filename extensions, click the View button in File Explorer and choose Show ⇨ Filename Extensions.

Raster images typically have a .gif, .heif, .jpeg, .jpg, .png, .psd, or .tiff extension. Vector images have .svg, .eps, or .ai. You don't need to know all the intricacies of how each file type stores its information, but it is helpful to know that different apps work for different file types. For example, in Paint and Photos, you can open most raster images but not vector images.

If you need to know more about an image file type or what image types are compatible with a particular app, just ask Copilot.

Getting pictures from a camera or phone

Getting photos from a digital camera or other device into your computer is often a simple matter of following the onscreen instructions. Turn on the phone or camera and connect it to the computer with its transfer cable. If you have only a memory card from the phone or camera, slide it into an appropriate slot on the computer, or connect the card to the computer with a USB adapter. If you see a message asking what you want to do with the item, choose the option to Import Photos and Videos and follow the onscreen instructions to completion.

If you don't get a prompt to import photos, make sure the device is turned on and connected. Then try using the Photos app instead:

1. **Open the Photos app.**

2. **Click Import near the upper-right corner, and then choose your phone, camera, or SD card.**

3. **In the window that opens, select the photos to transfer to your computer.**

4. **Click the Add button in the top-right corner.**

5. **If you want to change the folder to which the images will be saved, click the Change button and navigate to the folder to which you want to import the photos.**

6. **Click Confirm, and then click Import.**

   Depending on how many images you're importing, the process may take a few minutes to complete.

If you hit any snags, consider asking Copilot for help with your specific phone or camera. For example, you might ask Copilot, "In Windows 11, how can I download photos from my iPhone?" If you get an error message on the screen along the way, you can also ask Copilot to explain the error message.

Taking screenshots

When you request tech support, the techie on the phone might ask you to send a screenshot. A *screenshot* is like a photograph of your computer screen, only you don't use a phone or camera to take the picture. You use the Print Screen (PrtSc) key on your keyboard, as follows:

1. **On your keyboard, press the Print Screen (PrtSc) key to capture the entire screen, or press Alt+Print Screen (PrtSc) to capture just the active window.**

    If pressing the Print Screen key opens Snipping tool, skip the following steps below and use Snipping Tool instead (as described in the next section).

2. **Open the Paint app (click the start icon and choose Paint).**

3. **Choose Edit ⇨ Paste.**

4. **If the image is too large, reduce the magnification by using the slider in Paint's lower-right corner.**

5. **To print the screenshot, choose File ⇨ Print.**

6. **Choose File ⇨ Save to save the screenshot to any folder on your computer.**

Using Snipping Tool for screenshots

Windows 11 2024 Update includes a screen capture app called Snipping Tool that offers more options than the Print Screen key. Click the start icon and choose Snipping Tool, or start typing the word *snip* in the Search box near the start icon and then click Snipping Tool App when you see that option.

To take a screen shot using Snipping Tool, click the snip icon, which looks like a regular camera (not a video camera). Then click the down arrow on the snipping mode icon to reveal the options shown in Figure 17-2.

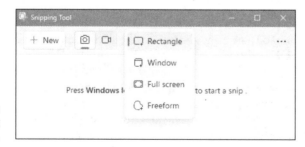

FIGURE 17-2:
The Snipping
Mode menu.

GETTING PHOTOSHOP POWERS FOR FREE

You may have heard the term *photoshop* in references to a modified image, for example, "That image has been photoshopped." The word *photoshop* comes from the Adobe Photoshop image-editing app. That app is probably too expensive for non-professional users.

Fortunately, Paint and Photos can do a lot of what Photoshop can do, so there's a good chance you'll never need anything more. However, if you have advanced graphics-editing skills and need to work with Photoshop PSD files, you can use the free Photopea app. You don't download or install anything. Just browse to https://photopea.com. The app has its own Learn module, and you can find plenty of free tutorials online. Just search YouTube or Bing videos (https://bing.com/videos) for *Photopea tutorial* to see what's available.

Click the mode that best describes what you want to capture:

>> **Rectangle:** Capture any rectangular portion of the screen.

>> **Window:** Capture a single open app window on the screen.

>> **Full Screen:** Capture the entire screen.

>> **Freeform:** Capture any portion of the screen in any shape.

Arrange your screen to show whatever you plan to capture in your screenshot. If you're capturing a single open window, click that window to bring it to the forefront. Then click New on the left side of Snipping Tool.

Your screen will darken. If you chose Full Screen, the screen will return to normal automatically. If you chose Window, click the title bar of the window you want to capture. If you chose another option, drag the mouse pointer around the area you want to capture, and then release the mouse button.

You'll see a notification in the lower-right corner, indicating when your image is ready. The screenshot is saved to the Screenshots folder in your Pictures folder.

Editing images with the Photos app

Windows 11 comes with two free imaging-editing apps. Like the famous Photoshop app, these apps let you edit (change) photos and other images. Photos is the default app for working with images, so if you double-click the icon or thumbnail for an image file, it will most likely open in Photos. However, if you (or someone else) changed the default for the type of file you're opening, you can still open the image in Photos by right-clicking the file's icon and choosing Open With ⇨ Photos. Figure 17-3 shows an example of an image open in the Photos app.

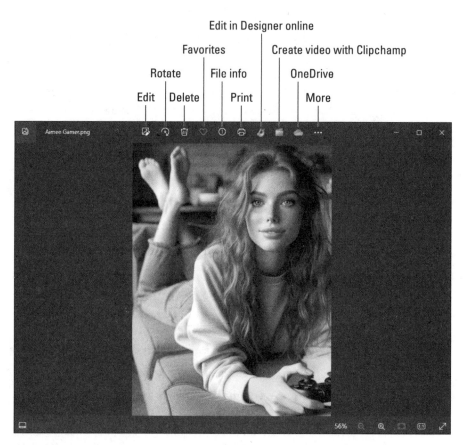

Edit in Designer online

Favorites

Rotate | File info

Edit | Delete | Print

Create video with Clipchamp

OneDrive

More

Aimee Gamer.png

56%

FIGURE 17-3:
An image
opened in the
Photos app.

Use the controls in the lower-right corner to zoom in and out, view the image at its actual size, or show the image full screen. When the image is full screen, press Esc to return to the previous view.

Icons centered at the top of the Photos app do the following:

» **Edit:** Alter the image in ways described after the list.

» **Rotate:** Rotate the image clockwise 90 degrees.

» **Delete:** Delete the image from its current folder and move the image to the recycle bin.

» **Favorites:** Add the current photo to the Photos app's Favorites album. To review your favorites, click the heart icon in the left column.

» **File info:** Display detailed information about the image file.

» **Print:** Print the image to paper.

>> **Edit in Designer online:** Open the image in Microsoft Designer, where you can create professional-grade graphic designs without a Graphics Arts degree. Add text to the image to create ads, social media posts, signs, and more.

>> **Create video with Clipchamp:** Open the Clipchamp app (see Chapter 18) and put the image file in the Media bin to use in a slideshow or video.

>> **OneDrive:** Open the Pictures folder in OneDrive (if you've set up a OneDrive account).

>> **More:** Present more options for resizing and saving the image.

Don't worry about memorizing the names of the icons because you can see the name of any icon by touching it with the mouse pointer.

 Clicking edit (shown in the margin) switches the Photos app to editing mode, where you can do Photoshop-style editing. Icons across the top of the app window represent tools for modifying the image, as shown in Figure 17-4. Touch the mouse to an icon to see what the tool does.

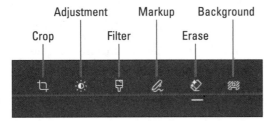

FIGURE 17-4: Editing mode in the Photos app.

Here is a quick overview of what each option offers:

>> **Crop icon:** Display sizing handles around the image. Drag the top, side, bottom, or corner handle to crop the image.

>> **Adjustment icon:** Change the brightness, contrast, color, or other aspects of the image.

>> **Filter icon:** Change the color tone of the image, convert a color image to black and white, or click Auto Enhance to let the built-in AI decide how best to adjust the colors.

>> **Markup icon:** Draw lines on the image to underline or circle parts of the image.

>> **Erase icon:** Remove objects (or people) from the image using generative AI object removal. For details, see the next section.

» **Background icon:** Remove the image background. You'll see options to fill, remove, or blur the background. If you want a transparent background, choose Remove. Then save the file as a PNG. (JPEG doesn't support transparency, and BMP and GIF are older formats that aren't great for photo-quality images.)

Use the Save Options button near the top right of the Photos app to save your changes. A Save As dialog opens. Change the filename so you don't overwrite the original image.

Removing Objects from Photos

NEW

AI object removal (also called *generative erase*) is a technology that allows you to remove unwanted objects (and people) from photographs and other images. To use the technology, you *mask* the item that you want to remove by holding down the mouse button while brushing over the item.

To remove an object from an image, open File Explorer. Then right-click the image file's icon, and choose Open With ⇨ Photos to open the file in Photos. Before you start making changes, click Save Options ⇨ Save As Copy and save the image with a different filename to protect the original photo from any mistakes you might make while learning this new technology.

Next, click the edit icon (shown in the margin). Then click the erase icon, as shown in Figure 17-5.

TECHNICAL STUFF

The name *generative erase* stems from the fact that this tool uses *generative AI*, the technology that allows AI to write your documents and generate your images. After you remove an object from an image, AI generates (creates) what was most likely behind the object, filling the empty space.

You can use generative erase in two ways: with Auto Apply turned on and with Auto Apply turned off. Experiment with both methods to see which gives you the best results. If you leave Auto Apply turned on, you simply hold down the mouse button, brush over the object you want to remove, and release the mouse button. AI removes the object immediately. You can repeat this process as many times as necessary.

If you turn off Auto Apply, the Add Mask and Remove Mask buttons appear. They allow you to brush over an object in multiple steps. If you miss a spot when brushing, you can brush some more. If you go too far and brush too much, click Remove Mask to remove your last brush mask. The object won't be erased until you click the erase icon (shown in the margin).

Erase icon

FIGURE 17-5:
AI generative
erase in the
Photos app.

Before you brush over an object, use the Brush Size tool (refer to Figure 17-4) to adjust the size of the brush. It's fine to go a little outside the edges of the object you want to erase, as I did with the robot in Figure 17-6. Just don't go so far outside the edges that you start removing other items. For example, you wouldn't want to remove the woman's elbow.

FIGURE 17-6:
Masking the area
to remove using
generative erase.

If you left Auto Apply turned on, the object will be erased as soon as you release the mouse button. Otherwise, click the erase icon when you're ready to erase. If weird remnants or markings were left behind, you can usually fix them by going over the area again. Turn on Auto Apply and use a small brush size to brush over the remnant until you are satisfied.

If you really make a mess of things, click Undo or press Ctrl+Z as many times as necessary. Generative erase technology isn't perfect, but with some patience and perseverance, you may be able to get exactly the look you want.

Creating and Editing Pictures in Paint

The Paint image editor has been a part of Windows for many years. The updated Paint version in Windows 11 2024 adds new AI capabilities that rival those found in Photoshop and other expensive image-editing apps. You can even draw or paint images in Paint using only your words, which is a boon to people like me, who can't draw worth beans.

Open Paint by clicking the start icon and then clicking Paint. Or start typing the word *paint* in the Search box and choose Paint App when it appears. You see the window shown in Figure 17-7. The toolbar below the menu bar displays various icons, representing tools you can use in the Paint window. As always, you can touch the mouse pointer to any toolbar icon to see the tool's name.

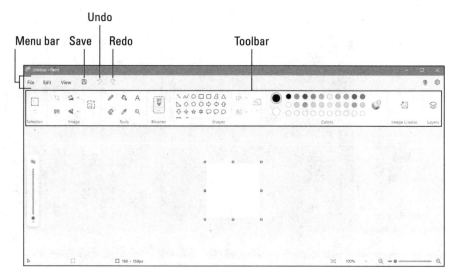

FIGURE 17-7:
The Paint app.

Creating AI images

The rectangle in the middle of the Paint app is a canvas for drawing. The suggested canvas might be 768x630 pixels. If you need a different image size, you can change those dimensions as follows:

1. **Click the resize and skew icon (labeled in Figure 17-8).**

Resize and skew

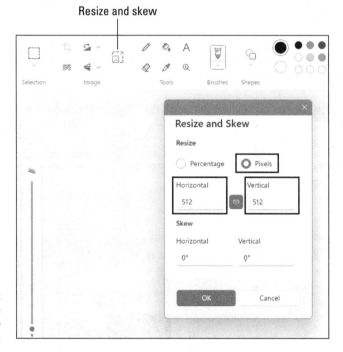

FIGURE 17-8:
Setting the
canvas size to
512x512 pixels.

2. **In the dialog that appears, choose Pixels, and enter** 512 **for both the height and the width. Or enter** 1024 **for a larger image.**

   TIP

   Most AI-generated images are square for technical reasons involving how AI is trained. So make sure the height and the width are equal when you specify a size. Both 512 and 1024 are common sizes for AI-generated images.

   If changing one number forces the other number to change, click the chain link icon between the numbers to unlink them. Then try again.

3. **Leave the Skew numbers both set to 0.**

4. **Click OK.**

To fill the canvas with an AI–generated image, just follow these steps:

1. **Click Image Creator in the toolbar.**

   The Image Creator window opens in Paint.

2. **In the first text box, describe your desired image.**

   I wrote, *A steaming hot pepperoni pizza, fresh from the oven.*

3. **Under Choose a Style, indicate the type of image you want.**

   I chose Photorealistic because I wanted the image to look like a photograph. Other options are Charcoal, Ink Sketch, Watercolor, Oil Painting, Digital Art, Anime, and Pixel Art.

4. **Click Create.**

   Be patient because it might take a few seconds for thumbnail images to appear. Eventually, you'll see two or more thumbnail images in the Image Creator pane.

5. **Click a thumbnail to see the image on the larger canvas, as shown in Figure 17-9.**

FIGURE 17-9:
An Image Creator picture on the Paint canvas.

6. **If you don't like the images, generate a new batch of images by clicking Create again.**

   Before clicking Create, you might want to change the wording in your description or choose another style for your image.

7. **To save the image currently on the canvas, choose File ⇨ Save or press Ctrl+S. Choose a folder, give the image a filename, and click Save.**

As you generate images, you'll notice that the number next to the Create button decreases. When your credits drop to zero, image creation takes much longer. You can earn credits through various tasks and promotions offered by Microsoft. To get the latest info on credits, just ask Copilot, "How do credits work in Image Creator?"

TIP

Microsoft Image Creator on the Bing website produces some of the best images around. The credits on that site refresh each day, so you can generate a lot of free images over time. To try the online version of Image Creator, open Microsoft Edge and browse to `https://bing.com/images/create`.

Editing images

Paint offers many tools for altering images. To edit an image, choose File ⇨ Open from Paint's menu bar and open your image. Optionally, navigate to the image's icon in File Explorer, right-click the image thumbnail or icon, and choose Open With ⇨ Paint.

When your image first opens, you might want to change the magnification to make it fit nicely in Paint. For a quick fit, choose View ⇨ Zoom ⇨ Fit to Window (or press Ctrl+1). You can also zoom in and out using the drop-down menu and slider in Paint's lower-right corner.

It's a good idea to work with a copy of your original image. That way, no matter how badly you mess up, you'll always have your original image. To make a quick copy, choose File ⇨ Save As. If you plan to make any part of the image transparent, choose PNG as the file type. (JPEG doesn't support transparency.) Name the file and then click Save. The filename of the current image appears in Paint's upper-left corner, so you always know which image you're currently working on.

Tools for altering the image are in the toolbar, as shown in Figure 17-10. To see the name of any tool in the toolbar, touch the tip of the mouse pointer to the tool's icon. If a tool is dimmed, the tool isn't relevant at the moment. For example, the crop tool is disabled until you select an area to crop.

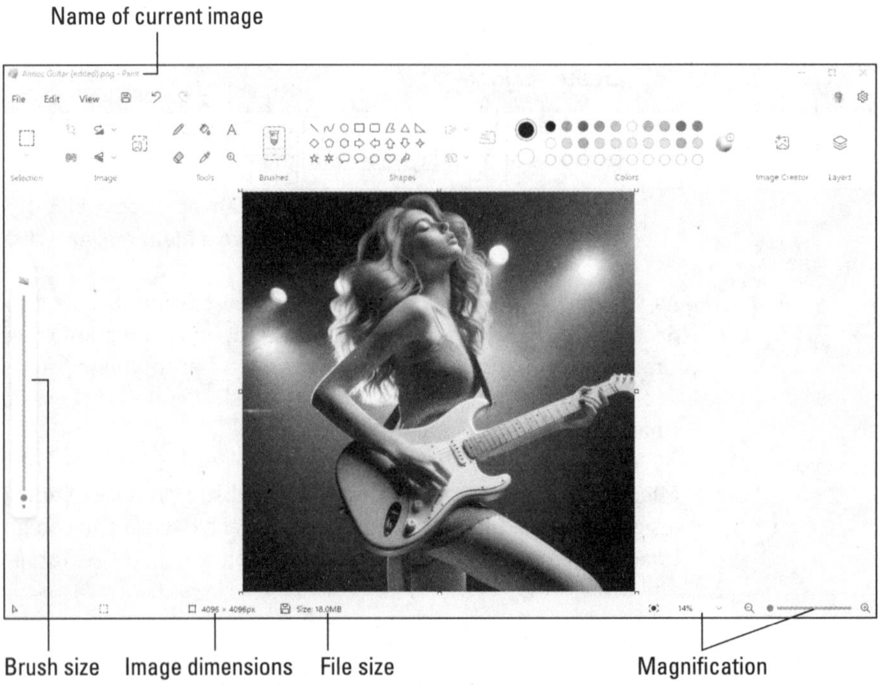
Name of current image
File
Edit
View
Brush size
Image dimensions
File size
Magnification

FIGURE 17-10: Areas in Paint.

Choosing text and shape colors

The pencil, fill, text, and shapes tools enable you to write or draw on the image. Before you use such a tool, choose a foreground and background color for the tool. To choose a foreground color, click the top-left circle in the Colors section (labeled in Figure 17-11). Or to choose a background color, click the bottom-left circle. Whichever you click will be selected (circled) so you know which color you're defining.

Next, choose a color using the smaller color circles. If you want to match a color in the image, click the Color Picker tool and then click the color in the image that you want to match. If you're familiar with defining your own colors, click Edit Colors, define your color in the Edit Colors window, and then click OK.

Annotating an image

You can annotate an image by adding lines, arrows, boxes, and text labels. Just to the following:

1. **Choose your color(s).**
2. **In the Shapes box, click the shape you want.**

   Once you choose a shape, the shape outline, shape fill, and size tools are enabled.

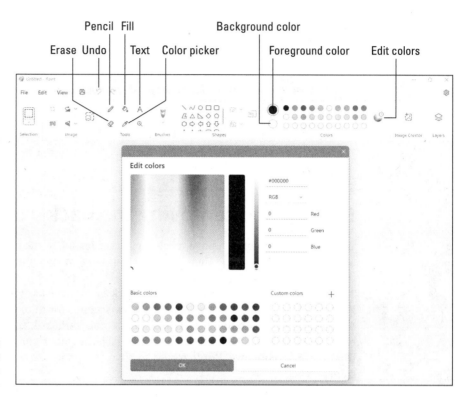

Pencil Fill

Erase Undo Text Color picker

Background color

Foreground color Edit colors

3. **Specify the shape outline, fill color, and line thickness of the shape.**

4. **Drag out your shape on the image.**

    When you're using the line, circle, or rectangle tool, you can hold down the Shift key while dragging to get a straight line, a perfect circle, or a perfect square. If you make a mistake, click the undo icon (labeled in Figure 17-11) or press Ctrl+Z, and try again until you get exactly what you want.

5. **To add text to the image:**

    a. *Click the text tool.*

    b. *Choose a font, a font size, boldface, italics, and strikethrough as desired.*

    c. *If you want, left align, center, or right align the text within its box.*

    d. *If you want the text to have an opaque background color, select the Background Fill check box. Leave it deselected for a transparent background.*

    e. *Click inside the image and type your text.*

    f. *To size the text, drag the handles on the box's corners and edges.*

    g. *To move the box, put the mouse pointer in the center of the box and drag. If you make a mistake, click the undo icon or press Ctrl+Z, and try again.*

6. **To draw freehand on the image:**

   a. *Click the pencil tool.*

   b. *Select a brush style by clicking the Brushes drop-down arrow.*

   c. *Specify your brush size by using the tall slider on the left side of the Paint window.*

   d. *To draw, drag through the image. As always, if you mess up, click the undo icon and try again.*

Erasing and removing the background

To erase a portion of an image, click the eraser icon. Use the brush size slider to set your eraser width, and then drag over anything you want to erase.

NEW

To remove the entire image background, click the remove background icon, which is labeled in Figure 17-12. It might take a few seconds for AI to analyze the image. But then the background should look like a checkerboard, to indicate that the background is now transparent. If the removal isn't quite right, use the eraser tool to erase any remnants. Don't forget to save the image as a PNG to retain the transparency.

Remove background

FIGURE 17-12: The checkboard indicates transparent portions of the image.

If you can't get a good transparent background in Paint, open the image in Photos, click the edit icon, and then use the remove background tool there. Once the background appears, you'll be given the option to blur it, remove it (making it transparent), or fill it with solid white. When editing an image in Photos, the erase icon supports AI object removal, where you can erase an object or a person from the photo and have the background filled in automatically to match the rest of the background.

Cropping an image

When you *crop* an image, you eliminate a portion of the image. For example, in Figure 17-13, the left image is the original and the right image is the cropped version, which focuses on the person without the extraneous background.

FIGURE 17-13:
An original image (left) and the cropped version (right).

To crop an image, open it in Paint. To retain your original image, save the current image with a different filename. Then click the selection tool's down arrow and choose Rectangle. In the image, drag out a frame surrounding the portion of the image you want to keep. If you make a mistake, click outside the selected area and try again. When you're happy with the selection, click the crop tool in the toolbar (refer to Figure 17-4).

Combining and layering images

NEW

Combining multiple images is sometimes called *layering* because you can put one image on top of another. If you layer an image with a transparent background onto another image, the image on top looks like it's part of the original image.

To illustrate, Figure 17-14 shows two images that have not been layered yet. I cropped the eagle from another image and gave that cropped image a transparent background.

FIGURE 17-14:
Two separate images.

To stack two or more images, first open the background image in Paint. In my example, that's the image of a woman taking a picture of the sky. Then, to bring in another image, layered, choose File ⇨ Import to Canvas ⇨ From a File, and open the image you want to stack on top. In my case, that's the image of the eagle with the transparent background. The imported image lands in the upper-left corner of the larger image.

Next, drag the imported image to a new position in the larger image. Size the imported image by dragging the size handles around the image's border. Once the image is in place, click outside the imported image. The result is that the two separate images now appear to be a single image, as shown in Figure 17-15.

You can have a lot of fun playing around with layers in pictures. But it does take some practice and patience to become good at it. As always, you can get Copilot to help. Older versions of Paint don't have all the capabilities described in this chapter, so be sure to start your Copilot prompt with, "In the Windows 24h2 Paint app, how do I"?

Asking Copilot about Your Screen and Pictures

NEW

AI has no eyes (nor a brain, for that matter), so it can't see pictures like we can. Yet AI can tell you about most pictures. You can ask about something you see on your screen right now or about a picture in an image file. Here's how:

1. **Open Copilot in Windows by clicking the Copilot icon in the taskbar.**

2. **In the Ask Me Anything box, type** What is this? **but don't submit the question yet.**

3. **Do one of the following:**

   - *To ask about something on your screen:* Click the Add a Screenshot tool (labeled in Figure 17-16), and then drag a selection frame around the object of your curiosity.

   - *To ask about something in an image file:* Click Add an Image, and then open the image you're curious about.

4. **Click the submit icon, and let Copilot think about it for a bit.**

You may be pleasantly surprised to see just how much, and how fast, you can learn about things you see on your computer screen by using this method!

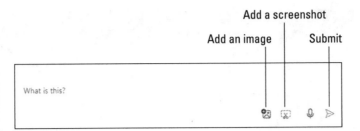

Add a screenshot

Add an image   Submit

FIGURE 17-16:
Asking Copilot
about something
on your screen or
in an image file.

What is this?

Chapter **18**

Fiddling with Video and Music

You have many ways to acquire video and audio for your computer. You can download videos you've shot with your phone or a digital video camera to your computer, just like you download photos. You can download songs from online services such as Amazon Music and iTunes. You can download video and audio from free services such as pexels.com and pixabay.com as well as paid services such as Adobe Stock and Shutterstock.

In addition, new sites for creating music and video from text with AI are popping up all the time. Just ask Copilot, "Where can I create AI music online?" or "Where can I create AI video online?"

In this chapter, you explore tools built into Windows 11 2024 Update that will help you create and work with video and music files.

Recording Your Computer Screen

You can record your computer activity into a video. You might want to record your screen to make tutorials or to share with tech support people remotely. Everything you need to record your screen is built into Snipping Tool, which comes with Windows 11.

To record your screen, do the following:

1. **Click the start icon and then choose Snipping Tool.**

   If the Snipping tool isn't pinned to the Start menu, click the All Apps button and then choose Snipping Tool.

2. **Click the record icon, which is labeled in Figure 18-1.**

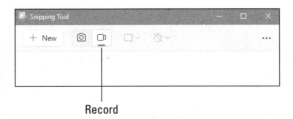

FIGURE 18-1:
Use the record icon in Snipping Tool to record your screen activity.

Record

3. **Click the + New button.**

4. **Drag a frame around the area of the screen (or the entire screen) that you want to record.**

5. **Click Start.**

   A 3-second timer starts counting down.

6. **When the countdown ends, perform that activity you want to record.**

7. **When you've finished recording, click the red stop icon in Snipping Tool.**

   The stop icon is in the same location as the record icon. The recording opens in a Snipping Tool window.

8. **To save the recording as a video file, click the save as icon (labeled in Figure 18-2).**

   The video file is saved with the .mp4 extension.

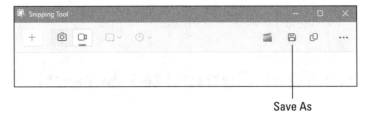

FIGURE 18-2:
The save as icon in Snipping Tool.

Save As

You can now post the video online, if you like, or use it in any video-editing software to make a larger presentation.

Making Videos with Clipchamp

Video-editing apps enable you to create movies incorporating your videos, photos, and audio files. Most of the videos you see on YouTube and other social media sites were created using video-editing software. However, professional video-editing apps are expensive. Before you spend any money or time downloading third-party apps, start with Microsoft Clipchamp, which comes with Windows 11 2024 Update.

Entire books have been written about video creation and video editing. I don't have that much room, but I can show you how to get started with Clipchamp and where to find more information on video editing with Clipchamp.

To take Clipchamp for a spin, start it as you would any other app. Click the start icon and choose Microsoft Clipchamp. Or, if Clipchamp isn't pinned to the Start menu, click the All Apps button and choose Clipchamp. The Clipchamp app opens to its home page, as shown in Figure 18-3.

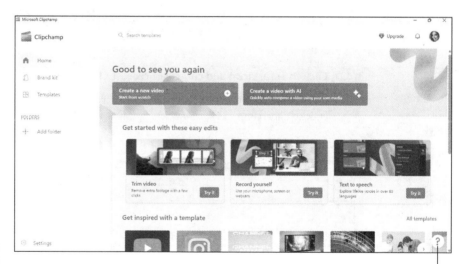

FIGURE 18-3:
Clipchamp
home page.

Help icon

To get to the free tutorials, click the question mark icon in the lower-right corner and choose Help and Learning. In the new page that opens, shown in Figure 18-4, click the Get Started icon. Then work your way through other topics to the right — Add Media, Editing Features, and so forth — as time permits.

If you want to take a shot at cranking out a quick video or slideshow from your own files, without studying or learning anything, try Clipchamp's AI capability, as discussed in the next section.

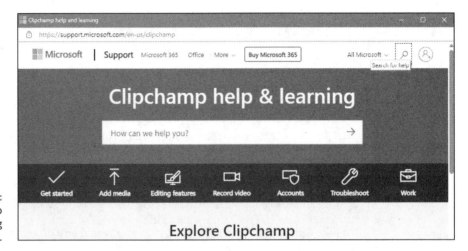

FIGURE 18-4:
Clipchamp Help
and Learning
section.

Letting AI create your video

If you let AI create a video for you, you can get started with video editing without investing a lot of time. Simply choose one or more of your videos or photos or both. Photos in a video are displayed as a slideshow. Here's how to get started:

1. **Click the start icon and choose Microsoft Clipchamp.**

   If Clipchamp isn't pinned to the Start menu, click the All Apps button and choose Clipchamp.

2. **Click Create a Video with AI.**

   The window shown in Figure 18-5 appears.

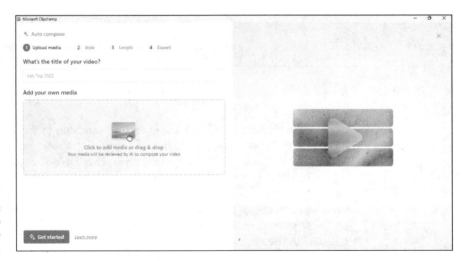

FIGURE 18-5:
The Auto
Compose page
in Clipchamp.

3. **Type a title for your video.**

4. **In the Add Your Own Media section, add the photos and videos you want to use in your production.**

   To add files, you can drag them from File Explorer. Or click the Click to Add Media or Drag & Drop link, and navigate to and select the files you want to use. Each file you add will appear as a thumbnail.

5. **When you've finished adding media, click Get Started.**

   The next page, shown in Figure 18-6, provides styles to choose from.

6. **Cycle through the styles, clicking the thumbs down icon to reject a style or clicking the thumbs up icon for any style you think might work. Then click Next.**

   To see more styles, click Style near the top. Or click Choose for Me to let AI decide on a style.

   The last style you like before clicking Next is used to create the video.

7. **Choose an *aspect ratio*, (orientation) and then click Next.**

   Your choices are Landscape (wide) or Portrait (narrow). Most TVs and computer screens have a landscape orientation, but TikTok videos, YouTube shorts, and some other sites use portrait.

8. **Under How Long Should Your Video Be, choose a length and then click Next.**

   If you're using only a few pictures or short videos, Full Length will likely be your only choice.

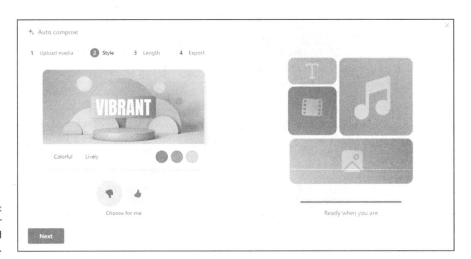

FIGURE 18-6: Choose a style for an AI-generated video.

9. **Click > in the Music box to see the available background music.**

Click the preview arrow under each music name to hear how it will sound if you use that music in your video.

10. **Leave your preferred music selected (highlighted), and then click the back arrow next to the Music heading to return to the previous page.**

11. **Click > on the right of the Font box, and then click the font you want to use.**

12. Optionally, you can click Edit in Timeline, and edit the video prior to exporting, using video editor tools and techniques described later in this chapter.

For this first try you might want to skip this step.

13. **Click Export.**

It might take a few seconds for AI to create your video. But eventually you'll see the page shown in Figure 18-7. The finished video is sent to your Downloads folder. The file name of the video is usually whatever title you provided followed by the .mp4 filename extension.

Optionally, you can save a copy of the generated video to OneDrive, YouTube, TikTok, or any other site listed on the page, just by clicking the pertinent option and following any onscreen instructions.

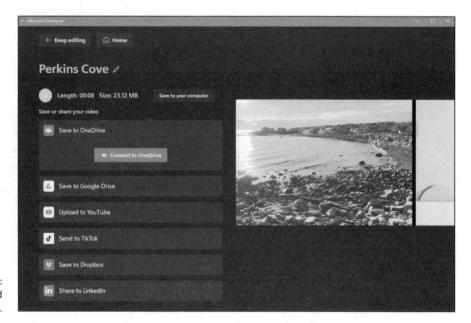

FIGURE 18-7:
The finished
video.

To watch the video, double-click the file's icon. You also have a copy of the video suitable for editing with Microsoft Clipchamp. Click Keep Editing in the upper-left corner to get to the video-editing page of Clipchamp. Or, if you've closed Clipchamp, just open it again, and then click the video's thumbnail under Your Videos.

Understanding video editing

Should you decide to edit your AI-generated video or create a video from scratch, you can do so in Clipchamp's video-editing page, which is shown in Figure 18-8. Video editing involves arranging clips along the timeline. The left side of the timeline represents the start of the video, and the right side of the timeline represents the end of the video.

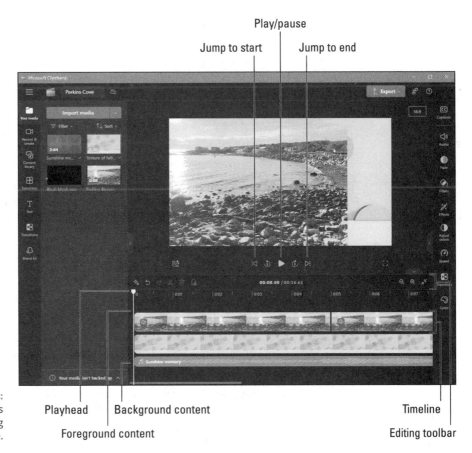

The bottom of the timeline presents background content, such as background music or spoken narration. Text, arrows, stickers, and any other smaller content that should play in the foreground are closer to the top of the timeline.

You can watch the video in Clipchamp by clicking the play icon (which turns into a pause icon when the video starts playing). The playhead moves along the timeline to show which part of the video is currently playing.

You can drag the playhead left and right to any portion of the timeline to make changes to that part of the video. For example, to split a clip at the playhead's position, click the scissors icon in the editing toolbar. Drag a clip left or right to change its position along the timeline. Click any clip to select it; the selected clip gains a colored border. Press Delete to delete the selected clip.

On the left side of the Clipchamp window are icons representing more tools for creating your video masterpiece. Starting at the top left, here's what they offer:

>> **Your Media:** Display the media bin for the current project, where you import content to use in the video. To add a clip to your video, drag it to the timeline, or click the clip and then click the plus sign (+) that appears. Remember, clips that are lower in the timeline are in the background, and clips near the top of the timeline are in the foreground.

>> **Record & Create:** Record the screen, yourself, or your voice, or convert a written script to spoken narration using one of several male or female AI voices.

>> **Content Library:** Include content (free and not free) in your video, such as stickers, shapes, backgrounds, frames, borders, cartoons, sound effects, photos, and stock footage.

>> **Templates:** Start with existing content, rather than from scratch or AI. Templates usually aren't used to edit an existing video.

>> **Text:** Add text with special effects to your video.

>> **Transitions:** Add transition special effects between any two clips by dragging the seam between two video clips in the timeline.

>> **Brand Kit:** Specify a default logo, brand colors, and fonts for videos. However, these features are optional and are available only to paid subscribers.

Down the right side of the Clipchamp window are tools for adding special effects to individual clips. To use them, first click the clip to which you want to apply the effect. To select multiple clips, hold down the Ctrl key as you click. Then use the following icons to apply effects to the selected clip(s):

>> **Captions:** Add automatic written captions for spoken text, if your video contains spoken narration.

- **» Audio:** Control the volume of sound coming from the clip. Or detach the audio from a video clip so you can work with the audio in its own track on the timeline.

- **» Fade:** Apply a fade in or fade out (or both) to the clip, and use the sliders to control the duration (in seconds).

- **» Filters:** Apply a special effect to the selected clip. You can choose warmer or cooler colors, black and white, a retro effect, and more. After you click an effect, use the Intensity slider to control the strength of the effect.

- **» Effects:** Apply zoom, slow-motion, glitch, or other special effects to the selected clip.

- **» Adjust Colors:** Adjust the exposure, contrast, saturation, and other visual aspects of the selected clip.

- **» Speed:** Control the speed at which the clip plays for fast and slow motion effects.

- **» Color:** Add color to the background. You see this option if a selected clip contains empty background space.

If you like being creative, you'll probably love making videos. I strongly encourage you to work your way through the Clipchamp Help and Learning tutorials.

Enjoying Music

These days, many people get their music from streaming services such as Spotify, Apply Music, or Amazon Music. You can also download music and play it by double-clicking its icon.

Getting music from CDs

If you have music on CDs, you can copy those songs to your computer, provided your computer has an optical drive. If your computer has no such drive, you can buy an inexpensive external drive. Search Amazon or another online retailer for *external optical drive for Windows 11.*

When you put a music CD into the drive, Windows pops up a notification asking what you want to do with the disc. Choose the option to *rip* (copy) songs to your computer. The songs will be saved to your Music folder, unless you specify a different location. If you need help, just ask Copilot, "How do I copy music from CDs in Windows 11?" If Copilot's initial answer doesn't tell you enough, look at some of the external resources that Copilot recommends.

Copying music to USB drives for your car

Unlike a CD, which can hold a dozen or so songs, a USB drive can store thousands of songs. If your car supports music from a USB drive and you have a music collection on your computer, it should be easy to create a music drive for your car.

TIP

If the music you want to hear is already on your phone, you may not need to copy the songs to a USB drive. Use a cable or Bluetooth to connect the phone to the car stereo, and see if your car can play music right from your phone.

The first step is to check the car's manual to find out the format for the USB drive: FAT, exFAT, FAT32, or NTFS. For a music USB drive, exFAT is usually the preferred format. You also need to know the size of the USB port in your car, which is typically the larger (and older) USB-A size but could be the more modern and smaller USB-C size.

The size of your USB drive determines how many songs the drive will hold. A drive that holds 16GB can store well over a thousand songs, so you probably won't need to invest in a pricey high-capacity USB drive. You need to format the drive first, which means erasing everything already on the drive. I suggest you purchase a new USB drive or use one that contains files that you no longer need. Then follow these steps:

1. **Insert the USB disk into a USB drive on your computer.**

2. **If prompted, choose the option to display the disk contents.**

3. **Open File Explorer, right-click the icon for the USB drive, and choose Format, as shown in Figure 18-9.**

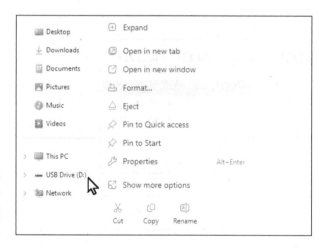

FIGURE 18-9:
Right-click
the USB drive
icon and
choose Format.

4. **Choose ExFAT (or whatever format your car supports).**

   The formatting might take a minute or two to complete.

5. **Copy any songs you want from your hard drive to the USB drive by dragging the song's icon or by copying and pasting.**

After you plug the USB drive into the appropriate USB slot in your car, you may need to use the car's controls to select the USB drive as the source of your music. Refer to the car's manual if you need help.

Keep in mind that your trusty Copilot knows about videos, music, and even Microsoft Clipchamp. If you ever feel stuck, ask Copilot for help.

6

Getting Help

IN THIS CHAPTER

» **Getting Copilot to fix your problem.**

» **Restarting the computer**

» **Checking out troubleshooters**

» **Reviving deleted files and folders**

» **Dealing with forgotten passwords**

» **Fixing stuck apps and frozen screens**

» **Discovering what to do when all else fails**

Chapter **19**

The Case of the Broken Window

S ometimes you have a vague sense that something's wrong. Your computer displays an odd screen that you've never seen before, or Windows starts running more slowly than Congress.

Other times, something's obviously gone haywire. Programs freeze, menus keep popping up, or Windows constantly nags you with an incomprehensible error message every time you turn on your computer.

Many of the biggest-looking problems are solved by the smallest-looking solutions. This chapter points you to the right solution for the most common problems.

Asking the Know-It-All

If your computer can start and get online, your first step should be to ask Copilot for help. Copilot is like your annoying know-it-all friend.

Open Copilot, explain your problem as best you can, and see what it has to offer. In some cases, you may have to carry on a conversation with Copilot to zero in on the problem. But if you're lucky, Copilot may be able to steer you in the right direction and help you solve the problem.

Restarting Your Computer

Getting back to a clean slate, rather than having a ton of apps and files open, might solve the problem. This process is referred to as *rebooting,* or *restarting,* the computer. If your mouse is still working, click the start icon, click the power icon in the lower-right corner of the Start menu, and choose Restart.

If only your keyboard is working, press Ctrl+Alt+Delete, and then keep pressing Tab until the power icon in the lower-right corner of the screen is selected. Press Enter, use the arrow keys to move to the Restart option, and press Enter again.

If you're prompted to save your work, choose Yes. Then follow any other instructions that appear on the screen. Eventually, the screen will turn off and the computer should start back up.

Using a Troubleshooter

Windows 11 has *troubleshooters,* which are apps designed to help with specific issues, such as internet or sound problems. To access the troubleshooters, follow these steps:

1. Click the start icon and choose Settings, or press Windows+I.

2. In the left pane, click System.

3. Scroll down and click Troubleshoot.

4. Click Other Troubleshooters.

   A partial list of troubleshooters appears, as shown in Figure 19-1. Scroll down to see them all.

5. When you find the troubleshooter that best describes the area in which you're having a problem, click its Run button.

6. Follow the onscreen instructions that appear on your screen.

   With luck, the troubleshooter will be able to fix the problem on its own.

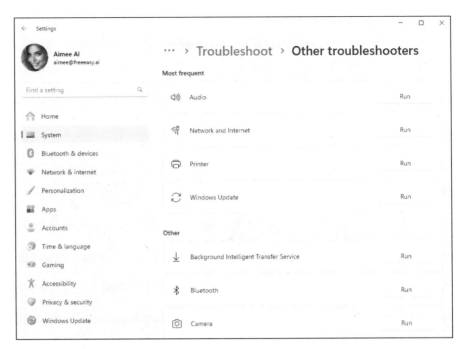

FIGURE 19-1:
Windows 11
troubleshooters.

Using File History to Restore a Backup

If you used the File History app to back up your files (as described in Chapter 13), you can recover any personal files that you've backed up.

To browse through your backed-up files and folders, restoring the ones you want, follow these steps:

1. **Click the Search box next to the start icon, type** File History, **and then click File History (Control Panel) on the Start menu.**

   The age-old Control Panel appears, open to the File History section.

2. **Click the Restore Personal Files link from the section's left side.**

   The File History program appears, as shown in Figure 19-2, displaying the folders you've backed up: your main folders, desktop, contacts, and favorite websites, as well as the Music, Documents, Videos, and Music folders, among others.

   Feel free to open the folders inside the File History window. You can also peek inside the files you find there to see their contents.

Date and time of currently viewed backup

Move up one folder   Number of available backups   Settings

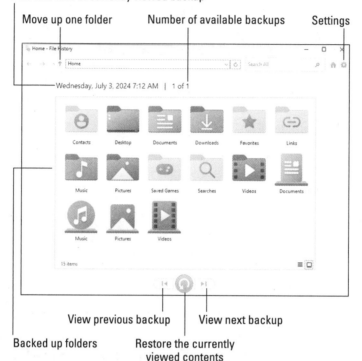

Wednesday, July 3, 2024 7:12 AM | 1 of 1

Contacts   Desktop   Documents   Downloads   Favorites   Links

Music   Pictures   Saved Games   Searches   Videos   Documents

Music   Pictures   Videos

15 items

FIGURE 19-2:
The File History
program lets you
restore backups
from any of your
main folders.

View previous backup   View next backup

Backed up folders   Restore the currently
viewed contents

3. Choose what you want to restore.

Point and click your way through the libraries, folders, and files until you spot the item or items you'd like to restore:

- *Folder:* To restore an entire folder, open it so you're viewing its contents.

- *Files:* To restore a group of files, open the folder containing them, so that the file icons are onscreen. Then select the file(s) you want to restore.

- *One file:* To restore an earlier version of a file, open the file.

4. Move forward or backward in time to find the version you want to restore.

To browse through different versions of what you're currently viewing, choose the left-pointing arrow at the bottom, as shown in Figure 19-3. To see a newer version, choose the right-pointing arrow.

As you move forward and backward through time, click open folders or individual files as necessary until you're looking at the version that you want to retrieve.

Not sure whether a folder contains your sought-after item? Type a word or two from your document in the Search box in File History's upper-right corner.

TIP

WHAT ARE LIBRARIES?

A *library* is a collection of folders, typically containing similar file types. Libraries were introduced in Windows 7, but they never caught on and have all but vanished in Windows 11. However, if you used File History in Windows 7 to back up your files, your libraries were backed up too. Those same libraries will still be in File History so you can restore them to your Windows 11 computer.

You access Libraries through File Explorer in Windows 11. If you restore some libraries but don't see them in Windows 11, right-click an empty spot in File Explorer's navigation pane and choose Show Libraries. All available libraries will be accessible under This PC in the navigation pane.

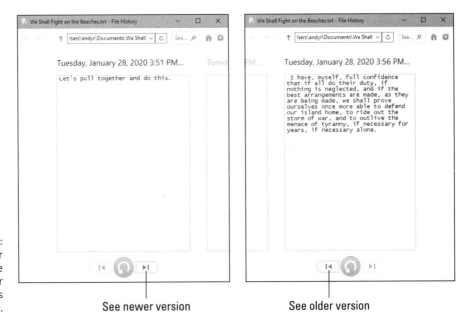

FIGURE 19-3: Click the left or right arrow to see newer and older versions of the file.

See newer version   See older version

5. **Click the restore icon (shown in the margin) to restore your desired version.**

   Whether you're looking at an individual file, a folder, or an entire library's contents, the item is moved back where it used to live.

6. **If Windows notices a naming conflict with the item you're trying to restore, choose how to handle the conflict, as shown in Figure 19-4.**

   - *Replace the File in the Destination.* Click this option only when you're sure that the older file is better than your current file.

- *Skip This File.* Click this if you don't want to restore the file or folder. This option returns you to File History, where you can browse other files.

- *Compare Info for Both Files.* Often the best choice, this option lets you compare the files' sizes and dates before choosing which one to keep, the replacement file or the current file. Or, if you want, this choice also lets you keep *both* files: Windows simply adds a number after the name of the incoming file, naming it Notes (1), for example.

7. **Exit File History by clicking X in the upper-right corner.**

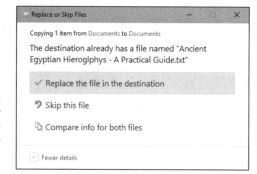

FIGURE 19-4:
Choose whether to replace the existing file, skip the file, or which file to keep.

Fixing Broken Apps

Windows makes it fairly easy to repair apps, which are almost always downloaded from the Microsoft Store. If an app no longer seems in good health and you'd like to reset it and start from scratch, follow these steps:

1. **Click the start icon, and choose Settings from the Start menu.**

   The Settings app appears.

2. **Click the Apps icon in the left column (and shown in the margin), and then click Installed Apps.**

   The Installed Apps page appears, listing your apps alphabetically.

3. **Scroll down, if necessary, until you find the app that's giving you trouble. Or use the Search Apps box to search for an app by name.**

4. **Click the three dots to the right of the app name, choose Advanced Options, and then click the Repair button.**

   Windows repairs the app, if possible, preserving your settings and data.

5. **If Repair doesn't fix the problem, click the adjacent Reset button.**

   When you choose Reset, Windows deletes and reinstalls the app from scratch, retaining your preference settings and sign-in details.

I Forgot My Password

Forgetting your password is one of the most annoying and most common computer problems. The first thing to do is to make sure the Caps Lock key is off because many passwords are case-sensitive. If you use multiple keyboard layouts, make sure you choose the correct layout for your password's language.

If the Caps Lock key or keyboard layout wasn't to blame, your only other recourse is to click I Forgot My Password at the password prompt and follow the onscreen instructions to reset your password. This process typically involves going through the unpleasant rigmarole of proving your identity and coming up with another password.

If you have a Microsoft Account, you can use that account to change and recover some other Windows 11 passwords. Browse to `https://microsoft.com` and see if your user account name appears near the top-right corner. If not, click Sign In to sign into your Microsoft Account. If you can't because you forget your Microsoft Account password, choose I Forgot My Password right there, and give yourself a new Microsoft Account password. Make sure you write the password down this time!

Once you've signed into your Microsoft account, click Support in the menu near the top. Type *passwords* in the How Can We Help You? box and then press Enter. You'll see options for dealing with a variety of password problems. Click whichever one best describes the problem you're trying to solve.

My App Is Frozen!

Eventually, one of your apps may freeze, leaving you in the cold with no way to reach the app's close command. The following steps will extricate the frozen program from your computer's memory (and the screen as well):

1. **Right-click the Start menu and select the Task Manager option from the pop-up menu, or press Ctrl+Alt+Delete.**

   The Task Manager program appears, and its Apps section lists the names of currently running programs.

2. **Click the name of the frozen app or program.**

   If you don't spot your program's name, click the More Details link to reveal everything currently running on your PC.

3. **Click the End Task button, and Windows whisks away the frozen program.**

   If your computer seems a bit groggy afterwards, play it safe by restarting it.

My Computer Is Frozen Solid

Every once in a while, Windows drops the ball and wanders off somewhere to sit under a tree. You're left looking at a computer that just looks back. Panicked clicks don't do anything. Randomly tapping the keyboard does nothing or, worse, makes the computer beep at every keypress.

When nothing onscreen moves (except, perhaps, the mouse pointer), the computer is frozen. Try the following approaches, in the order shown, to correct the problem:

➤ **Approach 1:** Press Esc twice. This action rarely works, but it's a quick first salvo that can't hurt anything.

➤ **Approach 2:** Press Ctrl+Alt+Delete simultaneously, and choose Start Task Manager from the menu that appears.

  • If you're lucky, Task Manager appears with the message that it has discovered an unresponsive application. Task Manager lists the names of currently running programs, including the one that's not responding. On the Processes tab, click the name of the program that's causing the mess and then click the End Task button. You lose any unsaved work in that program.

  • If that doesn't do the trick, press Ctrl+Alt+Delete again and click the power icon in the screen's lower-right corner (and shown in the margin). Choose Restart from the pop-up menu. Your computer should shut down and restart.

➤ **Approach 3:** Turn off the computer by pressing its power button. If that merely brings up the Turn Off the Computer menu, choose Restart, and your computer should restart.

➤ **Approach 4:** Keep holding down your computer's power button long enough (usually about 4 to 5 seconds) for the computer to eventually stop resisting and turn off.

When All Else Fails

If the computer won't start, first make sure that you don't have a dead laptop battery. Charge the battery for a little while if you see no indication of power. Or if it's a desktop PC, make sure the computer is plugged in. Look for a little power switch near where the computer plugs in, and make sure that switch is turned on.

If this simple solution doesn't help, be aware that the rest of this section isn't for the technologically fainthearted. If your problem is too severe for any of the previous sections to help, a repair shop may be your safest bet. But if that's not an option for you, read on.

WARNING

If you created a recovery drive, as described in Chapter 13, you may be able to restore Windows from that drive and get the computer going again. Note that you will likely lose all your personal files by using this method. You won't lose any files on OneDrive or any backups you've made.

If you have no choice but to recover from a recovery drive, follow these steps:

1. **With the computer turned off, insert the recovery drive into a USB port on your computer.**

2. **Hold down the Shift key (don't let go until I tell you) and turn on the computer.**

   If holding down the Shift key doesn't display any boot options, you may have to contact your computer manufacturer and get specific instructions for your make and model computer.

3. **When you see something on the screen, release the Shift key. Use the arrow keys to highlight USB Boot, and then press Enter.**

4. **Follow the onscreen instructions.**

Once you get Windows up and running again, you should be able to get your files on OneDrive. Or, if you used File History to back up files, restore files from there as discussed in the "Using File History to Restore a Backup" section. If you have Microsoft 365 with Word, Excel, and other Office apps, logging into Office 365 should get those apps going again. Any other missing apps can probably be downloaded from the Microsoft Store again.

Chapter **20**

Getting Strange Messages

E rror messages in real life are easy to understand. A blinking digital clock means you need to set the time. A parked car's beep means you've left the key in the ignition. A spouse's stern glance means you've forgotten something important.

But Windows error messages may have been written by a Senate subcommittee, if only the messages weren't so brief. The error messages rarely describe what you did to cause the event or, even worse, how to fix the problem.

When you see a message on your screen that you don't understand, your first step should be to ask Copilot about the message. Click the Copilot icon on the taskbar. If you've been carrying on conversations in the past, click New Topic next to the Copilot title near the top-left corner. Then type your question and include the words from the confusing message. For example, "What should I do when I see a message telling me to enter my network credentials?" Or "What should I do about a message for a file or folder for which I don't currently have permission?"

If you don't get a satisfactory answer, carry on the conversation with Copilot. Sometimes it takes a little back-and-forth conversation to zero in on the problem and come up with a good solution.

In this chapter, you learn how to deal with some of the most common Windows error messages. Find the message that matches what you see on screen and then read how to handle the situation as gracefully as Windows will allow.

Add Your Microsoft Account

Meaning: The exact wording of messages about your Microsoft account may vary, but they all mean the same thing — you must sign in with a Microsoft account, as shown in Figure 20-1.

FIGURE 20-1:
To take advantage of some Windows features, you must create a Microsoft account.

Probable causes: You may have tried to buy an app from the Microsoft Store, access OneDrive from the internet, or activate the Windows Family Safety controls, which all require a Microsoft account.

Solution: Sign in with your Microsoft account. If you don't have one, sign up for a free Microsoft account, as I describe in Chapter 2.

Choose What Happens with This Device

Meaning: Windows wants to know what to do with the device you've just plugged into your computer, so a message like the one shown in Figure 20-2 appears in your screen's lower-right corner. When you click the window in Figure 20-2, the window in Figure 20-3 appears in the screen's upper-right corner.

FIGURE 20-2:
Click to tell
Windows how to
react when you
connect a device
to your computer.

FIGURE 20-3:
Tell Windows
what to do with
the item you've
just inserted into
your computer.

Probable causes: You just slid a *flash drive* (a stick of memory) into your computer's USB port, attached a phone or camera, or connected another device to your computer.

Solution: Click the message in Figure 20-2 to tell Windows how to react when you reconnect the device in the future. You can always change this decision by visiting the Settings app's Bluetooth and Devices page and choosing AutoPlay from the right pane. Click any listed device, and a drop-down menu lists all your choices. (I prefer the Ask Me Every Time option, when it's available, so I can always choose the action I prefer.)

Deleted Files Are Removed Everywhere

Meaning: When you delete a file from OneDrive, it is no longer available to your other devices. To remind you, Windows sends the message shown in Figure 20-4.

Probable cause: You're deleting a file stored on OneDrive.

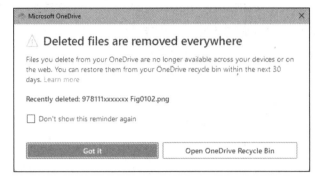

FIGURE 20-4:
Deleting files
from OneDrive
removes
them from
the OneDrive
folder of all
your devices.

Solution: Feel free to delete the file from OneDrive if you no longer need it there but be sure to keep a copy on the local hard drives of computers that require the file. If you delete a OneDrive file, it goes to the OneDrive recycle bin, where it stays for 30 days. To retrieve a mistakenly deleted file, click the message's Open OneDrive's Recycle Bin button, select the mistakenly deleted file, and click the Restore button. For more on OneDrive, see Chapter 5.

Do You Want to Allow This App to Make Changes to Your Device?

Meaning: In Figure 20-5, Windows is asking whether you're sure that the software is free from viruses, spyware, and other harmful things?

FIGURE 20-5:
Do you think this
software is safe?

Probable cause: You're trying to install downloaded software or a driver, and Microsoft's security app is asking if you trust the source of this download enough to allow it to make changes.

Solution: If you're downloading from the Microsoft Store or your computer manufacturer, click the OK, Yes, or Install button. But if this message appears unexpectedly or you think it may not be safe, click the Cancel, No, or Don't Install button to prevent installation. I cover safe computing in Chapter 11.

Do You Want to Save Changes?

Meaning: When an app is about to close but you haven't saved your work, you see the dialog shown in Figure 20-6.

Notepad ✕

Do you want to save changes to
C:\Users\andyr\Desktop\The Fine Art of
Belching.txt?

Save | Don't Save | Cancel

FIGURE 20-6:
Do you want to save your work?

Probable causes: You're trying to close an application, sign out, or restart your computer before telling the app to save your work.

Solution: If you opened a file in the wrong app and the file's contents look like gobbledygook, click Don't Save. But if you were working in the app and want to save your changes, click Save to save your work and let the app close.

Enter Network Credentials

Meaning: Windows isn't letting you access a particular file or folder, so it sends you the message shown in Figure 20-7.

Probable cause: You're trying to access a file or folder on a network or on another user account where you don't have permission.

Solution: If you're trying to access a shared resource on a private network, the person who shared the resource needs to log into the computer that's sharing the resource by using a Microsoft account, not a PIN or other method. See Chapter 15 for more information.

Let's Finish Setting Up

Meaning: Figure 20-8 is Microsoft's way of making sure that you know about all the new features in Windows 11, including features you have to pay for.

Probable cause: Owners of new or recently upgraded computers see this message a lot.

Solution: Click Dismiss to put off the task, or click OK to let Windows complete the task. The task might take a few minutes to finish, during which time you can't use the computer.

Select to Choose What Happens with Removable Drives

Meaning: Windows sends the message shown in Figure 20-9 when it wants to know what to do when you plug a hard drive or flash drive into your computer's USB port.

FIGURE 20-9:
Windows wants
to know what to
do with a
new drive.

Probable cause: You've plugged a new hard drive or flash drive into your computer's USB port.

Solution: You can ignore the message, and it will go away with no harm done. If you click it, Windows lets you choose one of the following actions:

>> **Configure Storage Settings:** Opens the Settings app's Storage settings, few of which have to do with portable drives. (Previously, Windows would offer to let you use the drive as a backup device.)

>> **Open Folder to View Files:** Lets you view the contents of your newly plugged-in drive.

>> **Take No Action:** Stops sending pointless messages like this. When you want to see what's inside the drive, open File Explorer to view the drive's contents.

Threats Found

Meaning: When the built-in Windows antivirus program finds a potentially dangerous file on your computer, it lets you know with the message shown in Figure 20-10. Windows then removes the file so it can't harm your computer or files. Like most notifications, this one appears in the screen's lower-right corner.

Probable cause: A potentially dangerous file — *malware* — probably arrived through email, a flash drive, a networked computer, or an evil website. Windows is removing the file so it can't do any harm.

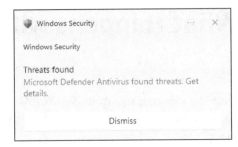

FIGURE 20-10:
Microsoft
Defender
Antivirus has
found and
removed a
potentially
dangerous file on
your computer.

Solution: Microsoft Defender Antivirus is already removing the offender, but try to remember what action forced Microsoft Defender Antivirus to clean up the problem. Then, if possible, try not to repeat that action. It wouldn't hurt to tell Microsoft Defender Antivirus to give your computer a full scan and to scan any storage device you just connected. (I explain Microsoft Defender Antivirus in Chapter 11.) Then click the Dismiss button, breathe a sigh of relief, and continue with your work.

You Don't Currently Have Permission to Access This Folder

Meaning: If you spot the window in Figure 20-11, Windows won't let you look inside the folder you're trying to open. A similar message appears when Windows won't let you look inside a file.

FIGURE 20-11:
Find someone
with an Adminis-
trator account to
open the
folder or file.

Probable cause: The file or folder belongs to someone with a different user account.

Solution: If you hold an Administrator account, you can open files and folders from other people's user accounts by clicking Continue. If you don't have an Administrator account, you're locked out.

Your Privacy Settings Blocked Access to Your Location

Meaning: Something in Windows is asking permission to know your current location, as shown in Figure 20-12, and Windows wants to know whether you want to allow that.

FIGURE 20-12:
Click Settings and
give the app
permission to
know your
location.

> ⛊ Privacy   ⋯   ✕
>
> Your privacy settings blocked access to your location.
> If you want to change these settings, go to Settings,
> Privacy, App permissions, Location

Probable cause: Your Privacy settings in Windows 11 are set so that apps are not allowed to know your location.

Solution: To change your Privacy settings, open the Settings app from the Start menu. Then head for the Privacy and Security section. There, you can choose which apps can access information that many people consider private. I cover the Settings app in Chapter 12.

Chapter **21**

Moving from an Old PC to a New Windows 11 PC

When you bring home your exciting new Windows 11 computer, it lacks the most important thing of all: the stuff from your old computer. How do you copy your files from that dusty old PC to that shiny new Windows PC? How do you even find everything you want to move?

This chapter explores your options and compares their degrees of difficulty.

TIP

Here's a timesaver: If you're just upgrading your relatively new Windows 10 PC to Windows 11, you can skip this chapter. When you upgrade, Windows 11 leaves your personal files, apps, and desktop programs in place.

Avoiding File Transfers

If you store your personal files in a cloud drive, you won't have to transfer files at all. Cloud drives such as OneDrive, Google Drive, Dropbox, and iCloud store your personal files in a private place on the internet (generally referred to as a *cloud*). You can access the files from any internet-connected computer or device; you don't need to move, copy, or transfer any files.

In Windows, if you store your files in the built-in Documents, Pictures, Music, and Videos folders on OneDrive, those files will be available on your new computer when you sign in to OneDrive on the new computer. Signing into your account on any other cloud drive service you use also makes files stored in those services available on your new computer.

If you're not familiar with any of the services I've mentioned, ask Copilot for more information. (And if you need help asking Copilot questions, see Chapter 3.)

Transferring Files on a Private Network

When two or more computers share the same Wi-Fi network for internet access, they automatically become members of a *private network*, which means you can share files and folders on one computer with other computers (and devices) on the same Wi-Fi network.

By default, the private network is turned off and invisible. You need to set up the private network and activate Network Discovery to be able to share files among the computers on the network. See Chapter 15 for details.

Once your new PC is a member of the private network, it can access any shared resources through File Explorer (as explained in Chapter 15). To copy a file on the private network to your new PC, just use standard copy techniques, as described in Chapter 5.

Transferring Files Using an External Drive

Using an external drive as an intermediary to copy files from one computer to another is a viable alternative to cloud drives and private networks. If all your personal files are in your Windows Documents, Pictures, Music, and Video folders, you can find out how much storage you'll need on the external drive to copy them all in one step.

To see how much storage space you'll need to transfer all your files, follow these steps:

1. **Open File Explorer by clicking its icon on the taskbar or by using the Start menu.**

2. **In the navigation pane on the left, expand This PC by clicking its right arrow. Do the same for Local Disk (C:).**

3. **Right-click the Users folder and choose Properties.**

   The Properties dialog opens.

4. **Click the Details tab.**

   The amount of space used by all files in all user accounts appears next to Size on Disk, which is 41.4 GB in Figure 21-1. For this example, you'd need a USB drive or external hard drive with at least 42 GB of free space to store all the files from all the user accounts in your Users folder.

FIGURE 21-1:
Size on Disk shows how much space the Users folder is taking up on the hard drive.

Of course, you don't have to transfer all the files at once. You could transfer them in batches to, perhaps, your Documents folder first, your Pictures folder next, and so forth, until you've copied and transferred all the files you want on your new computer.

TIP

If you use the File History app (see Chapter 13) to back up your files to an external drive, you can use File History on your new computer to restore files on your new computer.

Using a Third-Party Solution

If none of the options described previously are viable, try a third-party solution such as PCmover, available for free from the Microsoft Store. The free version is limited to 500MB, so it might not be for everyone. But even if you need to transfer more that 500MB, you can use the free version to test things out and get the paid product later.

To open Microsoft Store, click its icon in the taskbar, or click the start icon and choose Microsoft Store. You could also type *microsoft store* in the Search box next to the start icon and click Microsoft Store (System) in the Start menu.

Once you're in the store, search for *pcmover* and look for the free Windows Store edition.

You don't need to use a cable or external drives to transfer files with PCmover. But your old and new computers must be using the same Wi-Fi network and must have PCmover installed. You'll also be limited to transferring files 500MB at a time, which could be time consuming if you have a lot of large picture and video files. Paid versions of PCmover, available at `https://laplink.com`, can transfer larger files more quickly.

If the solutions discussed so far still are beyond your tech abilities, a computer repair shop should be able to transfer the files for you.

IN THIS CHAPTER

» Getting instant help

» Using Windows built-in
help resources

» Asking for help from the Windows
Community website

Chapter **22**

Help on the Windows Help System

H ere are the quickest ways to make Windows dish out helpful information when something on the desktop leaves you stumped:

» **Ask Copilot:** Copilot is your every-ready, free tech nerd. You can ask it anything. See Chapter 3 if you need help asking Copilot questions.

» **Press F1:** Press the F1 key in Windows or any desktop app.

» **Click the Get Help icon:** Click the start icon and then click the Get Help icon.

» **Click the question mark:** If you spot a question mark in a window's upper-right corner, pounce on it with a quick click.

In each case, Windows fetches help, either by going online, fetching built-in instructions, or leading you to a built-in tutorial. This chapter explains how to take advantage of the help Windows 11 has to offer.

Getting Started with Windows 11

The Get Started app offers a short guided tour to Windows 11. It appeals to the same people who enjoy reading book introductions, setting the mood for what's coming. To find the app, type *get started* in the Search box next to the start icon, and then click Get Started on the Start menu. The screen shown in Figure 22-1 appears.

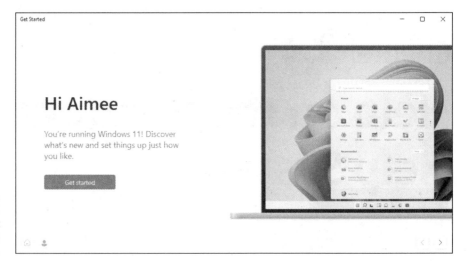

FIGURE 22-1:
The Get Started app offers a short introduction to Windows 11.

Click the Get Started button. The rest of the app is interactive. You'll see a list of possible interests and the different ways people use their computers. Set the toggle on for any category that interests you. Then click > near the bottom-right corner of the screen to continue through the interactive app.

The Get Help App

Windows 11 comes with an app that simplifies finding the help you need. Called simply Get Help, the app works much like those phone robots that make you press different numbers until you're routed to the proper department.

The Get Help app needs some help of its own: It works only when you're connected to the internet. If you're not connected, the app simply displays an error message.

To summon the Get Help app and begin routing yourself to someone or something to help you with your computer's problem, follow these steps:

1. **Click the start icon, click the All Apps icon, and then click Get Help.**

   The Get Help app appears, as shown in Figure 22-2, and fetches a Virtual Assistant (a robot) to answer your problem.

2. **Type your question in the box.**

   The robot searches Microsoft's online stash of answers for matches and presents the results. If any of the results answers your question, you're through!

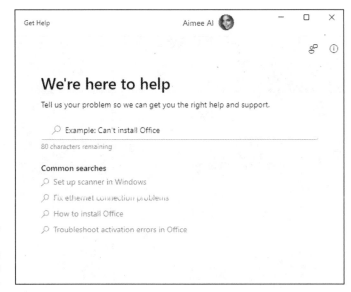

FIGURE 22-2:
The Windows 11 Get Help app tries to guide you to an answer.

If you still have questions, interacting with a human (gasp!) might be your best bet, as described in the next section.

Ask the Microsoft Community

For free support, your best bet is the Microsoft Community website. It's an online gathering place for confused owners, knowledgeable tech enthusiasts, and an occasional Microsoft employee.

After you get to the website, you choose your category, type your question. Sometimes a Microsoft employee will answer, but usually someone who had a similar problem will chime in. The more people who respond, the more likely everyone will find a solution to a common problem. Remember, though: The forums are for only Microsoft products.

To visit the Microsoft Support Community, follow these steps:

1. **Visit the Microsoft Community website at** https://answers.microsoft.com.

   The Community page opens, looking something like Figure 22-3. Websites change often, so don't be surprised if the page you see is slightly different.

FIGURE 22-3:
Search the
community for
your question
or problem.

2. **In the Search the Community box, type a few keywords explaining your question or problem, and then press Enter.**

   Browse the results to see if any solutions work for your computer's particular problem. If you find a solution, you're finished with these steps.

3. **If you don't see an answer, copy your original question by triple-clicking it and pressing Ctrl+C.**

4. **Click Get Started (near the top of the page), and then click Ask a Question in the menu that appears.**

5. **If prompted, sign into your Microsoft account.**

6. In the Question box shown in Figure 22-4, paste your original question by pressing Ctrl+V.

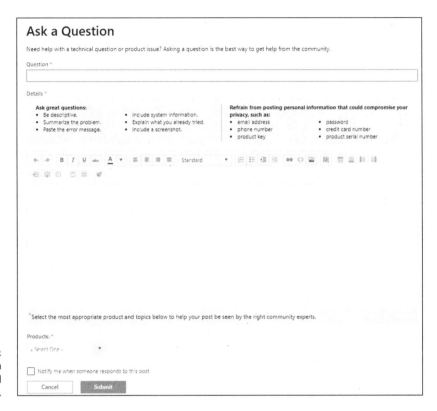

Ask a Question

Need help with a technical question or product issue? Asking a question is the best way to get help from the community.

Question *

Details *

Ask great questions:
- Be descriptive.
- Summarize the problem.
- Paste the error message.

- Include system information.
- Explain what you already tried.
- Include a screenshot.

Refrain from posting personal information that could compromise your privacy, such as:
- email address
- phone number
- product key

- password
- credit card number
- product serial number

Select the most appropriate product and topics below to help your post be seen by the right community experts.

Products: *

- Select One -

☐ Notify me when someone responds to this post

Cancel   Submit

FIGURE 22-4:
Page for asking a more detailed question.

7. In the Details section, provide as much relevant information as you can.

Follow the guidelines under Ask Great Questions for the best results. Also check out the list at the end of the chapter.

8. On the Products drop-down menu, choose Windows.

9. Select the Notify Me When Someone Responds to This Post check box.

10. Click Submit.

Now you wait. When someone responds, a notice appears in your email with a link to your posted message and the response.

11. Click the emailed link to revisit the forum, where you can begin a correspondence that may solve your problem.

The Microsoft Community website is free, and although it's not guaranteed to provide an answer, it's definitely worth a try. I've found quite a few solutions just by browsing the answers to previously asked questions.

For the best results, keep these tips in mind when posting a message on the Microsoft Community website:

>> **Don't rant.** Most members of the Microsoft Community aren't paid. Many are confused souls trying to piece together solutions, just like you. Computer nerds also hang out here and are more likely to solve problems when persuaded by logic rather than emotion.

>> **To attract the best responses, be descriptive.** If you see an error message, list it in its entirety, without typographical errors. Also include your computer's make and model.

>> **If possible, list the exact steps to reproduce the problem.** If your problem can be reproduced on other people's computers, it's much easier to solve.

>> **Keep an eye on your email, and respond to people who try to help.** The information you're exchanging will live on inside the forum for years. Even if you can't solve your immediate problem, you're leaving a trail that can help others solve the problem down the road.

Most of the best answers come not from Microsoft's paid technicians but from strangers who have the same problem, perhaps even the same make and model of computer, and who want to swap tips to make things better for you both.

7

The Part of Tens

IN THIS CHAPTER

» **Using AI to enhance your photos**

» **Removing objects (and people) from photos**

» **Cropping images to specific aspect ratios**

» **Changing and removing photo backgrounds**

» **Converting written text to spoken voice**

Chapter **23**

Top Ten Tips for Content Creators

C ontent creation is all about creating pictures, videos, ads, social media posts, and more for self-publishing online. Many tools are available to help you create professional-quality content for posting on YouTube, TikTok, Instagram, Facebook, X, and elsewhere. Some of these tools are expensive and difficult to learn. But as you discover in this chapter, Windows 11 2024 Update has free AI tools for content creators.

Enhancing a Photo with AI

NEW

If you have a photo that's faded or doesn't have enough pizzazz, let AI take a shot at enhancing it. Simply follow these steps:

1. **Open your Photos app from the Start menu, and double-click the image you want to enhance.**

   If the image isn't in your Photos app, open File Explorer, navigate to the folder that contains the image, right-click the image's icon, and choose Open With ⇨ Photos.

2. **Click the edit icon in the upper-left corner of the Photos app.**

3. **Click the filter icon, labeled in Figure 23-1, and then click Auto Enhance.**

Filters

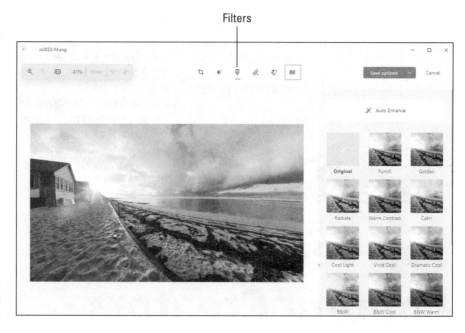

FIGURE 23-1:
The filter icon in
the Photos app.

4. **Drag the Intensity slider left and right to choose an intensity.**

   The farther you drag to the right, the more intense the enhancement.

5. **(Optional) Click a color effect such as Punch, Vivid, or Black & White.**

   Each effect has an Intensity slider you can use.

6. **When you're happy with the effect, click Save Options, click Save As Copy, and provide a new file name for the image.**

   Or you could save the file to a different folder and keep the same filename. By typing a new file name or saving to a different folder, you retain the original photo.

When modifying and experimenting with photos, it's a good idea to save your changes under a new name, or separate folder, so you still have the original photo to work with.

TIP

Removing Objects and People from a Photo

Once in a while we take a great photo that's ruined by an unwanted person or object. Perhaps a beautiful landscape is compromised by a junk car in the foreground. Or a stranger appears in a family photo. AI is pretty good at removing unwanted items and people from photos. The Photos app in Windows 11 has this capability built right in, so you can use it for free any time you like. Here are the steps:

1. **In the Photos app, find and double-click the image.**

If the image isn't in your Photos app, open File Explorer, navigate to the folder that contains the image, right-click the image, and choose Open With ⇨ Photos.

2. **Click Edit in the upper-left corner, and then click the erase icon, labeled in Figure 23-2. Make sure Auto Apply is on.**

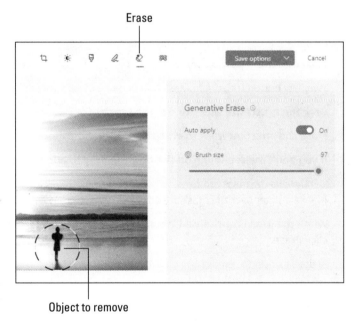

Erase

Object to remove

FIGURE 23-2:
Most of the object to erase is inside the circle.

3. **Move the mouse pointer over the photo.**

The circle that appears is the brush.

4. **Drag the Brush Size slider to size the brush so that all or most of the item to erase is contained in the circle.**

5. **Click and wait a few seconds.**

   AI attempts to remove the object.

6. **Repeat Steps 3 through 5, as necessary, until all traces of the unwanted item are gone.**

   If the object is too large to be contained in the circle, try the method in the next set of steps.

7. **When you're happy with the results, save the image by clicking Save Options. To retain the original photo, choose Save as Copy, and save the image with a new filename or to a different folder.**

If you can't remove the object or person using the preceding steps, click Cancel to undo your current changes and exit without saving. Then, try the following steps, which use the same erase tool but without the Auto Apply option. With this pro-cedure, you *mask* the item you want to remove by dragging the mouse pointer over the item:

1. **Follow Steps 1 and 3 in the preceding list.**

2. **Click the Auto Apply option off.**

   Two new buttons titled Add Mask and Remove Mask appear.

3. **Drag the Brush Size slider to size the brush.**

4. **Mask the area you want to erase by dragging the mouse pointer over it.**

5. **If you don't mask enough on the first try, drag to add more mask.**

   If you make the mask too big, you can click Remove Mask and then drag the mouse pointer over the mask area that you want to remove.

6. **When the item is entirely within the mask, as shown in Figure 23-3, click Erase.**

   AI does its best to remove the masked object.

7. **If the item is only partially removed, continue to mask and erase the remaining areas as necessary.**

   You can always click Cancel if your efforts do more harm than good.

8. **When you're satisfied with the results, click Save Options, choose Save As Copy, and save the copy with a new file name.**

Object to remove

Cropping an Image

When using an image in social media or a printed document, you might need the image in a certain aspect ratio (shape) to fit properly. Or you might want to eliminate a distracting background by cropping the image. You can do both by using the Photos app. Here are the steps:

1. **In Photos, double-click the image.**

   Or right-click the image's icon in File Explorer and choose Open with ⇨ Photos.

2. **Click Edit in the upper-left corner of the Photos app.**

3. **Click the crop tool, which is labeled in Figure 23-4.**

4. **If you need a specific aspect ratio, click Free (near the bottom of the screen) and then click the aspect ratio you want to use.**

5. **Drag the image as needed to position it in the frame. To change the size of the frame, drag a corner or an edge.**

   Anything inside the frame will appear in the final image. Anything outside the frame will be cropped out (deleted).

6. **When you're happy with the results, click Save Options, click Save as Copy, and give the image a new file name.**

You can also change the size of the image by using the Paint app, as described in the next section.

Crop   Aspect ratios

FIGURE 23-4:
Cropping an
image in Photos.

REMEMBER

The aspect ratio defines the *ratio* of the image's width to its height. It doesn't define the size of the image. To make the image larger or smaller, at the current aspect ratio, you *size* the image.

Sizing an Image

The size of an image can be expressed by its *dimensions,* the height and width in pixels. If you touch the mouse pointer on a picture's icon in File Explorer, as shown in Figure 23-5, you'll usually see the image dimensions. You can also right-click an image's icon in File Explorer, choose Properties, and then click the Details tab to display the dimensions in the Properties dialog.

FIGURE 23-5:
Touch the mouse
pointer on an
image to see its
dimensions.

Mountain Background.png

Item type: PNG File
Dimensions: 1280 x 720
Size: 1.17 MB

To change the size of an image, follow these steps:

1. **Right-click the image's icon in File Explorer and choose Open with ⇨ Paint.**

   The image's dimensions appear near the bottom of the app window.

2. **Click the fit to window icon, labeled in Figure 23-6, to set the magnification so that the image fits inside the app window.**

Resize and skew

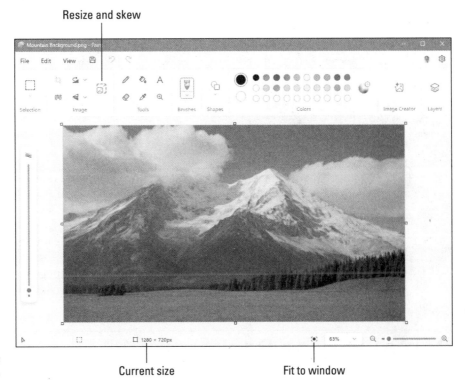

FIGURE 23-6:
An image in Paint.

Current size   Fit to window

3. **Click the resize and skew icon.**

4. **In the dialog box that appears (see Figure 23-7), specify the new size for the image.**

   If you change the aspect ratio of the image, you'll distort the image, like a funhouse mirror. To change the size without changing the shape, first choose either Percentage or Pixels. For example, to double the size of the image, click Percentage and set both Horizontal (width) and Vertical (height) to 200 (for 200 percent). If you need a specific size, click Pixels. Then type the dimension in pixels for either Horizontal or Vertical in pixels. The other dimension will adjust automatically to retain the current shape of the picture.

5. **When you're finished, click OK.**

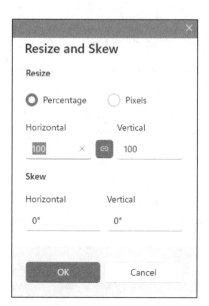

FIGURE 23-7:
Resize and Skew
dialog in Paint.

REMEMBER

If you make a mess of things, you can undo your most recent change by pressing Ctrl+Z. Or just close the Paint app and choose No when asked if you want to save your changes.

TIP

If you try to enlarge a small image too much, it will become blurry. To get around this problem, you need to *upscale*, rather than just resize, the image. Unfortunately, Windows doesn't have a built-in tool for upscaling images. However, you can find sites online that let you to upscale images for free, such as https://dgb.lol.

Removing the Background

NEW

AI can help you remove the background from an image. This feature is helpful if you want one picture in front of another, such as when putting a picture of yourself in the foreground of a YouTube thumbnail or social media post, as shown in Figure 23-8.

A plain background is easier to remove than a complex one. If you're planning on removing the background from a photo of yourself, start by taking a photo with a plain wall in the background. Or better yet, use a green screen, which works both for photos and videos. Search Amazon or a similar online retailer for *video green screen.* For general information about green screens in videography, ask Copilot, "What is a green screen in video?"

FIGURE 23-8:
Photo of a person
superimposed on
a thumbnail.

To remove the background from an image, you might first want to start with an image that's been cropped so there will be less extraneous background to remove. Use the method described in the "Shaping and Cropping an Image" section. Then, follow these steps:

1. **In the Photos app, double-click the image from which you want to remove the background.**

   Or in File Explorer, right-click the image and choose Open with ⇨ Photos.

2. **Click Edit in the Photos app's upper-left corner.**

3. **Click the background icon and then click Remove, as shown in Figure 23-9.**

   The gray-and-white checkerboard in the resulting image shows the transparent part of the image, where the background has been removed.

4. **If AI was only partially successful, click to enable Background Brush Tool and erase any remnants that were left behind.**

5. **Click Save Options, and then choose Save as Copy.**

   The Save As dialog appears.

6. **Choose png (*.png) as the Save as Type, choose the folder in which you want to save the image, and give it a new file name.**

When you place the image with the transparent background onto another image, the transparent parts will be invisible. In the next section, you see how to do that in Paint.

Background

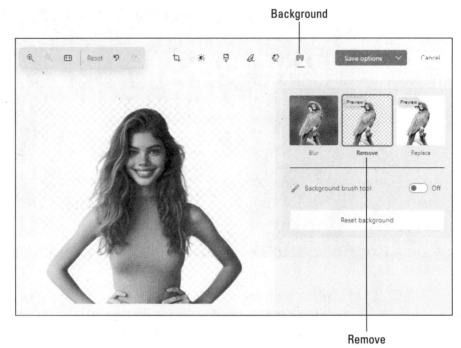

FIGURE 23-9:
Background
removed in
Photos app.

Remove

Changing a Picture's Background

NEW

To change the background of an image, your best bet is to layer two images. You choose one photo for the background. Then you place a photo with a transparent background in front of the background photo. You can do both steps in the Paint app. Here's how:

1. **Right-click the background image, and choose Open with ⇨ Paint.**

2. **Click the fit to window icon (refer to Figure 23-6), so you can see the entire image.**

3. **In Paint, choose File ⇨ Import to Canvas ⇨ From a File, and then open the foreground image (the one with the transparent background).**

   The foreground image is the one you created in the preceding section.

4. **Size the imported image by dragging a sizing handle, as shown in Figure 23-10.**

5. **Move the entire imported image by placing the mouse pointer in the middle of the image until you see a four-headed mouse pointer and then dragging the image.**

FIGURE 23-10:
Transparent
background
image in front of
back-
ground image.

Transparent background image   Sizing handles

6. **When the foreground image is in place, choose File ⇨ Save As, and then save the image with a new file name to any folder you want.**

   The newly saved file will contain both images combined into a single image.

Converting Text to Voice

NEW

If you need spoken narration for a video but keep tripping over your own words, you can write a script and have an AI read it aloud for you. You can do so for free right from Windows, choosing from a variety of voices.

For the script, work in chunks of 100 to 300 words (a minute or two of speech) at a time. You can write the script or ask Copilot to write it for you. You can store the script in a simple text document using Notepad (which comes with Windows), Word, Google Docs, or another editor.

After you have your words on paper, follow these steps:

1. **Open Microsoft Clipchamp from the Start menu or by using the search box.**

   The Clipchamp home page appears.

2. **Under Text to Speech, click Try It.**

3. **When the Clipchamp editor opens, click Text to Speech in the left column, as shown in Figure 23-11.**

Project name   Voice   Language

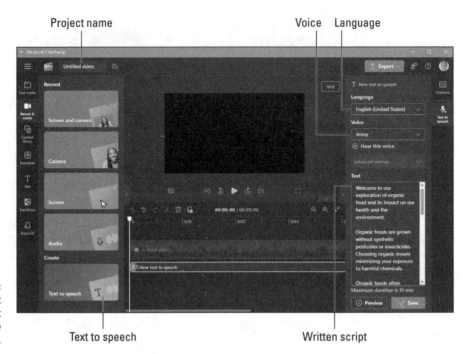

FIGURE 23-11:
Written script
in Microsoft
Clipchamp to be
read aloud.

Text to speech   Written script

4. **Click the Untitled Video box in the upper-left corner, and type a new name that describes your script.**

5. **In the Language drop-down menu (on the right), choose the language for the AI voice to speak.**

6. **In the Voice drop-down menu, choose a voice. Click Hear This Voice to listen to a sample.**

7. **Copy and paste your typed speech into the Text box.**

8. **Click the Preview button to listen to the script.**

9. **If necessary, you can change the text by editing it in the Text box.**

10. **(Optional) Click Advanced Settings and adjust the emotion, pitch, and pace of the voice.**

11. **When you're happy with the spoken text, click Save to save the script as a project in Clipchamp, and then click Export to export the voice to a separate file. When asked, choose 720p or 1080p.**

   The spoken voice is saved to your Downloads folder with the filename you provided in Step 4, and the .mp4 filename extension.

To listen to the narration, open the Downloads folder and double-click the exported mp4 file. If you need the voice file in mp3, flac, or another audio format, consider using a free online conversion site such as www.online-convert.com or www.zamzar.com.

Creating Pictures from Words

NEW

If you need a picture of something but can't find one for free, try creating it yourself using only words. Note that you need to have a Microsoft account for this to work. Also, the number of images you can create in one day is limited because AI image generation uses a lot of computing horsepower.

Windows 11 2024 Update supports AI image generation in the Paint app that comes with Windows. Here's how to use it:

1. **Open Paint from the Start menu.**

   If you don't see Paint in the pinned area, click the All Apps button and then click Paint.

2. **Click the Image Creator icon, as shown in Figure 23-12.**

FIGURE 23-12: Image Creator in Paint.

3. **In the box, describe the image you want.**

   Be as descriptive as possible. You don't need to type any special commands. For example, in Figure 23-13, I gave it the prompt, "Cute baby unicorns and bunnies playing in a green field of waterfalls and rainbows under clear blue sunny skies."

4. **Under Choose a Style, select the kind of image you'd like (Photorealistic, Watercolor, Oil Painting, and so forth).**

   I chose Watercolor for my example, to give the image a soft appearance.

5. **Click Create.**

   After a few seconds, Paint displays the generated images as thumbnails under Explore Variants, as shown in Figure 23-13.

Crop   Generated images

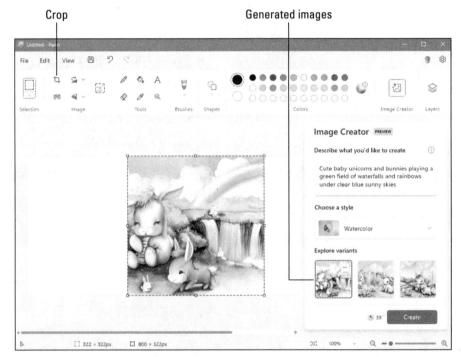

FIGURE 23-13:
Viewing a generated image in Paint.

6. **Click a thumbnail image to enlarge it.**

   If the generated image seems to be layered on top of a blank canvas or a previous image, click the crop icon to delete the extra background.

7. **When you find an image you want to save, choose File ➪ Save As and save the file.**

After you have your image, you're free to do with it as you please. There are no copyright restrictions, so you can use it in your social media posts or other content you create.

Making AI Images with Image Creator

The Paint app, which is described in the preceding section, uses Microsoft Image Creator to create images for you. As an alternative to Paint, you can use the Image Creator website to generate images. Many people feel the images they get from the website are better in quality than the images they get through Paint.

Unlike Paint, Image Creator won't prompt you for a style, such as watercolor or anime. But you can be specific about the style, mood, medium, and settings of your desired image. The more detailed your prompt, the better results you're likely to get. For example:

> Photograph of a young Hawaiian woman surfing a huge wave at Banzai Pipeline

> An abstract charcoal drawing of a bearded old man who has seen his share of hard times

> Watercolor of baby unicorns and cute bunnies frolicking in a landscape of water-falls and rainbows

> Oil painting in the style of Van Gogh of a spooky carnival at night

> Pencil sketch drawing of a young woman smelling a rose

> iPhone selfie taken by a young woman dressed in costume at an Anime Cosplay Convention

> Digital photograph of a Maine forest at the peak of autumn colors taken from atop Mt. Desert at the golden hour

You need a personal Microsoft account to access Image Creator. To get to the website, browse to `https://bing.com/create`. Websites change often, so I can't say exactly what you'll see when you get there. But there will likely be a box for you to type your prompt, some instructions, and some sample images, as shown in Figure 23-14.

The instructions section of the Image Creator home page provides some tips and useful information for generating images. Sample images appear under the Explore Ideas heading. Touch the mouse pointer to any sample image to see the prompt used to generate the image.

To create an image, type your prompt into the box near the top of the page, and then click the Create button to the right of the box. Be patient. Within a minute or so, you should see from one to four sample images (see Figure 23-15).

Type your prompt here

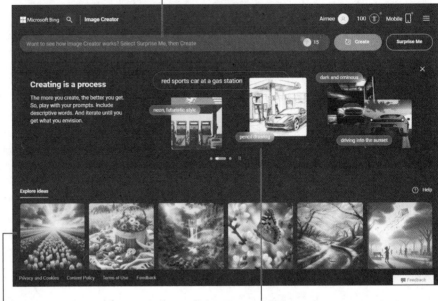

FIGURE 23-14:
Microsoft
Image Creator
home page.

Examples   Instructions

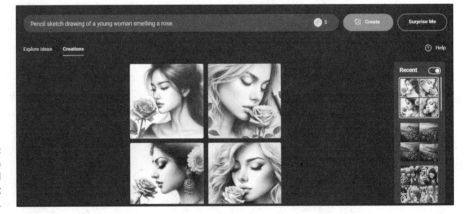

FIGURE 23-15:
Pencil sketch
images created
with Microsoft
Image Creator.

Click an image to enlarge it for a closer look. Click < and > at the sides of the enlarged image to browse through all the images that were created. Use options to the right of the image you're viewing, as shown in Figure 23-16, to do any of the following:

>> **Share:** Provides a web address (URL) that others can browse to in order to see your image.

>> **Save:** Saves the image to your collections, which you can find by browsing to `www.bing.com/saves`.

>> **Download:** Downloads the image to your computer (to your Downloads folder by default).

>> **Customize:** Opens the image in Microsoft Designer, where you can do additional AI editing and enhancing.

>> **Resize:** Switches from the square aspect ratio (1:1) to a landscape aspect ratio of 4:3.

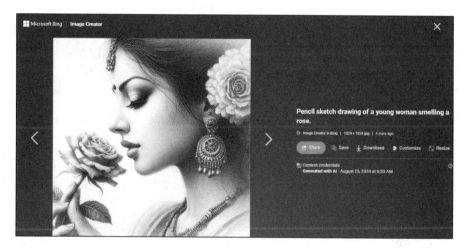

FIGURE 23-16:
An AI-generated
pencil sketch.

When you start creating images, a Creations heading appears next to Explore Ideas on the Image Creator home page. Click Creations to see your recent creations. As you create new images, older images will be removed from the page, so make sure you download any images you want to keep. Or at least save those images so you can return to them in the future on the `www.bing.com/saves` page.

Designing Like a Pro for Free

Microsoft Designer is a graphic design tool that allows you to create professional-quality social media posts, ads, printed business materials, and more without knowing graphics design. If you have a Microsoft 365 account (which is not free), you can download Microsoft Designer from the Microsoft Store. If you don't have a Microsoft 365 account, you can use the Microsoft Designer website instead. Just browse to `https://designer.microsoft.com`. If you're not logged in automatically when you browse to the site, log in with your personal Microsoft account.

On the Microsoft Designer website, you'll see a box where you can state exactly what you want to create, as shown in Figure 23-17. Or click Create with AI to see different types of designs you can create, such as Greeting Cards, Icons, Social Posts, Invitations, Stickers, Avatars, and Emojis. Use the scroll arrows on the left and right to see more options. Then click the type of design you want to create, and follow the onscreen instructions.

FIGURE 23-17:
Microsoft
Designer
home page.

You can also work with existing images. Click Edit with AI, and you see options to edit the image, frame the image, and more. Click the option you want to try, and follow the onscreen instructions. For example, the Restyle Image option enables you to create different types of illustrations from a photo or other image, as shown in Figure 23-18.

To try out the Restyle Image feature, first browse to the Microsoft Designer home page. Then follow these steps:

1. **Click Edit with AI.**

2. **Click Restyle Image.**

3. **If you see a prompt warning that you might be disappointed, click I Agree.**

   AI is still rough around the edges, so don't expect the quality to equal that of a human artist.

FIGURE 23-18:
Original image
(top left) and
restyled
variations.

Original

Claymation

Doodle Art

Modern Cartoon

Pop Art

Stylized 3D

4. **Click Add an Image, click the Add Image button, and then browse to and select the image to upload. Then click Open.**

   If the image is on your hard drive, click From This Device and navigate to the image's folder.

5. **Under Media on, click the image you just uploaded and then click Select.**

6. **Click Style, and then click the style you want to apply.**

   Scroll through the options by clicking the arrows on the left and right sides.

7. **If you want something specific in the background, such as balloons or fireworks, click Background Elements and describe what the background should display.**

8. **Click Generate.**

   After a minute or less, you see up to four thumbnails of your restyled image. In Figure 23-19, I created a Claymation version of a person from a photo. Below the Claymation image are thumbnails of other restyled versions of the same image.

To download a restyled image, click its thumbnail, and then click the download icon that appears in the upper-right corner of that thumbnail. All restyled images are available on the My Creations tab.

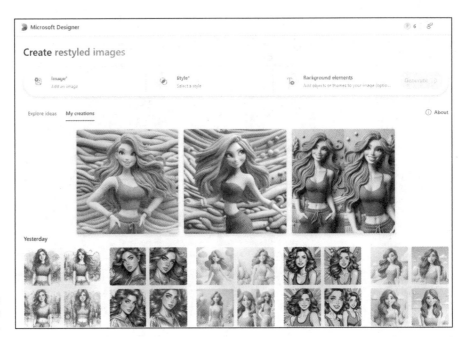

FIGURE 23-19:
Restyled image
thumbnails.

The third major section of Microsoft Designer is Design from Scratch. Clicking this option on Designer's home page gives you many choices for designing your creation. Scroll thought the options, both vertically down the page and horizontally across each category. Following is a small sample of the types of designs that Designer can help you create:

>> Brochure

>> Invitation

>> Gift certificate

>> Flyer

>> LinkedIn post

>> Instagram story

>> Facebook ad

>> Pinterest story

>> X (Twitter) post

Click the type of content you want to create, and then follow the onscreen instructions to start designing. If you get stuck, ask Copilot for help. In your prompt, tell Copilot that you want help with Microsoft Designer. You can also browse to `https://support.microsoft.com` and search for *Microsoft Designer*. And for more fun ways to work with AI and images, see Chapter 17.

Chapter **24**

Top Ten Tips for Thriving in the Age of AI

indows 11 2024 Update brings the power of modern artificial intelligence (AI) to everyone for free. Most AI capabilities are in the Copilot app, which you can open by clicking the Copilot icon in the taskbar. Think of Copilot as a know-it-all best friend who never gets tired of answering your questions. In this chapter, I give you some tips on how to start taking advantage of Copilot and AI, right now.

Chatting with Copilot

When you search the web with Google, Bing, or another search engine for a term or subject, you get a ton of references for content related to your topic. You're on your own to sift through the results. Copilot — and AI in general — doesn't work that way. Instead, you engage in a conversation. You ask Copilot a question, and you get an answer. If the answer isn't quite what you expected, you can continue asking questions until you zero in on the information you need.

You can open Copilot in several ways: Click its taskbar icon, as shown in Figure 24-1; click the start icon and then click the Copilot icon, if it appears in the Pinned section; or click the start icon, click All Apps, and then click Copilot.

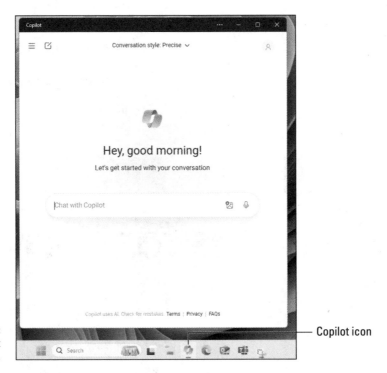

Copilot icon

FIGURE 24-1:
The Copilot chat window.

Once the app is open, simply type your question in the Chat with Copilot box. Then press Enter or click the submit icon, as shown in Figure 24-2.

Your answer will arrive shortly. But if that answer isn't exactly what you were expecting, you can continue chatting, just as you would if speaking to another person. Perhaps change some aspect of your question or provide more information. You can keep the conversation going until you get exactly what you're looking for. For example, you might start with a general question such as

What are some common ways to make money online?

You may get a long answer with many options. If so, you could ask for more details about one of the options, such as

What is affiliate marketing?

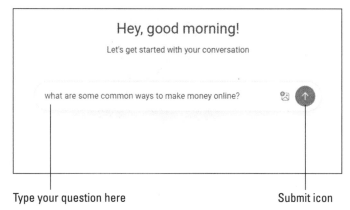

Hey, good morning!

Let's get started with your conversation

what are some common ways to make money online?

FIGURE 24-2:
Asking Copilot
a question.

Type your question here   Submit icon

After you get your answer, you could follow up with another question, such as

Where can I get affiliate marketing links?

Most people find this process quicker and easier than searching the web. When you've finished your conversation and want to start a new conversation, just click the new chat icon near the top of the Copilot window (labeled in Figure 24-3).

New chat

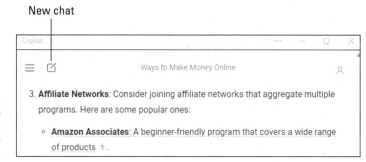

Copilot

Ways to Make Money Online

FIGURE 24-3:
Click the new
chat icon to
start a new
conversation.

3. **Affiliate Networks**: Consider joining affiliate networks that aggregate multiple programs. Here are some popular ones:

○ **Amazon Associates**: A beginner-friendly program that covers a wide range of products 1 .

Copying and Pasting Copilot's Answer

After Copilot answers your question, you can copy its answer and paste it into any app that lets you type text, such as Notepad (which comes with Windows), Microsoft Word, and Google Docs. Move the mouse pointer down near the bottom of the answer, and icons appear. Click the copy icon (labeled in Figure 24-4) to copy Copilot's answer.

FIGURE 24-4:
Copy icon below
Copilot's answer.

Copy

Then navigate to where you want to paste the text, and do one of the following:

>> Press Ctrl+V.

>> Right-click and choose Paste from the menu.

>> Choose Edit ⇨ Paste from the app's menu bar.

For more information about working with text, see Chapter 16.

Asking Questions about Pictures

If you're curious about a picture on your screen, you can usually get more information about it by asking Copilot, "What is this?" or "Where is this?" For privacy reasons, Copilot blurs the faces of people in pictures, so often it won't identify people in photos. If you submit a photo of a person and ask "Who is this?" you'll likely end up with an answer like, "I apologize, but I cannot identify or make assumptions about people in images."

To ask a question about a picture, follow these steps:

1. **Right-click the image and choose Copy Image, as shown in Figure 24-5.**

2. **Open Copilot by clicking its icon on the taskbar.**

3. **Type** What is this? **or** Where is this?

4. **Click the add an image icon, which is labeled in Figure 24-6.**

5. **Press Ctrl+V to paste the copied image.**

6. **Click the submit icon (blue arrow that appears after you paste the image).**

    Copilot does its best to analyze the picture and come up with an answer.

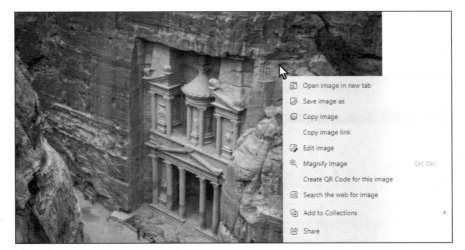

FIGURE 24-5:
Right-click the
picture and
choose
Copy Image.

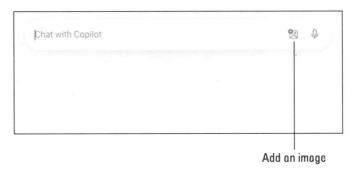

Add an image

FIGURE 24-6:
Add a screenshot
to a Copilot
prompt.

Getting Instant Tech Help

If you're stymied by something on your computer screen, remember that you can always ask AI to define the term. If you're trying to accomplish a specific task, ask AI. For the best results, include as much specific information as you can.

If you don't get the answer you were expecting on the first try, keep the conversation going, as described at the beginning of the chapter. You can ask just about anything. For example:

What does right-click mean and how do I do it on a tablet?

What are files and folders in Windows?

What are apps, programs, files, and documents in computers?

What is the internet, exactly?

What is a PDF and how do I view one?

What is Bluetooth?

How do I copy and paste text?

Asking questions like these as they come up is an easy way to educate yourself on-the-fly. Don't worry about memorizing the answer. If you forget it, just ask the question again.

Letting AI Solve Math Problems

Copilot can solve most day-to-day math problems with ease. Just type your prompt as though you were asking a person to solve the problem. For example:

What is 145.89 with 6 percent sales tax added?

If my front yard is 10 x 20 feet and my back yard is 8 x 20 feet, how many square yards is that?

I have a circle that's 8 feet across. How many square feet is that?

What's 214.15 divided by 11?

If I have a right triangle with side A of 20 and side B of 15, what is the hypotenuse?

What is the square root of 11.3?

What is the sum of squares for 11, –4, 91, –44, 70, -2?

For more complex equations, you can ask using a screen shot, such as the one in Figure 24-7 of a web page in Microsoft Edge.

Do the following to have Copilot in Windows solve the equation:

1. **Open Copilot for Edge by clicking its icon near the top-right corner of Edge's app window.**

2. **If you're on the Compose tab, click Chat.**

3. **In the Ask Me Anything box, type** solve this.

4. **Click the add a screenshot icon (scissors).**

5. **Drag a frame around the equation, and then click the green check mark to add the equation to your prompt, as shown in Figure 24-8.**

6. **Press Enter or click the submit icon (blue up arrow) in the prompt box.**

   Copilot shows you how to solve the equation (if it's solvable) and gives you the correct answer.

Chat   Copilot in Edge

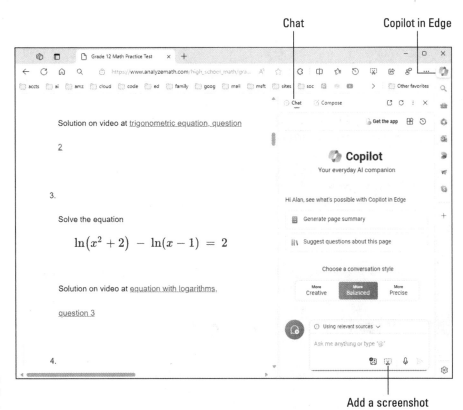

FIGURE 24-7:
Math equation on
the screen.

Add a screenshot

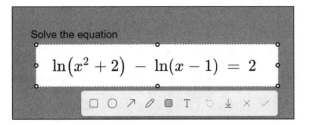

FIGURE 24-8:
Isolating the
equation to solve
in a screenshot.

Planning Trips with AI

AI can be a handy tool when planning to travel. For example, you can get distances and advice in particular places you want to visit by posing a something like this:

> I'm traveling south to north in Maine, and want to visit Bar Harbor, Belfast, Camden, Castine, Kennebunkport, and Ogunquit. In what order should I visit, and how many miles are there between each location?

You can also ask

> How long does it take to drive from San Diego, California to Ashland, Oregon on the Pacific Coast Highway?

If you're traveling to a foreign country with a different currency, you can do instant currency conversions. For example:

> What is 10,000 Mexican pesos in US dollars?

You can do quick translations too:

> How do I say Good Morning in French?

Basically, whatever question pops into your head, consider asking AI.

Writing Like a Pro with AI

Many of us struggle with getting words down on paper. And even when those words are finally written, we might not be sure if the punctuation, spelling, and grammar are correct.

AI can help. Simply do the following:

1. **Use a text editor or word processor (such as Notepad in Windows or Microsoft Word) to type your text.**

2. **Select and copy that text by pressing Ctrl+A and then pressing Ctrl+C.**

3. **Open Copilot.**

4. **Type** Improve this: **(include the colon) and press Ctrl+V to paste your copied text.**

5. **Click the submit icon (blue up arrow) and wait a few seconds.**

   Copilot checks your writing, fixes any errors, and might even suggest other ways to improve the text.

Feel free to copy what Copilot wrote and paste it into your own document.

Letting AI Do All the Writing

Do you need to write an email, a social media post, a blog post, a homework assignment, a poem, or something else, but you don't even know where to start? Tell AI to write it for you. Although Copilot in Windows can certainly write anything you ask, you'll get more control using the Compose feature in Microsoft Edge. Here's how:

1. **Open Microsoft Edge from the Windows Start menu.**

2. **Click the Copilot icon in the upper-right corner.**

3. **If Chat is selected (underlined), click Compose (see Figure 24-9).**

Copilot in Edge

FIGURE 24-9:
Copilot Compose
in Microsoft Edge.

4. **In the Write About box, type the subject of your writing.**

5. **Under Tone, choose a tone for your writing: Professional, Casual, Enthusiastic, Informational, or Funny.**

   If you don't see a tone you like, click + and specify a tone, such as song lyrics or romantic.

6. **Under Format, choose Paragraph (for regular text), Email, Ideas (for a list or an outline), or Blog Post.**

7. **Under Length, click Short, Medium, or Long.**

8. **Click Generate Draft.**

If you need a specific type of document, such as a script, a poem, song lyrics, or a haiku, include that in your Write About prompt. For example:

> Write a poem about pizza and beer.
>
> Write a video script about how to record your computer screen in Windows.
>
> Write lyrics for a sad song about leaving your cat at home while you're on vacation.

For longer, more formal documents and books, consider working in stages. For example, under Write About, you could type:

> Write an outline for a research paper about the debate over the threats of a technological singularity.

Set Tone to Professional, Format to Ideas, and Length to Long. Click Generate Draft. Copy and paste the outline into a Word document (or whatever app you use for writing). Then you can have AI write each section as paragraphs, one section at a time. For example, if one of your headings is "Definition of Technological Singularity," go back to the Compose tab and tell Copilot to

> Describe what a technological singularity is, and add citations in APA format.

(or MLA format, if that's what's required). Make sure you use the Paragraph format. Repeat the process for each item in your outline. You'll need to treat everything AI provides as a draft, but it's a great way to quickly get all your facts and ideas down on paper.

Summarizing and Simplifying Web Pages and PDFs

Sometimes when you're searching for information online, you end up with a lot more than you bargained for. Perhaps you get a Wikipedia page that reads like a technical manual for engineers, when all you're looking for is basic information. Or perhaps you need to summarize a lengthy PDF file you downloaded or received from someone. Either way, Copilot in Edge can be your best tool:

1. **For a PDF, right-click the PDF file's icon and choose Open in Edge. For a web page, browse to the page in Microsoft Edge.**

2. **Click the Copilot icon in Edge's upper-right corner.**

3. **If Compose is selected (underlined), click Chat (see Figure 24-10).**

4. **Do one of the following:**

   - *If you see a Generate Page Summary button, click it.*

   - *If you don't see a Generate Page Summary button, type @ in the Ask Me Anything box or click the drop-down menu at the top of the box and select This Page as your source.*

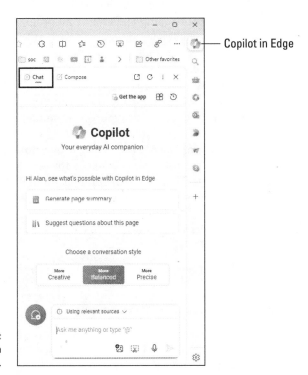

TIP

Typing @ in the Ask Me Anything box lets you choose between using the internet (Relevant Sources), the page currently appearing in Edge (This Page), or the current web site (whose URL appears in the address bar).

It might take a few seconds for Copilot to generate your summary, so be patient.

5. **If you're not too thrilled with the summary you get the first time, type** Try again **and click the submit icon (up arrow).**

Copilot takes another shot at summarizing the page. You can tell it to try again as many times as you want.

Learning to Code with AI

All apps and websites you visit are created by people writing computer code in various languages with names like HTML, CSS, JavaScript, and Python. The people writing that code are commonly called *developers* (or *computer programmer* or just *programmer*). AI knows all about coding and almost all programming languages, so it can easily write most of your code for you.

You'll still need to learn the terminology and concepts that go along with coding. For instance, if you tell AI, "Write an app that will go viral and make me a billion-aire so I can live in the lap of luxury for the rest of my life," that won't work. Sadly, we don't all get to be billionaires by typing AI prompts.

However, once you start learning to code and can pose questions using the correct terminology, you can get AI to write chunks of code for you. Just make sure you tell AI the language you're working in as part of your prompt. For example, the following are all valid questions that can produce computer code that works:

Write an HTML page with header, nav, main, and footer sections and a link to an external style sheet.

Write a CSS external style sheet with style rules for body, header, nav, main, and footer.

Write a Python image classifier app that uses Pytorch.

Write a Java class that includes a default constructor and main method.

Obviously, you're not going to be able to think up and ask questions like that without training in software development. But I hope you can see that the ability to ask questions like these, and get immediate answers, could speed up the learn-ing process considerably.

Index

About the Author

Alan Simpson is the author of more than 100 books on web design, database design, and software development. His books have been published throughout the world in dozens of languages and have sold millions of copies. Alan also teaches online college courses on web development and programming.

Dedication

To Susan, Ashley, and Alec.

Acknowledgments

Many thanks to Margot Maley, Steve Hayes, Susan Pink, Guy Hart-Davis, and everyone else at Wiley who helped get this book into your hands.

Publisher's Acknowledgments

Executive Editor: Steve Hayes

Project Editor: Susan Pink

Copy Editor: Susan Pink

Technical Editor: Guy Hart-Davis

Production Editor: Saikarthick Kumarasamy

Cover Image: © APCortizasJr/Getty Images